BOOKS BY
FORD MADOX FORD

IT WAS THE NIGHTINGALE
PARADE'S END
THE GOOD SOLDIER
PROVENCE
ETC.

IT WAS THE
NIGHTINGALE

IT WAS THE NIGHTINGALE

"It was the nightingale and not the lark
Which pierced the envious hollow of thine ear"
ROMEO AND JULIET

FORD MADOX FORD

II

THE ECCO PRESS · NEW YORK

Copyright © 1933 by Ford Madox Ford
Copyright renewed 1961 by Katherine Lamb
All rights reserved
First published by The Ecco Press in 1984
18 West 30th Street, New York, N.Y. 10001
Published simultaneously in Canada by
George J. McLeod Limited, Toronto
Printed in the United States of America

Library of Congress Cataloging in Publication Data
Ford, Ford Madox, 1873-1939.
It was the nightingale.
Reprint. Originally published: 1st ed. Philadelphia & London:
Lippincott, 1933.
I. Title.
PR6011.05318 1984   823'.912   83-16570
ISBN 0-88001-034-7

TO

EUGENE PRESSLY, ESQUIRE

My dear Pressly:

You have read every word of this book; thus you are the only man in the world of whom I can say for certain—or shall ever be able to say for certain!—that he has read every word of it. . . . To whom can a book be more fittingly dedicated than to its only reader?

I hope you have liked it. If it upholds too noisily for your tastes the banners of the only perfect republic and the only permanent kingdom, forgive that. That is nothing against diplomatists. The Kingdom of the Arts has many subjects who have never employed for expression the permanencies of paper, canvas, stone or catgut, reed and brass. And unless a diplomatist be an artist in those impermanencies, the fates and boundaries of nations, he is no true ambassador. Indeed it is amongst the prouder records of your temporal republic—along with that of France—that it has not infrequently employed and still employs creative artists as its communicating links with other lands. And, since I notice that two of the typed pages of this book have an eagle for their watermark, may I not pride myself on the fact that I thus become, as it were microscopically, a floor-sweeper in the embassy of our lord Apollo, sovereign over Parnassus.

They say every man has it in him to write one good book. This then may be my one good book that you get

5

dedicated to you. For the man's one good book will be his autobiography. This is a form I have never tried—mainly for fear of the charge of vanity. I have written reminiscences of which the main features were found in the lives of other people and in which, as well as I could, I obscured myself. But I have reached an age when the charge of vanity has no terrors as against the chance of writing one good book. It is the great woe of literature that no man can tell whether what he writes is good or not. In his vain moments, he may, like Thackeray, slap his forehead and cry: "This is genius" . . . But in the dark days when that supporter abandons him he will sink his head over his page and cry: "What a vanity is all this!" . . . And it is the little devil in human personality that no man can tell whether he is vain or not. He may—as you certainly have every reason to—assert that at least he has a good nose. But if I advanced the same claim? Or a man might limit his boasting to saying that he was a good trencher-man, and yet be vain since he may delight in wolfing down what, in the realm of the haute cuisine, *is mere garbage.*

I have tried then to write a novel drawing my material from my own literary age. You have here two ad-ventures of a once jeune, homme pauvre—*a poor man who was once young. In rendering them, I have em-ployed every wile known to me as novelist—the time-shift, the* progression d'effet, *the adaptation of rhythms to the pace of the action. If then it is a bad book it is*

6

merely because of my want of skill, or because my canons are at fault.

I woke this morning, as is my habit, just before dawn and lay looking, through the mosquito-net, at the harbingers of day and thinking of what I was going to write now. . . . These words! I saw, in the fantasmagoric way in which one perceives things at dawn when one's thoughts are elsewhere—something gross descending the trunk of the oak whose boughs overhang my bed. From there the nightingale has awakened me just before every dawn for how long now! . . . It was a rat, and the nightingale, as it moved, glided down, just three inches from its eyes.

It seemed a fantastic and horrible conjunction, that of rat and nightingale. But after all, all poets are at outs with . . . let us say, their bankers. Having been, as you see, an editor, I dislike saying that editors are all the same as rats. . . .

I was filled with horror until in a moment peace descended on me. The cat of the house jumped from the roof to a lower roof and so to the path beside me. And at once there went up the long warning note of the male and the answering, croaking menace of the female nightingale when she sits on her eggs. They were then safe. . . . It is as futile for a rat to try to rifle the nest of the nightingale who is nyctalops *as for a banker to ruin the home of a poet. The birds, seeing in the dark, will fly at the rat's weak eyes until the discomfited quadruped shuffles away down the trunk and the female bird again sits in triumph and peace. . . .*

As for the banker, the poet—be it Bertram de Born or Mr. Pound or Mr. Hemingway—will address to him some immortal sirventes or pop him into a novel so that he will never again hold up his head. . . .

Then as soon as it was light I went down into the garden to plan out, in the pitiless, Mediterranean drought, the irrigation of the day. The semi-tropical plants and trees—the oranges, lemons, peppers, vines and the rest can do without water for a long time. Musk- and water-melons must have a little water and the Northern plants that for his sins the pink Nordic has imported here—the peas, beans, string beans, cabbages, carrots, and such gross, over-green matter, must have a great deal or incontinently die. It was a whole campaign of irrigation channels that I had mentally to arrange for a day given up entirely to writing and the affairs of the parched earth.

As I went back up the hill to sit down and write this I saw, drinking at opposite ends of my sinking cistern, the great snake who is three foot longer than my six-foot stretch and the emerald green, vermilion spotted lizard that is as long as my arm. I felt satisfaction. These creatures one only sees drinking in the magic hour between darkness and day. They looked at me with their fateful indifferent glances as I passed, and went on drinking.

For me the great snake, messenger of Aesculapius to whom the cock is sacred, represents Destiny, the scarlet-spotted lizard, the imps of discomfort and the little devils of doubt that beset one's daily path. I know that

8

writer's cramp will make me have to lay down my pen often today and the femme de ménage *will be more than usually like a snake in the kitchen. These are the reminders that Fate sends us so that in our baked sanctuary our stomachs be not too haughty or too proud . . . But I know that the great snake will soon swallow the rat. It is true that, being inscrutable and august, it will eventually rifle the nightingale's nest. But it is fitting that Lilith should ruin poets. . . .*

So you see that, to date, this fairy-tale has found its appropriate close. The persons of the transatlantic drama are scattered but all active. You, it is true, are in Paris with Katherine Anne, and Mr. Glenway Westcott is still faithful to the great Faubourg; Mr. Pound is Professor of Economics in Rapallo; Mr. Hemingway is writing a novel in Key West if he is not momentarily shooting lions in Arkansaw or diving to recover bottles of Perrier Jouet from a sunken rum-runner. Mr. Nathan Ash is somewhere in the State of New York; Mrs. Rodes is shiningly directing the interior decorating of the chief but not capital city of that State; the conscientious objector is on the other side of the frontier near here; the White Russian Colonel is I don't know where; Mrs. Foster is in Schenectady. And so the city sitteth solitary and the round table is dissolved. . . .

But all, all the Knights, be sure, in their fastnesses seek the Holy Grail. . . . I read in the newspapers that Mr. Pound—momentarily in Paris—announces that his opera Cavalcanti—*more power to his* bâton!—*will be broadcasted in a month or so. From time to time he writes a line of poetry, too.*

The flood of laymen will in the end submerge us all and dance on our graves. The layman hates the artist as the atrocious Mr. Hitler hates learning. Indeed the layman regards the artist as a sort of Jew. But, to the measure of the light vouchsafed, my late comrades shine in their places and may be content. The pogroms will come but, even as Heine, the greatest of German poets, they have lit beacons that posterity shall not willingly let die.

I had intended to continue this novel to the edge of the abyss of 1929. But I found that subsequent events are too vivid in my mind. I cannot get them into any perspective. Moreover it is inexpedient to write of living people in their too near presents. It is all right to write of a man in his hot youth. He will regard the record with complacency, knowing that he has now neared perfection. But write about their immediate presents and not only will you find yourself in a hornet's nest—which is so much my normal situation that it would leave me fairly indifferent—but they will be deeply and really grieved—which would be hateful! I once said to the beautiful and how much regretted poet, Elinor Wylie, that that day she was looking radiantly beautiful. As she was. She said to me with fury:

"That is because you thought I looked like a hag yesterday!" and she never spoke to me again. That grieved me because she and her husband used to be very good friends of mine because, she said, she and Mr.

Benet got engaged over reading one of my poems. But—what was worse—she was mortally hurt by that remark and, I have heard, never got over the idea that it had suggested to her. So, for my novel about the years immediately preceding super-Armageddon you will have to wait another decade. . . . And glad of it! says you. . . .

I don't wonder. During all these months you, as Benedict, should have been squiring Katherine Anne Porter-Pressly to Maxim's, or the Moulin Rouge, or the Chat Noir . . . I see a smile of polite irony come over your diplomat's inscrutability: but what do I know or care about the transpontine night life of the Ville Lumière today!—Instead you have rushed home from your embassy at the days' ends and have spent the hours with Katherine Anne poring over my minute and indecipherable script. It is a scandal and I a real scoundrel to have let you do it. . . . Youth and beauty should be better served though the sky fall in on the manuscripts of all novels.

But there is this: Whilst you sat quiet at home Katherine Anne has written some more of her exquisite short stories. Thus what youth, beauty and the night club lost on the fugitive swings, Literature has gained for her roundabouts that are eternal. . . .

And there is this too . . . I daresay that, in the course of this novel I have rendered humanity as a little chequered. People who owe one a little gratitude or a little consideration now and then fall short. One's ewe lamb will shew the terrible teeth of the lamb in

Turgenev's story. . . . But you have done that heavy and monotonous work—I dare not say "for the love of God"—but then without any faint hope of any return. For what return could I possibly make you except to subscribe myself

With infinite gratitude

FORD MADOX FORD

CAP BRUN

ON THE FEAST OF ST. EULOGIUS

MCMXXXIII

CONTENTS

PART ONE
"DOMINE DIRIGE NOS"
15

PART TWO
"FLUCTUAT NEC MERGITUR"
153

PART THREE
"E PLURIBUS MULTA"
257

PART ONE

"DOMINE DIRIGE NOS"

PART ONE

CHAPTER ONE

THERE WAS NEVER A DAY SO GAY FOR THE
Arts as any twenty-four hours of the early 'twenties in
Paris. Nay, twenty-four hours did not seem sufficient
to contain all that the day held of plastic, verbal and
harmonious sweets. But I had a year or so to wait before
that ambience was to enfold me. I begin with the day
of my release from service in His Britannic Majesty's
army—in early 1919.

Naked came I from my mother's womb. On that day
I was nearly as denuded of possessions. My heavier
chattels were in a green, bolster-shaped sack. All the
rest I had on me—a worn uniform with gilt dragons on
the revers of the tunic. . . . All that I had once had
had been conveyed in one direction or the other. That
was the lot of man in those days—of man who had been
actively making the world fit for . . . financial disaster.
For me, as writer I was completely forgotten and as
completely I had forgotten all that the world had before
then drummed into me of the art of conveying illusion
to others. I had no illusions myself.

During my Xmas leave in a strange London I had
gone to a party given at the French Embassy by M.

Philippe Berthelot, since ambassador himself and for long principal secretary to the French Foreign Office. I swam, as it were, up the Embassy steps. Then I was indeed a duck out of water. . . . The party was given for the English writers who with the implements of their craft had furthered the French cause. And there they all were, my unknown confrères. It was seven years since I had written a word: it was almost as many since I had spoken to a man of letters. Unknown faces filled the considerable halls that were misty under the huge chandeliers. There was a fog outside. . . . Unknown and queer!

I cannot believe that the faces of my British brothers of the pen are really more pallid and misshapenly elongated than those of any other country or of any other sedentary pursuit. But there, they seemed all unusually long, pale, and screwed to one side or the other. All save the ruddy face of Mr. Arnold Bennett to which war and the years had added. He appeared like a round red sun rising from amongst vertical shapes of cloud. . . .

But I was not on speaking terms with Mr. Bennett and I drifted as far from him as I could.

Just before the Armistice I had been summoned from my battalion to the Ministry of Information in London. There I had found Mr. Bennett in a Presidential chair. In my astonishment at finding him in such a place I stuttered out:

"How fat you've got!"

He said:

"You have to write about terms of peace. The Ministry has changed. France is not going . . ."

We immediately disagreed very violently. *Very* violently! It was a question of how much the Allies ought to secure for France. That meeting became a brawl. Sir W. Tyrrell got introduced into it at first on the telephone and then personally. He was then Secretary to the Foreign Office and is now British Ambassador in Paris. I have never seen any look so irritated. The chief image of that interview comes back to me as a furnace-hot flush mounting on a dark-bearded cheek. And Mr. Bennett lolling back augustly in his official seat like a marble Zeus on a Greek frieze. I suppose I can be very irritating, particularly when it is a matter of anyone who wants, as the saying was, to do France in the eye. That responsible diplomat uttered language about our Ally! I should think that now, when in his cocked hat he passes the sentry at the door of the Elysée, he would have little chills if he thought of what he then said. I on the other hand had come straight from a company of several million men who were offering their lives so that France might be saved for the world.

When he had stormed out I asked Mr. Bennett if he still wanted my article about the terms of peace. A Chinese smile went over his face. Enigmatic. That was what it was.

He said:

"Yes. Write it. It's an order. I'll have it confirmed as such by the Horse Guards if you like."

I went back to my regiment where, Heaven knows,

the work was already overwhelming. I wrote that article on the top of a bully-beef case in between frantic periods of compiling orders as to every conceivable matter domestic to the well-being of a battalion on active service. The article advocated giving to France a great deal more than Mr. Lloyd George's government desired to give her. A great deal more! As I have said elsewhere, that article was lost in the post—a fate that must be rare for official documents addressed to a great Government department. A week later I received through my Orderly Room an intimation that, as an officer of His Britannic Majesty's Army I was prohibited from writing for the press. And I was reminded that, even when I was released from active service, I would still be an officer of the Special Reserve and a paragraph of the Official Secrets Act was quoted to me. I could not think that I was in possession of a sufficiency of Official Secrets to make that intimation worth while but at that point I had understood Mr. Bennett's queer smile.

I like what the Boers call slimness and usually regard with pleasure acts of guile practised against myself. I fancy it must make me feel more real—more worth while!—if a Confidence Trick man attempts to practise on me. But at that party at the Embassy I felt disinclined to talk to Mr. Bennett. Dog should not, by rights, eat dog.

But patriotism and the desire of Dai Bach's Government to down the French covered in those days hundreds of sins in London town. *Dai Bach*—David darling!—was the nickname given to the then Prime Minister in the Welch Regiment for which in those days I had the honour to look after many intimate details. It pleases me still to read the "character" that decorated my Soldier's Small Book on my resigning those duties:

"Possesses great powers of organisation and has solved many knotty problems. A lecturer of the first water on military subjects. Has managed with great ability the musketry training of this unit."

I notice on the day on which I begin this book that Mr. George has attained the age of seventy and that his message to humanity is stated as being, on that occasion, that what is needed to save the world is men who know how to save the world. I could almost have thought that out for myself. . . .

I stood then alone and feeling conspicuous—a heavy blond man in a faded uniform in those halls of France. Pale faces swam, inspectantly, towards me. But, as you may see fishes do round a bait in dim water, each one checked suddenly and swam away with a face expressing piscine distaste. I imagined that the barb of a hook must protrude somewhere from my person and set myself to study the names and romantic years of the wines that M. Berthelot had provided for us.

Their juice had been born on vines, beneath suns of years before these troubles and their names made fifty sweet symphonies. . . . It had been long, long indeed, since I had so much as thought of even such minor glories as *Château Neuf du Pape* or *Tavel* or *Hermitage*—though I think White Hermitage of a really good vintage year the best of all white wines. . . . I had almost forgotten that there were any potable liquids but *vins du pays* and a horrible fluid that we called Hooch. The nine of diamonds used to be called the curse of Scotland, but surely *usquebaugh*—which tastes like the sound of its name—is Scotland's curse to the world . . . and to Scotland. That is why Glasgow on a Saturday night is Hell. . . .

A long black figure detached itself from Mr. Bennett's side and approached me. It had the aspect of an undertaker coming to measure a corpse. . . . The eyes behind enormous lenses were like black pennies and appeared to weep dimly; the dank hair was plastered in flattened curls all over the head . . . I decided that I did not know the gentleman. His spectacles swam almost against my face. His hollow tones were those of a funeral mute:

"You used to write," it intoned, "didn't you?"

I made the noise that the French render by "!?!?!"

He continued—and it was as if his voice came from the vaults of Elsinore. . . .

"You used to consider yourself a literary dictator of London. You are so no longer. *I* represent Posterity. What I say today about books Posterity will say for ever." He rejoined Mr. Bennett. I was told later that that gentleman was drunk. He had found Truth at the bottom of a well. Of *usquebaugh*! That was at the other, crowded end of the room.

That reception more nearly resembled scenes to be witnessed in New York in Prohibition days than anything else I ever saw in London. It must have given M. Berthelot what he would call *une fière idée de la Muse*, at any rate on Thames bank.

Eventually Madame Berthelot took pity on my faded solitariness and Madame Berthelot is one of the most charming, dark and witty of Paris hostesses. . . . *Et exaltavit!* . . .

A month or so later I might, had it not been too dark, have been seen with my sack upon my shoulder, approaching Red Ford.

That was a leaky-roofed, tile-healed, rat-ridden seventeenth century, five-shilling a week, moribund labourer's cottage. It stood beneath an enormous oak beside a running spring in a green dingle through which meandered a scarlet and orange runlet that in winter was a river to be forded. A low bank came down to the North. At the moment it loomed, black, against the bank and showers of stars shone through the naked branches of the oak. I had burned my poor old boats.

My being there was the result of that undertaker's mute's hollow tones at M. Berthelot's party. I had told Mme Berthelot, to her incredulous delight, that as soon as the War was finished I should go to Provence and, beside the Rhone, below Avignon, set out at last as a tender of vines and a grower of *primeurs*. In the lands where grow the grapes of *Château Neuf du Pape*, of *Tavel* and of *Hermitage*! That had of course been the result of seeing those bottles on the long buffet. For years and years—all my life—I have wanted to live in that white sunlight and, at last, die in a certain house beside the planes of the *place* in Tarascon. I cannot remember when I did not have that dream. It is the whiteness of the sunlight on the pale golden walls and the castle of the good king René and, across the Rhone, the other castle of Aucassin and Nicolette. . . .

But when at last I was released from service I found myself in a rat-trap. They refused me a passport for France.

I cannot suppose that Mr. George's government feared that with my single eloquence I should be able to stampede the Versailles Congress into giving France the whole of both banks of the Rhine from Basel to the Dutch frontier. But that singular interference with the liberty of a subject had that aspect—as if they were determined that no Briton should speak for France. . . .

A queer, paradoxical rat-trap. If I cannot say, like Henry James, that I love France as I never loved woman, I can lay my hand on my heart and swear that I have loved only those parts of England from which you can see and most easily escape into the land of Nicolette. And, what was queer, whilst I had been the chained helot that the poor bloody footslogger is supposed to be, I had crossed over to France more times than I can now remember and had passed more time than I now like to remember in parts of Picardy and French Flanders that I should have been very glad to get out of. Now I was free. . . . But I was chained to the kerbstone on which I stood, forbidden to make a livelihood and quite unfit to stand the climate in which I found myself.

I paid of course no attention to my being forbidden to write. I did not believe that even with the Defence of the Realm Act at its back Authority could have enforced that prohibition. I was quite ready to chance that and did indeed chance it. . . . If you have been brought up in England you find it difficult to believe in the possibility of interference with your personal liberty though if, outside that, Authority can hamper the Arts it will hamper the Arts. . . .

But the spectre at M. Berthelot's feast had told me that I was as good as dead as a writer; I had no one to tell me anything to the contrary and I was myself convinced that I could no longer write. I had proved it before Red Ford received me.

Some queer lunatics I had been with in the Army had started a queer, lunatic, weekly review. They had commissioned me to write articles on anything under the sun from saluting in the army to the art of Gauguin and the eastern boundaries of France. I had written the articles and those genial lunatics had received them with wild—with the wildest—enthusiasm. They had also paid really large sums for them. But I knew that they had been the writings of a lunatic.

At the same time the *Saturday Review* had asked me to write for it. I had been pleased at the thought. The *Saturday Review* still retained at any rate for me some of the aura that it had when Lord Salisbury who wrote for it had been known as the master of flouts and jeers, and some of the later aura of the days when, under the brilliant editorship of Frank Harris it had been written for by Mr. Bernard Shaw, Max, Mr. H. G. Wells—and indeed myself.

So I went with pleasure to the office to find the extremely dingy editorial room occupied by a plump, little, grey man who welcomed me uproariously. I do not remember his name but I know that he too seemed to me to be a lunatic. He was both querulous and noisy.

He exclaimed:

"You're the man I want. You're the very man to explode all this bunk and balderdash."

I said: "!?!?!?"

"All this bunk and balderdash," he repeated. "This heroism in the trenches legend! Explode it! We know it was all nothing but drunken and libidinous bean-feasting. Show the scoundrels up! Blow the gaff on them. You've been in it. You know!"

It was the first sound—like the first grumble of a distant storm—the first indication I had that the unchangeable was changing, the incorruptible putting on corruption. Over there we had been so many Rip van Winkles. The *Saturday Review*, the Bank of England, the pound sterling, the London County Council, the Lord Mayor and the Court of Aldermen along with the Marylebone Cricket Club—these things had used to be indubitable and as sure as the stars in their courses. And as unquestioned had been the thin red line!

Alas! I continued to regard that fellow as a lunatic, until, slowly, I realised that his frame of mind was common to the civilian population of London and of the world from Odessa to Seattle. It seemed to me that he was mad to want to turn the *Saturday Review* of all papers into an organ of what in my innocence I took to be pro-Germanism. So I declaimed to him the one ethical axiom that seemed to be still unshaken. Dog, I said, doesn't eat dog. I might have partaken of drunken and libidinous orgies but I was not the man to blow the gaff on them. . . . And I was so sure that he could not succeed in his wild project that I offered to write for him some articles on campaigns that I had not witnessed. I have never been able to make up my mind as to whether or no it was proper to write for organs of whose policy one disapproves. Your name may appear to endorse their mischiefs. But you may counteract some of their bad influence and at least you may occupy some space that otherwise might be given over to working evil. I suppose too that I wanted to try my hand at writing. I am not incorruptible!

He was disappointed but he accepted my offer.

I had been for the whole period of the war on the Western front with my nose so close to the grindstone of affairs that, as soon as I had any leisure, I really thirsted to know something about the events of war and of the world outside my own three inches on the map. So I read everything I could lay my hands on about the Hindenburg victory at Tannenberg. Then

I wrote an article about what I had read. It was of course a bad thing to do.

I went to the office of that journal to correct the proof. That rotund grey ball of a man was fairly bouncing in his shadows with all his feet off the ground over a long, narrow white slip of newsprint. It ran across and fell over the edge of the table in front of him. . . . I had thought it right to put into my article something about the sufferings that must have been undergone by the Russians and even by the Germans in those terrible marshes where hundreds of men went to their deaths. It seemed to me that though it might be immoral to suggest that my own comrades had found the trenches anything but gas and gingerbread —for of course on the playing fields of Eton and elsewhere one learns that one must never applaud one's own side—it might be licit at least to say that the men of our Enemy and of our Ex-Ally had had a bad time. . . . I learned there that I was wrong. I was so wrong that I was propelled out of that obfusc office as if by a soda-water volcano. It was shouted at me that I was never to come there again.

In the outer, sub-editorial room, very slim, tall and sempiternally youthful Mr. Stuart Rendal was depressedly holding up a long white slip. My article seemed to pain him as if it had been a severe neuralgia. I for my part was depressed to think that anyone, tall, slim and with the gift of eternal youth should serve as wage-slave under that explosive little ball of suet. And it was still more depressing that it should be a gentleman and scholar like Mr. Rendal. . . . As if we had not rendered the world free for heroes!

When I had last seen him he had been the all-powerful editor of the *Athenaeum*. I had always disliked the *Athenaeum*, for its grudging omniscience, its pomposity, its orthodoxy and its hatred of the new in letters. . . . But that an editor of that awful sheet should "sub" it for such an atomy was as if one should see an ex-president of the United States selling papers outside the White House. And with a sense of comradely affection I said:

"Is that article really so awful, Rendal?"

He said miserably:

"You used, you know, to write fairly. Not really well but at least grammatically." But this writing was rotten. When it wasn't rotten it was incomprehensible. He exclaimed: "What's the 'Narw Army'? Is *Narw* the name of a general or a river? I can't make head or tail of it."

I drifted slowly away in mute sign that I accepted his stricture. It was true enough. Whilst my thoughts had been working over that piece of writing they had seemed to me to have broken backs. . . . When a snake has its back broken the forepart glides ahead in waves, the rest drags in the dust. . . .

A few days later—or a few days before—for I am hazy as to this chronology—the other lunatic paper had ceased its hilarious career. Just after that earthquake, I paused with one foot off the kerb at the corner of the Campden Hill waterworks, nearly opposite the stable in which, thirteen years before, I had used to breakfast with Mr. Galsworthy. I was about to cross the road. But, whilst I stood with one foot poised in air, suddenly I recognised my unfortunate position. . . .

Quite a number of curious things have happened to me whilst I have been in that posture of preparing to cross a road; in particular I have taken a number of sudden resolutions with one foot suspended like that. . . . In 1923 a gentleman whom I will call the doyen of American letters invited me to lunch with him at the Brevoort. He telephoned that he was moving into a new apartment in the 50's and must be there at two o'clock at latest to meet his architect. Would I mind lunching with him at twelve? He must leave at 1.30.

I was stopping at that hotel so it was no trouble to be there at noon. He arrived at 1.15, which did not surprise me since that was New York. He said he was sorry but I knew what moving was. . . . In revenge we talked over luncheon till 4.30 by which time I imagine his architect knew what moving and New York were. . . . We talked about style. Yes, style!—the use of words minutely and technically employed. And I am bound to say that no-one with whom I have ever talked about the employment of words—with the possible exception of Joseph Conrad—no-one knew more about them than my friend. Indeed I am ready to aver that I could never have talked with any man for a solid three hours and a quarter on end unless he had a pretty good knowledge of the use of words.

We discussed every English or American author living or dead who could claim any sort of interest on account of his methods of writing—every writer we could think of except two. And we agreed very closely in all our estimates. The discussion continued up several blocks of Fifth Avenue. We reached East Fourteenth Street where he was to take a trolley. I knew there was another author whom I ought to have discussed, but I have my shynesses. . . . At last, with my foot in the air off the kerb I cleared my throat and opened my mouth. Before I could speak he said, also with one foot in the air:

"You know, I've read all your books and I like them very much."

I said:

"Well, you know, Dreiser, I've read all your books and I like them very much. . . ."

That is why I think that the act of taking a resolution in crossing roads may lead to other inceptions in the mind. At any rate I hope Mr. Dreiser spoke as truly as I did!

It is singular how Letters, for me, will come creeping in. I had intended to make this a chapter generally about farming and when I had written the last word of the paragraph above this one I said: "Now for the hoe and the nitrates!"

I went for a walk down through the dim Luxemburg Gardens of the end of January where they were putting iris plants in among privet bushes. It seemed a curious thing to do. But of course they know what they are about. I continued down the rue Férou which, it is said, Dante used to descend on his way from the Montagne Ste. Geneviève to the Sorbonne—and in which Aramis lived on the ground—and Ernest Hemingway on the top, floors. And how many between the musketeer and the toreador! And so across the Place St. Sulpice, more dimmed by the thaw than even the long alleys of the Luxemburg.

Terrible things—for those to whom terrible things occur in their lives—happen in the last days of January. The heavy drag of winter is then at its most dire and your courage at its lowest as if in a long four o'clock in the morning of the year. You seem to pass as if you yourself were invisible in the owl light of the deep streets. . . . Between dog and wolf, they say here. It is a good phrase.

Because, through such tenebrousnesses, I made my way to a café where I sat all alone and read that Galsworthy was dead. A week ago it had been George Moore. So the days between—the days of black frost twilight turning to crepuscular thaws—were days between dog and wolf. . . . Between their deaths!

I sat for a long time looking at the words:

Mort de John Galsworthy
La Carrière du célèbre Romancier. ·

It seemed wrong to be reading of his death in Paris. And, for me in tawdry light above tawdry *nouvel art* decorations of a café I much dislike, I saw through the white sheet of paper . . . dull green hop-lands rolling away under the mists of the English North Downs; the sunlight falling through the open door of the stable where he used to give me breakfast; the garden of the Addison Road house. It backed on the marvellous coppices of Holland Park and the pheasants used to fly from them into the garden.

He had a dog—an immense black spaniel—that seemed to be more to Galsworthy than his books, his friends, himself. A great, dignified, as if exiled-royal creature. That is why I say between dog and wolf. For, when it came to writing, George Moore was wolf —lean, silent, infinitely swift and solitary. But Galsworthy was the infinitely good, infinitely patient, infinitely tenacious being that guards our sheepfolds and farmsides from the George Moore's. Only, there was only one George Moore.

In one January week the Western World lost its greatest writer—and its best man! So it seems to be wrong to read about the death of Galsworthy here before the West begins. With George Moore it mattered less. He was as Parisian of the '70's to '80's as an Anglo-Irishman could be.

The last time I saw him was on the Quai Malaquais. He wandered along before the old book backs, under the grey branches of the plane trees, above the grey Seine. His pale eyes were unseeing in his paler face. They must have seen a Seine and book backs of fifty years before. Sexagenarian greynesses—as when I saw the news of the other death my eyes rested on thirty-year-old Kentish greennesses.

I stood with my hat in my hand for several seconds.
I always stood with my hat in my hand when George
Moore passed me in the streets and I think that writers
of English should stand with their hats in their hands
for a second or two on the anniversaries of a January
day in 1933. . . . On that day he was walking very
slowly and I waited—as one does when the King goes
by—until he was a little way away before I put my hat
on again. I don't think he so much as saw me though
he seemed minutely to acknowledge my salute with
the fingers of the hand that hung at his side.

It was as if a ghost had passed—the ghost of a High
Priest who had also been a King. I never go along the
quays just there without feeling slightly chilled when
I remember that it was there that I saw George Moore
for the last time. It was just there too that I had stood
to watch the orators over the coffin of Anatole France
. . . and immediately after that ghost had passed Miss
Nancy Cunard flashed, like a jewelled tropical bird
along the Quai, going to rejoin him.

At a British military funeral, after the Dead March
in *Saul*, after the rattling of the cords from under
the coffin, the rifle-firing and the long wail of the Last
Post suddenly the band and drums strike up "D'ye
ken John Peel?" or the "Lincolnshire Poacher"—the
unit's quickstep. It is shocking until you see how good
it is as a symbol.

I don't suppose Mr. Moore was really cutting me—
though he may well have been! A number of his inti-
mates disliked me a great deal. He told me that Mr.—

afterwards Sir Edmund—Gosse had advised him not to give me anything for the *English Review.*

I did not ever know Mr. Moore at all well. I must first have been in the same room with him in the gloomy house of Mr.—afterwards Sir Edmund—Gosse. It was on the banks of the Regents Canal and my father lived opposite across the canal. Mr. Gosse had at one time a subordinate position on a review that my father owned. I was brought up among admirers of Mr. Moore. My grandfather thought very highly of his writings on the French Impressionists; my father was one of the earliest to praise "Esther Waters" and later nearly all my young friends patriotically championed Mr. Moore in his claim to be the master of Guy de Maupassant. I did not go as far as that but I did believe—as I do now—that Mr. Moore was the only novelist of English blood who had produced a novel that was a masterpiece at once of writing and of form. So in one house or London club or the other when I found that Mr. Moore was there I always effaced myself as much as I could. If I had not had so great an admiration for his greatness, his clarity of mind and the chilliness of his temperament I might have got to know him well for I saw him often enough. . . .

At a later stage I was writing a preface to a volume of translations from Maupassant. Mr. Henry James had told me some singular details about the life and habits of the author of "La Maison Tellier." Conrad had said that these stories were all nonsense. I was not writing about the life or personality of Maupassant—only about his methods of writing. But I thought it might clarify my thoughts if I could get myself posted as to the matter upon which James and Conrad disagreed. Moore had lived in Paris in the great age of impressionistic painters and had known all the naturalistic writers of the last decades of the last century. It was a question of French manners and I do not intend to say what it was for a reason that will appear.

I wrote to Mr. Moore and asked him for information as to two succinct points so that he need take no more trouble than to answer "Yes" or "No." . . . He ordered me to go and see him. . . .

He was in a dressing gown, recovering from influenza in a darkish rather rich room that I found overheated. Before we had even sat down he said:

"So you want to steal my thunder!"

I was then young and that annoyed me. I denied that I had any intention of using anything that he said but he paid no attention. The interview continued disagreeably for me.

There is an early American folk song:

> So I sez to Maria, sez I:
> "Praise to the face
> Is open disgrace".

And I have never been able in the presence of the Great to express to them the admiration that I usually feel. I try to bide my time until I can slip into the conversation something like: "Your admirable 'Nets to Catch the Wind'" or whatever I judge to be the great one's favourite work. But Mr. George Moore never gave me the time to manœuvre for position. He said at once that Maupassant had pilfered his ideas in "Une Vie" and "Bel Ami" and hinted that he had made a very poor job of it as compared with "Esther Waters" and "A Modern Lover." . . . If you put it to me to-day that "Esther Waters" is a greater novel than "Une Vie" I do not suppose that I should deny it, for Maupassant, great as he may have been as a short story writer, was not a novelist *pur sang*. To state that is to deny the gods of my youth but I was then in the full heat of the Maupassant faith. . . . And Mr. Moore, if he was unobservant as to material details, was a perfect demon for detecting hesitancies of the voice.

It became worse later for I distinctly chilled him by obstinately stating that I preferred "A Drama in Muslin," he, quite properly thinking that "Esther Waters" was his masterpiece. But at the moment I had just finished reading the other and I had read it with a personal enthusiasm for its relative humanity whereas all the rest of the Master's novels left me—personally—cold. Intensely admiring—but repelled!

So I have that early image of him, standing rather rigid and grim, chilled and monacal in his long dressing gown. He was dismissing me with one hand on the door-knob of his dim, overheated room. I had at the moment for the first time the impression of his extreme pallor. That was owing, possibly, to a shaft of light coming from the passage. And he seemed as aloof as if he had been a denizen of another world, where there was neither sun nor wind. The impression was so strong that I was relieved that he did not remove his hand from the door-knob and offer it to me. . . . I gathered that he took me for an interviewer. I had told him again and again that I had no intention of printing anywhere anything that he might say but it had not seemed to make any impression on him. Before I came he had made up his mind that he was going to receive a reporter who would pick his brains and he was a man who had great difficulty in changing his ideas. In those days an interviewer was regarded in England at once with a sort of fearful fascination and at the same time as a being some degrees lower than the man who comes to check your gas meter.

So I remained with the impression of something at once querulous and etiolated. Etiolation is what happens to plants if you grow them in the dark. I felt as if a minor James had called on a blotted Flaubert. . . . I have already recorded elsewhere the repulsion that James said he had felt when Flaubert had opened his front door to Turgenev and himself—and in a dressing gown! And Flaubert had bellowed at James. . . . Mr. Moore had a servant to open his front door, and his voice was almost too faint, his dressing gown almost too elegant. Nevertheless he always gave me the impression of being a water colour drawing of the sage of Croisset that whilst it was still wet had been nearly bleached with blotting paper. . . .

It was, I fancy, a sort of nervousness engendered by this particular pallor that prevented my making any

effort to see any more of the author of "Esther Waters."
I called on him once more at his request and the visit
was even more of a failure. As I have said I had asked
him to give me something for the *English Review*. That
had been before Marwood and I had actually started
that periodical. His first words were:

"Gosse says I should certainly have nothing to do
with you. . . . What do you want of me?"

I never knew what I had done to Mr.—afterwards Sir
Edmund—Gosse, and I never enquired. It is natural to
dislike the sons of one's early patrons even more than
one dislikes in the end the patrons themselves. That
seems to be a law of humanity and I left it at that.
So I answered Mr. Moore's question. I explained that
Marwood and I wanted the review to contain the best
writing in the world so that naturally one came to Mr.
Moore at a very early date. We had secured promises
of work from Mr. James, Mr. Conrad, Mr. Meredith,
Mr. Swinburne, M. France. . . .

Mr. Moore said;

"Not of old Gosse?"

I said we were prepared to pay any price an author
asked, leaving it to his conscience not to ask much more
than his usual prices so as to leave something for the
others. That had worked very well so far.

He said:

"You must be in possession of gold like the floods of
Pactolus!"

I said: "No. Some authors asked preposterous prices

but some quite distinguished ones asked nothing at all, so it worked very well."

Then he asked me what sort of writing we wanted from him and we got once more to something like icy bickering. It was of course my fault. I had just been reading his reminiscences—"Ave Atque Vale," I think and I had felt such admiration for their beauty of expression and poetry that I said that I liked them infinitely better than anything else he had ever done.

You should never say to a novelist that you prefer his "serious" writings to his fiction though I find that such few novelist friends as I have always say that to me. But novel writing is a sport infinitely more exciting than the other form so that almost all writers would prefer to be remembered by their imaginations rather than by their records. . . .

I made it all the worse by telling that great man that his "Ave Atque Vale" was infinitely more imaginative than "Evelyn Innes." As imaginative even as "Esther Waters"! . . .

I was by then worked into a state of nervous inanity by his mere nearness to me. He was living then in Ebury Street, a neighbourhood that I have always disliked. And I kept looking aside at his pictures and missing what he said.

In the end he said that he was engaged in revising one of his novels but that if I would ask him again in a month or two he might do something for me. I think he really liked the idea . . . but to my lasting shame I forgot to write to him and I never saw him alone again.

I suppose it was his aloofness from life that made one always forget George Moore. I have never met a critic with any pretensions to knowledge of letters who would not acknowledge when challenged that Moore was infinitely the most skilful man of letters of his day. The most skilful in the whole world. . . . Yet in an infinite number of reviews and *comptes rendus* of the literature of the world that I have read—and written—George Moore was almost invariably forgotten. That was due perhaps to the fact that he belonged to no school in England; perhaps to his want of personal geniality, perhaps to something more subtle.

I was walking last night along a cold dark boulevard with a critic possessing a delicate discrimination in letters. He said, talking naturally of Galsworthy:

"He wasn't at least wicked like George Moore. . . ." Then he checked and exclaimed almost in mental distress: "I don't know why I say that George Moore was wicked. I know nothing against him personally. I have never heard anything against him and the 'Brook Kerith' is one of the most beautiful books in the world. But you know what I mean. . . ."

I knew what he meant. It was that something wicked seemed to distil itself from the pages of Moore's books so that whilst you read them you felt, precisely, mental distress. You felt even mentally distressed at merely remembering the writings of George Moore—as if you were making acquaintance with what goes on in the mind behind the glacial gaze of the serpent that is the Enemy of Man. . . .

I will make a personal confession. . . . It has been my fate to be mistaken for—or to be told that I resembled—three men that I particularly disliked resembling. . . . Whenever I have gone to public literary assemblies I have inevitably heard two or three people say: "Here's Gosse!" And two or three others would whisper: "Isn't that man like Oscar Wilde!" That I could just stomach though I should much have disliked to meet the fate of either of those writers. But when the late John Quin, the collector, said to me on our first meeting in Ezra's studio in the rue Notre Dame de Champs:

"Hullo, George Moore, how well you are looking!" I had hard work to refrain from knocking him down. I think I should have knocked him down if he had not had the sense to see that I looked well . . . for George Moore! I had so often been taken for Mr. Moore or told that I resembled him that, by that time; it had become an obsession.

There was nothing of that sort attaching to John Galsworthy. When you thought of him you thought of green fields in the cool, calm, bright weather of George Herbert. He had a sort of Greek aura as of perfect physical motion accompanying measured speculations in a halcyon atmosphere of eternal youth. . . .

I at least have never got over the feeling that he was, as Conrad called him, "young Jack" and I cannot bring myself really to believe that he ever had any perturbations of the spirit though actually I have known him have—and indeed I have accompanied him through, some dark periods. And even at this moment I cannot think of him as other than the Fortunate Youth—happy at once in the lines on which his life was laid and in the occasion of his death. For it is no sorrow to die amidst the still resounding acclamations of a whole planet—and in the same week as George Moore. You may have the feeling that however Fate may deal hereafter with your name you are at least one of twin pillars that were the terminal stones—the portals of an age.

I was some years younger than Galsworthy but he did not publish his first book until six years after I had published mine. In consequence, he being always unobtrusive and I overbearing, I got very early into the habit of considering him, and of treating him, as a much younger man. So that, when I read of his death it was almost as if I had lost a younger brother in the flower of his age.

I first saw him in a sporting club. They told of him there a curious anecdote; the fame of it hung over him like a curious legend so that, though I was not introduced to him for several years, I was accustomed to speculate as to what sort of a fellow he could be.

In those days he was the young man about town—at any rate to all appearances. He had eaten his dinners at the Middle Temple, which every young man of good position then had to do, so that he was an unpracticing barrister. He was moderate in everything, sedulous in the effort to pass unnoticed in the best places where young men about town shew themselves. He had a little bachelor establishment; kept a small stable; drank very moderately and dressed with the careful negligence that was then required of you. So he appeared always to be in harmony with his surroundings. He seemed to sink into his background—on the grand-stand of a good race-meeting, in the stalls of a good theatre, at an afternoon tea in the best of houses—as harmoniously as a thir-teenth-century madonna sinks into its gold background in a dim, twelfth-century, Italian church. He was never-theless marked out—perhaps because of his legend. I have heard elderly colonels say he was not "sound."

I do not know that I ought to tell that story. It is not derogatory to Galsworthy but it probably belongs to someone else and one should not tell other people's stories. But most of the people who once knew it must be dead by now and the tale is infinitely illustrative. It is this:

One night a young man—I think it must have been Earl Bathurst or one of the Bathursts—turned up in that club with another young man—Galsworthy. Bathurst wanted to borrow a fiver from somebody. The two had been to the Derby and had done rather well. In the train with them, coming back, there had been a thimble-rigger. Galsworthy had been perfectly aware that the fellow was a swindler. But he obstinately backed him-self to discover under which thimble was the pea—which was of course under none. . . . With the grim persistence that was the main note of his character he had backed himself, doubles or quits against the thim-ble-rigger and his confederates. He had lost his watch and chain, tie-pin, signet ring. So they had come to that

44

club to borrow money to redeem the watch which had sentimental associations for Galsworthy while the thimble-rigger waited in the hall. Bathurst had eventually got the money out of the club porter.

Grim persistence. . . . That was what it was. Galsworthy thought that the trick *ought* to be exposed for the benefit of the public. . . . "Ought": that was even then his great word!

His face seemed to be always just about to smile, the lines of a smile being always about his lips. Actually he smiled a real smile—the product of an emotion rather than of a generally benevolent attitude—only rarely. He was "Devonshire," and proud of being Devonshire and proud that the chief attribute of the Devonshire man is a surface softness under which lies the grimmest of obstinacies—the velvet glove on a hand of marble. . . . Nevertheless your main impression of Galsworthy would be his smile. . . . And his softness.

In his physique too he had those characteristics. He appeared gentle and inactive as if with a continuous pensiveness. But he had in his youth muscles of iron and, in athletics, the same persistence.

I do not suppose I shall ever forget my surprise just after my first introduction to him. It was at the Pent when Conrad was stopping with me. I was prepared for something remarkable by Conrad's really radiant expression when he said: "Jack wants to know if he may come down." For some days I heard then of "Jack." I do not know that I even heard his surname for Conrad had a trick of taking it for granted that you must know everyone whom he knew. Then, at the station appeared the smiling being of the sporting club. . . . That was already an astonishment.

I was driving a waggonette with a pretty good mare. He swung his grips over the side of the cart and would not get in because, he said, he wanted some exercise. The road from Sandling Junction goes immediately up a very steep bluff so he walked beside the box-seat, conversing as Englishmen of his station converse . . . about the properties on either side of the road—the Laurence Hardie of Sandling; the Deedes of Saltwood Castle; Earl Sondes a little farther on.

At the top of the bluff he would not get in. He said:

"Drive on. That will be all right. I need some exercise."

I said:

"If you mean to walk there is a kissing-gate in the hedge after the next ventways. On the left. . . . You cater the field. You'll be on Pent Land. You'll see the house."

He said:

"That will be all right. Drive on. I want some exercise."

I touched up the mare. She was a pretty good goer, aged, but with a strain of Wilfred Blunt's Arab blood. I did not expect to see that fellow again until a quarter of an hour after I got to the house. . . . But there he was, still beside the box-seat, trotting along with the utmost equanimity. And, as if we had been strolling down Piccadilly he continued conversing . . . about the land of the Pent which is a clayey loam in the bottoms till it runs into the chalk of the Downs; and about how the young partridges were coming on; and about Selby Lowndes the redoubtable Master of the East Kent Hounds who had once had a trencher fed pack in the Cleveland. Englishmen have to know all these things or they are not "sound." So he trotted the mile and a quarter to the Pent. I felt like Maupassant when the head of Swinburne rose out of the Mediterranean beside his canoe and the poet swam to shore beside him conversing joyously of Anacreon. . . . Conrad told me afterwards that Jack had held the mile record at Oxford for several years. That needs persistence.

I remember I once had a sort of portable pulpit built to write at. Someone had told me that the reason why painters usually live to be old men whilst writers die relatively young is that they stand at their work and do not lean over tables, compressing their stomachs and lungs. . . . When Galsworthy saw that pulpit he must have one too for he wanted to live at least as long as I. . . . I gave up my monstrosity in a very short time but he persisted with his for many years. . . . So that the image I have of Galsworthy at work is that of a painter before his easel. In those days he wore a painter's gaberdine when he wrote. He had once the idea of using different coloured pencils or ink for passages of differing character. He was always trying new devices. . . . So there he would be, an erect figure, thin, not very tall, blond, camped in front of his pulpit with a blue pencil between his lips; in his right hand a red pen

47

that he had just taken up and profusion of other pens and pencils and rubbers and gadgets along the ledge in front of him. . . . Poor Jack!

It is sad to have to say: "Poor Jack"! he being no longer there. But it comes naturally because whenever Conrad mentioned him in later years it was always as "Poor Jack." That was because Galsworthy was so worried about his writing. It did not go very fast in the early days. The life social still had its lure for him; he was not very sure of where, as a writer, he was going. He was grimly determined to produce novels but he was at first hampered and a little depressed by the influence of Conrad who knew well enough where *he* was going. . . . "Jocelyn" is a palish study in the manner of the early Conrad—the Conrad of the "Outpost of Progress." Then Turgenev gripped Galsworthy as he must grip every serious writer and he produced the "Villa Rubein" which is a very charming, young book, with, as it were, the face of Turgenev smiling up through every page. . . .

He still however worried in our Campden Hill days. His friends and parents jeered at the idea of his writing. His father was a Tartar. I lived at one time next door to him and that was what the servants said of the old gentleman. Galsworthy *père* and *mère* separated, tired of seeing one another, at very advanced ages. There was something pixy-ish and hard about both those old people; the father ferocious, the mother young for her age, flighty, with bright coloured bonnet ribbons.

It was not a usual stock, that from which Galsworthy came.

Nevertheless, say in 1903, he still let social considerations weigh in a major degree in the arrangements of his life though the Arts began to occupy more of his thoughts. One of his sisters, a few yards away on the Hill was *mélomane* and gave wonderful concerts; the other was married to Sauter, the tough, dynamic, Austrian painter and lived just down the Hill. Campden Hill, in the royal borough of Kensington, was like a high class Greenwich Village in which all the artists should be wealthy, refined, delicate and well-born. It was high in the air. In its almost country roads you met ladies all of whom wore sable coats—or at least sable stoles; and admirable children all bursting with health; and Whistler and Abbey and Henry James. . . .

I lived myself in a house on the very top of the Hill, Galsworthy in a stable just on the other side of the great, covered-in reservoir. It was of course a converted stable; very beautifully appointed and suitable for a young bachelor of means and slightly romantic tastes. Here he used to give me those admirable English breakfasts two or three times a week to the accompaniment of gleaming silver and hissing tea urns with, as I have said, the sunlight shining in through the open door. For myself I have always hated comfort and all its accompaniments but here something ascetic mingled with the tempered luxury and I used to sit there feeling like a pleased fish wife who had got into the basement of a palace. . . .

Galsworthy however was still worried. He was preparing to break with Society but his life was still an energetic round of concerts, receptions, race-meetings, richer studio teas, theatres, dinners and the rest. We used to dispute very vigorously—mostly about writing, I being clamorous and he very determined over his kidneys and bacon. I used to declare that a writer can learn no more of Turgenev than he can of Shakespeare, both being temperaments rather than writers with methods to be studied. That used to pain Galsworthy. He would declare that no one could avoid being benefited by contact with that temperament of infinite pity and charity. . . .

There came the mental crash. He crossed his Rubicon. I can place the very agitating day and after that Galsworthy was no more the young bachelor about town even in appearance. Nor was he any longer Poor Jack. He had got religion and his path was plain.

He never looked back and gradually our ways parted. I still saw a great deal of him. We still lived close together but now down the Hill. I could see the beggars and hardcases from my windows, going from my office of the *English Review*, round the corner, to Galsworthy's doorstep that was never without its suppliants. My hardcases were all of the literary sort, such as come to the office of a journal and go on to a Galsworthy. But he had innumerable others. His charities were inexhaustible.

He was helpful with the *English Review* but I always thought he was not very approving. That organ

was too distinctly literary and in no way either philan-
thropic or propagandist of social re-organisation. I used
to go for morning constitutionals with him and Gilbert
Cannan. Occasionally with Ezra too, across the park to
Hyde Park Corner. And always Galsworthy would be
rather wistfully suggesting that I should print the work
of someone who wanted to reform something—the poor
laws, the relations of the sexes. . . . Marwood also was
too Tory for him. He used to spit with indignation
over Galsworthy's humanitarian suggestions so that my
life was not very easy when Marwood walked with us
and when the blameless tool of the Reformers who had
by then got the control of the *Review*, Galsworthy, was
induced to sit in my editorial chair, I had really a difficult struggle to prevent Marwood's assaulting him.
. . . Galsworthy of course was completely innocent of
any intrigue and the incident caused no shadow to fall
between us. I had gone for a week's rest—which I immensely needed—to the countryside in Normandy. And
those Reformers having already a mortgage on the
Review had told Poor Jack that I had left the country
for good. . . . It was curious the difference there was
between his proposal for a number and that that I eventually printed. You would have said that it was impossible that Literature could have two such opposed faces.

The difference was that Galsworthy believed that
humanity could be benefited by propaganda for virtue
of a Christian order whereas I believed that humanity
can only be brought to ameliorate itself if life as it is
is presented in terms of an art. And the business of Art

is not to elevate humanity but to render. . . . Those
are the two schools of thought that have eternally divided humanity and no one in the end will ever know
which will win out. It is not even certain that the
Eighteenth Amendment will be repealed—and the
Eighteenth Amendment was brought about by exaggerated imaginative statement.

Yet it used to fill me with amazement to see Galsworthy at work—the grim persistence with which he
made point after point, the dog-like tenacity with which
he held to his thesis. He would ponder for hours and
hours. Then the little rabbits would creep out to die
after the battues; the law-parted lovers would feel the
thumbscrews pinching tighter; the convicts batter on
their cell doors until the cruel stupidity of men and
their institutions was shown at its apogee—and beyond.

I think that that method is better for plays than for
other forms and possibly at long last it is by his plays
that Galsworthy will be remembered. At any rate for
me the "Silver Box" and "Joy" were things of rapturous delight when I first saw them and they remain
like bright patches in my memory after more than
lustres. In them his extraordinary genius for contrasting
antithesis with antithesis—his extraordinary gift for
sticking to a situation till the last shred of drama was
extracted from it—was never thrown away and never
grew monotonous. And the structure even of his propaganda plays was almost always impeccable.

He could even keep within his *cadre* with sureness
of touch. I remember that after the second performance

of the "Silver Box" he was a good deal worried about the curtain to one of his scenes—the one in which a child is heard crying, outside the house in which its mother has been arrested. He thought that this did not come over—that there was no *clou* to the scene. He sketched several endings and rejected them. The point was that a middle class woman, amiable but insensitive had had the mother of the child arrested on the wrongful suspicion of having stolen the silver cigarette box. The child finding that its mother did not come home hung to the railings outside the open window and cried for her and the scene ended on the sound of the wailing.

I finally suggested that the middle class woman might send the child out a slice of cake. For the first time in his life I found Jack become really heated. He came out of the depths of his abstraction to say that that was an atrocious suggestion. The woman was a decent, well-brought-up mother. Her maternal instincts—the maternal instincts of any woman—would let her know that a slice of cake was not a fitting substitute for a mother's care. . . . So perhaps his detachment from the class that he so constantly held up to scorn was not so absolute as it might seem. . . . He once told me that never, in his man about days, had he been absolutely in the inner circle. Something always marked him off a very little and he had always the feeling that he was a fish in not quite the right water. But the habits of thought of a youth spent in an atmosphere of so strong a flavour remain singularly in your subconsciousness.

On one of our walks I asked him—just when we were

crossing a road—what had become of someone we had both known years before.

He exclaimed:

"Oh, poor man, his sister's married a working man!"

But as soon as we were on the opposite sidewalk he said determinedly:

"Of course there is no reason why one's sister should not marry a working man. But with poor Dash's notions it is very disagreeable to him."

I do not mean that there was anything of the hypocritical about him. Heaven knows nobody could be further from the English governing class frame of mind than I am. I daresay if it were ascertainable that it might well appear that I am much more alien to that frame of mind than even Galsworthy ever was, if in a different direction. But if anyone suddenly asks me even now what is my opinion of someone I find myself replying with an estimate that is astonishingly like that of the great English public school that it was my privilege to attend.

I will try to put on paper the occasion of one of his real smiles. I came in on him once; in the later days in his house in Addison Road. He was reading a cutting from some paper. He had a humorous expression and read onto the end without speaking to me. He said:

"Those poor devils of penny-a-liners! What won't they say and where won't they get it from!" He tossed the slip to me.

The cutting described the early struggles with poverty, the long years of want of recognition; the bit-

ter sufferings that, according to the writer, Galsworthy
had gone through.

It was when he took it back and looked over it again
that he smiled—the real smile coming out over the one
that was always there, coming out very slowly as if the
emotion came from somewhere very deep and irresisti-
bly moved his features. He said:

"Considering that I never had less than several thousands a year I can't be said to have suffered. . . . And
I don't believe I was ever conscious of waiting. . . ."

It comes into my head that I did on another occasion
see him in a real temper. You might call it topical, but
it happened many years ago. He had remembered after
paying his income tax that he had not included a quite
considerable sum that he had received for near Eastern
productions of several of his plays. He had written to
the income tax authorities that he was prepared now
to pay this sum. They had answered that the accounts
for the year were closed and nothing could be done
about it. He had replied by sending a cheque for the
amount. . . . He had received a letter, returning the
cheque, and saying that the Lords Commissioners had
ordered that his correspondence must now cease. . . .

At that he was enraged. He asked: How could the
country be run? How could justice be done? How was
it possible to do anything with officials who took serious
matters with that levity. He went on being angry about
it and worrying officialdom about the matter for a long
time. His concern was so great because, he said: How
was it possible that the poorer classes should not be

unduly burdened when the comparatively wealthy like himself could escape as easily—even involuntarily!

I will conclude with a little, gay story.

I had gone to lunch at the Galsworthys' one day when he had had to go out to meet a theatre manager before the meal was quite finished. The door closed behind him and Mrs. Galsworthy sprang up and said:

"Now we're going to have treat!"

Galsworthy kept an admirable table but it was one relatively chaste when compared with my reprehensible culinary feats with garlic and condiments. So Mrs. Galsworthy produced from secret recesses in the sideboard a very wrapped-up Camembert. And when it was unwrapped. . . . Well, it was a Camembert! . . . She said:

"Poor Jack doesn't forbid *me* to eat things like this. But nothing so pagan must ever appear when he's at table."

When the cheese was quite unwrapped and oozing over our plates poor Jack put his head around the door with his slow, friendly air of reconnoitring. He wrinkled up his nose, smiled as if he had caught two children stealing jam.

"Isn't that," he asked, "what you would call being caught *en flagrant délit*? . . . Or is it fragrant delights?"

So he was not above making a pun on occasion.

The last time I saw him was at one of those attempts to establish an entente between Anglo-Saxon and French writers over which he admirably shed his aureole. Curiously enough it was in Paris. The French loved him for his admirable presence, his old world dignity, his aureole and his charming French that was hesitant only because of his modesty. And standing, dominating that crowd of hard-shelled Gallic writers as a white swan might float over an assembly of black herons he told them that if he had any skill in letters, it came from France. It came from a long discipleship to Flaubert and Maupassant and Anatole France . . . and to Turgenev and Conrad who themselves had learned all that they knew of writing from French writers.

It was curious and touching to hear that valiant pronouncement.

PART ONE

CHAPTER TWO

T HERE WAS ONE POOR FELLOW—A MOST HOR-
rible physical mess. I used to see him from the windows
fluttering like a smashed crow from my doorstep to
Galsworthy's. In 1911 that would be. I do not remember his name; it was something like Regan and his was
one of those cases that neither Galsworthy nor I could
do anything to relieve, rack our brains how we might.
He had one of those distorted faces that give the Irish
a reputation for humour though I never heard him make
a joke. He smelt of course of whiskey and his crushed
limbs were hidden in the folds of a black Inverness.

He had been for many years a reporter on a Sheffield
paper; then, for more years, on a Brighton afternoon
sheet. His record had been admirable. One day he had
been riding a bicycle on the Downs behind the city,
after some country news story. An automobile had
come on him from behind and passed over him. It had
broken both his legs and both his arms and had gone
on without doing anything to help him. All this as well
as the excellence of his character was confirmed by the
journalists' benevolent association to which I subscribed.

He had been for more than two years in hospital and

for two years more in a home. Now he could just drag himself along—a man of perhaps thirty-five. . . . During his absence from it one of those shake-ups that characterise the English journalist world had taken place. Provincial papers had been merged one into the other; London journals had split up or had disappeared. He found himself alone in a completely changed world. I don't know how he had been employed before he came to see me. Certainly he had acquired a craving for drink. How should he not have?

I was at that time running what appeared to be an opulent monthly, so I was being inundated with hard cases and the habitually mendicant. It was really a nightmare. Men came looking like blackmailers, looking like police sergeants, like Montmartre poets, like sailors ashore. They all began by saying:

"I'm a journalist myself, Mr. H——."

As such they tried to sell poems, or the family secrets of distinguished personages, or balls of opium or adolescent chorus girls. Usually I sent them on to the journalists' benevolent society. That may seem a cold-blooded course but I was overwhelmed with work and even to deal with the major hard cases was by itself exhausting. Henry James once said that I possessed an unrivalled knowledge of the *bas fonds* of journalism. I certainly did by the time that inundation had passed over me.

But Regan's seemed to me to be the hardest of all cases, for he was a man of intelligence and great shrewdness. Unfortunately his journalistic brilliance was of a sort that I could not employ in the *English Review*. I got Mr. Anderson Graham, the editor of *Country Life* to promise him a job. Mr. Graham was a great, kindly, grey, homespun Scot. He had plucked the fine gowans of Edinburgh nights with Henley and Stevenson and Whibley and that gang so he was not to be frightened, as others might have been, of addicts to *usquebaugh*, and the stories about him were innumerable. In his more expansive moments he used to say that, in the office, they called his periodical *Pig & Piffle* and edited it in their sleep. I was once calling on him when a reporter from the *Daily Mail* came in to ask if *Country Life* would oblige by saying when cub-hunting began. Cub-hunting is the process by which supernumerary fox-cubs are chopped out of coverts and young hounds blooded in the early autumn before regular fox-hunting begins and it opens at different dates in various hunts according as the corn crops are off the furrows. But no one in the office of that agricultural journal, nor to all appearances did any one in the offices of the great metropolitan daily, know that cardinal fact of the country year. In those days, yearly, on the 12th of August, the "festival of St. Grouse," the *Daily Mail* used to announce that the crack of the rifle would be heard on the Scottish moors. . . . But I am bound to confess that once when a detachment of the Welsh were stationed outside some French coverts near a place called Béhencourt I have disgracefully shot pheasants, at night, with a Morris-tubed rifle. . . . I suppose that now I shall never again be able to go to England!

At any rate *Country Life* was the first English journal to find that when its circulation exceeded a certain figure it lost money. I remember Graham's perplexity at being faced with that dilemma. Circulation they had to have in order to attract advertisers; but when the bulk of advertisements became enormous the paper began to cost more than a shilling to produce and the postage rate went up. . . .

We shared sub-editors, Anderson Graham and I, in the golden and decorative person of Mr. Douglas Goldring, then and still, the most elegant and youthful of traveller-novelists. So I had hoped that with Graham and Goldring and myself to keep an eye on him poor Regan might hold down his job.

But he never turned up in the offices of *Country Life*. Instead, after a week's drunk and a week to sober himself he once more visited me. He was bone-sober, reasonable, cajoling and his Inverness coat was torn. . . . It was then that I discovered that he was also tapping poor Galsworthy. It was obvious that with the small sum I had given him to get presentable clothes for his job he could not have paid for a whole week's alcohol. So I begged Galsworthy not to give him any more money without warning me; got someone in the office to take him and order some clothes from my own tailor, paid his bill for a week in advance at a temperance hotel and rang up Lord Northcliffe. Lord Northcliffe was the most generous of men and was perfectly ready to give Regan money. He said that since Regan had worked and had incurred his wounds in the service of papers that he, Northcliffe, had acquired it would be only decent to provide for him. But at last I persuaded him to give Regan a job on one of his domestic-interest papers.

For that week Regan wrote brilliantly about suburban festivities and under-linen. Then he was paid—and wrecked the office with the fireman's hatchet from the corridor. I tried him in my own office for a week—carrying out proofs. He left all the proofs undelivered except for one batch that he took to the printer's. At the printer's he nearly murdered a young compositor. I handed him over then to Galsworthy.

Galsworthy believed that the country would cure him and got him jobs successively with a gamekeeper, in a park lodge and as several things that I have forgotten. The end was always the same. As soon as he touched money the drink drove him to commit light-hearted but ferocious outrages so that it was a tribute to the goodness of heart of humanity that none of his victims ever handed him over to the police. And there was no way out of it. He was in perpetual physical pain from which only drink would give him oblivion. Once Galsworthy put him with a country doctor who doped him with cocaine or morphia for a longish period. But in addition to that he had to have drink. At last he was run over and killed by a heavy motor-lorry as he lay at night across a narrow country lane, outside a public house. . . .

So, on that early day of 1919, I stood on the kerb by the Campden Hill waterworks and suddenly believed that I saw Regan flutter brokenly in the shadows across the road. There were in those days an infinite number of Regans and for myself I knew that my mind had had both its legs and arms smashed.

London then was no place for me. The London that I had left had been gay, if only with the hectic gaiety that was supposed to distinguish Paris. It had shot defiant rays of light to the peak of Heaven and beneath them one had gone with insouciance on careless errands. One had had little sense of the values of life if indeed one had the sense that life had any values at all.

Now it was as if some of the darkness of nights of air-raids still hung in the shadows of the enormous city. Standing on the Hill that is high above that world of streets one had the sense that vast disaster stretched into those caverns of blackness. A social system had crumbled. Recklessness had taken the place of insouciance. In the old days we had seemed to have ourselves and our destinies well in hand. Now we were drifting towards a weir. . . .

You may say that every one who had taken physical part in the war was then mad. No one could have come through that shattering experience and still view life and mankind with any normal vision. In those days you saw objects that the earlier mind labelled as *houses*.

They had been used to seem cubic and solid perma-
nences. But we had seen Ploegsteert where it had been
revealed that men's dwellings were thin shells that could
be crushed as walnuts are crushed. Man and even Beast
. . . all things that lived and moved and had volition
and life might at any moment be resolved into a scarlet
viscosity seeping into the earth of torn fields. . . . Even
omnibuses had picked their lumbering ways, crowded
with obfusc humanity, dulled steel and bronze, between
pits and hillocks of the tortured earth until they found
the final pit into which they wearily subsided. It would
be long before you regarded an omnibus as something
which should carry you smoothly along the streets of
an ordered life. Nay, it had been revealed to you that
beneath Ordered Life itself was stretched, the merest
film with, beneath it, the abysses of Chaos. One had
come from the frail shelters of the Line to a world that
was more frail than any canvas hut.

And, more formidable than the frailness of the habita-
tions was . . . the attitude of the natives. We who returned—and more particularly those of us who had gone
voluntarily and with enthusiasms—were like wanderers
coming back to our own shores to find our settlements
occupied by a vindictive and savage tribe. We had no
chance. We were like poor Regan after his four years
in hospital. The world of men was changed and our
places were taken by strangers.

As to my own fate I was relatively unmoved. Very
early in life I had arrived at the settled conviction:
Homo homini lupus—man is a wolf to his fellow men.

And I have always believed that, given a digging fork and a few seeds and tubers, with a quarter's start, I could at any time wrest from the earth enough to keep body and soul together. I thought so when I was twenty; I thought the same when I stood on that Campden Hill kerb and I am again preparing to set out on that adventure at this moment of writing with the world seeming to crumble around us.

I wrote then, in the columns of that lunatic journal, that England had suffered more, at least in her mentality, than any other of the nations that had shared in the war. . . . We fought in the beginning and for more than half of the duration of the fighting with volunteer soldiers. Thus in 1919 England found herself in the position of Bulgaria at the end of the Balkan War of 1913. . . . Bulgaria had formed a battalion of *élite* troops out of all the educated men in that relatively illiterate country. This battalion she hurled against the barbed wire of the impregnable Turkish entanglements round Tchatalja. It was entirely wiped out and Bulgaria found herself deprived of *intelligentsia* and almost of men who could read and write.

In 1919 England was in an almost parallel position. It was not her *intelligentsia* that she had lost. They had *embusqued* themselves in government offices, in munition works, in prisons or in the posts vacated by fighting men. . . . But the most vigorous and alert of the young men had been killed or mangled—physically and mentally. It had been impossible for a young man sound physically and of healthy imagination not to volunteer in the years between 1914 and 1917. Those who remained and filled all the posts in 1919 were the physically unfit and the mentally frigid. So those poor boys came back; maimed and bewildered to a world administered by those born to detest them. . . .

When I stood on the kerb watching the shade of Regan creep past on the opposite side of the street I had just come back from a police-court. One of the younger officers of my battalion had been sentenced to a month's imprisonment. . . . At the beginning of the war he had been in a First Class Government Office. He was a remarkable Greek scholar and possessed an extraordinary, sardonic wit. He lost a leg and an eye at Gheluvelt. His Government Office refused to re-employ him because he had lost an eye. He might, they said, lose another, poring over papers in their halls. Then he would become a charge on the peaceable taxpayer. The taxpayer must be protected from men who had chosen to endanger their eyes and limbs. It was a First Class Office.

On being demobilised my poor young friend had gone with a number of other young, just-demobilised officers to a Regent Street café. Its doors of revolving glass are regularly smashed every Boat Race night by Oxford or Cambridge undergraduates. He and his young friends, all from one University or the other, had duly smashed those revolving doors—to commemorate the end of a Boat Race of a larger kind. The regular punishment for that offence is forty shillings or a month. It has been that since shillings were shillings. The magistrate gave the other young fellows the option of paying the fine. My young friend he sentenced to a month's hard labour—not because he had been a ring-leader but because he had two decorations for gallantry. The magistrate said that the public must be protected from a brutal and licentious soldiery. He used that actual *cliché* phrase. If you consider what that poor young man had been . . . protecting when he had lost his eye, his foot and his sense of the fitness of things you will find that those words are of a singular piquancy. The young man however went to the bad. He became a hopeless case. Worse than Regan.

I suppose the fate of England would not have been much better or England truer to her old self if public opinion had insisted on saving for the public service the poor flotsam of its best blood, its best sinews and best, normal, brains. Yet it would have been better. . . .

That savage, that hysterical determination to extirpate —as rats—the men to whom the very same public had been on its knees but a few months before . . . that St. Bartholomew's Day engendered in its victims a cynicism of the betrayed and in the others a still more fatal cynicism of the traitor that were alike of almost infinite detriment to the poor old ship of the British state.

That day, immediately after seeing that poor boy martyrised I wrote for my lunatic journal some comments on his case. That periodical welcomed it, as you might say, with cheers and tears but on the next day ceased to exist. The rest of the press naturally refused to print those words. They were engaged in applauding the magistrate for his courageous pronouncement. Thus those words never saw the light. I will here summarise what I said. It was by way of being a grave warning. . . .

England had paid a terrible toll of the most English of its youth. In Notre Dame there was—there still is—a small tablet not much larger than a sheet of the *Times* of New York or London. It was surmounted by the pretty royal arms of England and her Dominions and announced that it was there to the glory of God and to the memory of more than a million British dead who lay for the most part in the fields of France. . . . It is a fine piece of English swank that that solitary tribute should be so small and so restrained. It is the fitting tailpiece to the answer to the Scrap of Paper speech and if England had compassed nothing else she would be justified of her national and emotional rectitude. For myself I never come in the shadows on that lettering and those symbols in gold, azure and vermilion without feeling more emotion than—even in shadows—my British upbringing will let me express. . . . Those miserable things I myself had witnessed!

More than a million is a great many men. To them you may add twice as many more of those who were mentally warped by mutilations, rough living and subsequent betrayal. Add some couple of million children that those dead youths might have had. (I am dwelling on factors making for change in national characteristics and fortunes and we may postulate a certain inheritance of character in children.) So you arrive at a people

68

destined to be very markedly changed in aspect as in functioning in the comity of nations. You will arrive at a commonwealth whose youth will be cynical and lack initiative and whose rulers will be wearied *intelligentsia*. They will, these last, be theorists . . . and it was the very quality of such merits as England possessed that her lawmakers had always been empiricists. Pre-war England had not been a very satisfactory affair. She had been distinguished in her intellectual as in her material harvests by the dead hand of vested interests. Questioning and innovation had been very difficult. But there had been at least some youth, some intellectual clarity, some carelessness, some iconoclasts. And her laws had been made for men relatively free.

Most of that was to go. For a generation England was to sink back—I am quoting from the memory of my article—into a slough in which despondency and vested interests however changed in incidence must strangle all initiative. You cannot kill off a million of your most characteristic young men, cram your work-houses and gaols with all that they will hold of the rest and for ever disillusionise those that remained outside those institutions—you could not do all that without at least modifying your national aspect. A nation—any body of men—cannot flourish either as empire builders or poets, or in any department of life that lies between those extremes without cherishing its illusions. And in England of those days all the great words upon which are founded the illusions of life lay under the shadow of reprobation. . . . In London Town of those days it was more than unfashionable to speak with commendation of Faith, Loyalty, Courage, Perseverance, God, Consols, the London Police Force or the Union Jack.

It was a matter of reaction. War time England had been like a lunatic asylum. To go from London with its yells, posters, parades and exhortatory beanfeasts to Paris, dead, grey, silent, overshadowed, had been to go from a parrot house in Coney Island to a Cathedral cloister. The reaction had to come in both cases. In Paris—even as in Berlin—the reaction must be against negationalism. That we shall witness. In London it had to be towards it.

I got as far as that in my article. . . .

. . . I don't know that the large words Courage, Loyalty, God and the rest had, before the war been of frequent occurrence in London conversations. But one had had the conviction they were somewhere in the city's subconsciousness. . . . Now they were gone. So at least I felt, standing on the Campden Hill kerb. . . .

I don't, again, know that large words in conversations are indispensable to make me happy. I knew that, at that moment, all was over between me and London. I had loved that vast, quiet agglomeration as few men had loved it. If I had never been—except for the duration of the war—English, even when buried in the deep woods of Kent, I had always been a Londoner. A Cockney. Born within sound of Bow Bells and proud of it. . . .

You can be a Londoner and not in the least English,

just as you can be a New Yorker and remain quite un-American. It is curious.

. . . Years and years ago I was talking to Mr. E. V. Lucas. I hope he is now Sir E. V. L. . . . We were lying on the grass at Kent Hatch, looking out over the great view that goes away into West Kent. . . . Mr. Lucas was then publishing his Edition of Charles Lamb and I was abusing Lamb and De Quincey and Hazlitt and all the tribe of English essayists. I was saying that it was with their works—and particularly with those of Charles Lamb—that the English people anodyned what passed for their brains so that Pure Thought was a thing unknown in all that green country. It comes to me suddenly and for the first time after thirty years that I was not tactful!

But Mr. Lucas seemed most amiable. Like all English humorists he was of a mournful and taciturn cast. On the very finest days he carried an umbrella. He listened for a long time to me, slim, dark, puffing at his pipe and looking out over the view.

I said:

"Damn it all, Lucas, you are an intelligent fellow. How can you read this buttered-toast-clean-fire-clear-hearth-spirit-of-the-game-beery-gin-sodden sentimentalism? What can you see in it? For Heaven's sake tell me what you see in it!"

Mr. Lucas let ten puffs of his pipe eddy away towards the great, green-grey vale below us. . . . I kept on with invectives, asking him to tell me. Why wouldn't he at least tell me?

Between the tenth and eleventh of his next set of puffs he said:

"Because you wouldn't understand."

I said:

"Damn it all, why shouldn't I understand? Has not your servant eyes? Has not your servant ears? A tongue to savour meats? A belly for their digestion?"

Mr. Lucas gave four puffs at his pipe. He said:

" 'Belly' is not a very nice word."

I said fiercely:

"But why can't I stomach Lamb and Hazlitt and the whole boiling? Why?"

He removed his pipe from his lips to say:

"Because you use words that are not quite nice. Charles Lamb would never have used them. You remember that Thackeray speaking of Lamb, removed his hat and whispered 'Saint Charles.' "

I said:

"Lamb was a drunkard. His sister committed a murder. Wainwright, another English essayist, committed a murder and was hung. I never was drunk in my life. I never attempted to murder anybody. I was never hung. I detest buttered toast. Is that why I do not appreciate Elia? Or is there another reason?"

Mr. Lucas did something with his pipe. Perhaps he put it back in his mouth. At any rate his pipe like that of later British prime ministers was an integral and active part of the landscape. I said insistently:

"Why—cannot—I—appreciate—Charles—Lamb?"

Mr. Lucas, always the gentlest of human beings, said more gently than usual:

"Because you are not really English."

That hit me in the face like a discharge from a fireman's hose.

I said:

"Why am I not English? I play cricket not quite as well as you do but with as much pleasure. I play golf more often if not so well. I went to as great a public school as yours. I take a cold bath every morning. I know as much about flower-gardening and more about kitchen gardening, sheep, the rotation of crops, hops, roots and permanent pasture. I drop my aitches before words derived from the French. My clothes are made by a Sackville street tailor who made for my great-grandfather and has never fitted me too well. I never let anybody see me writing and deprecate as far as possible the fact that I follow an art. I shave every morning and have my hair cut every fortnight at the proper shop in Bond Street. Why then, am I not English?"

Mr. Lucas said with dejection:

"Because you do not appreciate . . ." He paused; I supplied:

"Charles Lamb?"

He said:

"No, I am thinking." He added: "*Punch*."

I exclaimed heatedly that I was the sole owner of the recipe for the world famous Prince Regent's brew.

It had been all that my great uncle Tristram Madox had had to leave my grandfather.

Mr. Lucas said that he did not mean the beverage. He meant the journal. A number of Englishmen had not read or heard of Lamb but no one who was not English could appreciate him. Equally no one who could not appreciate him after they had read him could be English. But every Englishman read, appreciated and quoted that journal unceasingly.

I daresay the diagnosis was correct. . . .

Till that day in 1898 I had never given the matter of my own nationality a thought. I gave it very little after that. There remained in my subconsciousness a conviction that must have grown stronger—that I was not English. Not English at all, not merely "not really English." I never had much sense of nationality. Wherever there were creative thinkers was my country. A country without artists in words, in colours, in stone, in instrumental sounds—such a country would be forever an Enemy Nation. On the other hand every artist of whatever race was my fellow countryman—and the compatriot of every other artist. The world divided itself for me into those who were artists and those who were merely the stuff to fill graveyards. And I used to feel in the company of those who were not artists the same sort of almost physical, slight aversion that one used, during the war, to feel for civilians.

I do not apologise for these dicta. Humanity must divide itself into capillary groups or the Arts and the Crafts must die. If the blacksmith ceased to say: "By

hammer and hand all Art must stand" or if the road-
mender no longer boasted: *"Les cantonniers ce sont
des bons enfants,"* we should have atrocious roads and
lame vehicles whose axles break in their ruts . . . and
indeed, since, say, bankers say worse than hang of
artists why should artists take it lying down?

That became my settled conviction an immense number of years ago. I remember writing it in a diary that
I kept in the washstand in the top back bedroom of my
grandfather—the artist's house. That was before I was
eighteen. "Every artist is my fellow-countryman," I
wrote—so early did that flame of patriotism burst out
in me. . . . Mr. Lucas had supplied the corollary. . . .

That was hardly necessary. Englishmen of both camps
declared—the one side with complacency, the other
with dejection—that none of the great artists of that day
was pure English. Conrad was a Pole, James an American, Hudson an American born in La Plata, Meredith
a Welshman, Yeats an Irishman, Whistler an American,
Sargent the same. Even Thomas Hardy was popularly
credited with French ancestry. . . . And indeed the
Englishman—the *homme moyen sensuel*—was more and
more assuming the attitude of the Imperial Roman
whose works of art were all produced by Greek slaves.
The tendency had begun even earlier indeed—with the
Art of Music. It was not merely conceded: it was part
of a passionate national belief that no Englishman could
be anything so effeminate as a musician—and that led
to the equally passionate conviction that if, for your
private ends, you desired to listen to music it must be

composed and purveyed by some sort of unwashed foreigner. With the acknowledgment of the French Impressionists it appeared evident that the plastic arts too were the province of the lesser breeds without the law —the people who do not appreciate Mr. Lucas's favourite journal. Writing was on the run.

It was the passion of Germany in those days to be able to explain that every great man and especially every great artist was of Teutonic descent. The discovery that Dante, as a supporter of the Guelfs was really a German and that the real name of Bertran de Born was Bernstein van Bornhofen caused little emotion in the shires. But, in the suburbs, great enthusiasm attended the announcement that Rossetti was really a German. "Rossetti" means "little red head" and everyone with a small red head to be found in Italy is obviously Teutonic. And when it came to the turn of Shakespeare—the spear is an Allemannic weapon and everyone whose ancestors shook spears is of German descent!—then indeed a sigh of relief went up from the Land's End to Berwick. . . .

I am writing much more than half seriously. The normal Englishman did in those days—say at the time of the Boer War or during the Fashoda incident—seriously believe that too much study of the Arts would make the youth of England effeminate or that we should fare badly in our next war with France. During the Boer War I lunched after a foursome at Rye with a provincial Lord Mayor and a London Alderman who had passed the chair—who had, that is to say, been Lord Mayor of London. It was shortly after the terrible disaster to

British troops at Spion Kop. The Londoner said that it had been proposed in the Court of Common Council to present a humble petition to Her Majesty praying that, for the duration of the war, all theatres, music halls, public libraries, picture galleries, and other places of amusement might be closed. That was to stimulate recruiting and to force the youth of the nation, to take a sterner view of life whilst employing its leisure exclusively on field sports. The proposal was not accepted by the Councillors of London City. One of them pointed out that, if the theatres were closed, Shakespeare could not be played. Shakespeare was one of the most patriotic of English writers.

The provincial Lord Mayor did not agree. All these fellows were pestilential and should be suppressed at once. They made young men effeminate and vicious. His son, very much against his wishes, had gone to Paris to study French. After the boy's return, the Lord Mayor had found, actually hung on the wall of the boy's bedroom, an indecent photograph. The Lord Mayor had confiscated it and it had caused a sensation when he had passed it round his court of Aldermen. The son had said that it was a photograph of a celebrated Greek statue in a State Museum in Paris—the Venus of something. All the Lord Mayor could say was that if that was the sort of filth they shewed in these places the sooner they were shut for good the better. . . . He was the typical Englishman of those days.

That being so it could not be wondered at if I did not feel very English. Indeed I do not know that I ever had a very strong sense of nationality at all. But till the moment of the early spring of which I am talking—go as far from London as I might or stay away as long as I would—I remained a Londoner. Indeed, once after I had lived in the country a number of years, making only the merest swallow flights to town, I wrote a book about London. It was a monument of affection, was received with rapture and remained for a time a classic.

To be a Londoner is a singular, amorphous state. It is a frame of mind rather than a fact supported by domicile. The passion for London is a passion for vast easinesses and freedoms in which you may swim as in a tepid and tranquil sea. You are surrounded by infinite multitudes yet you know that no eye will be upon you. You know that because you know how completely un-observant you yourself are whilst you walk the streets. I suppose one could say: "Now I will go and take a look around and see what I can see in the highways and byways of London." It would "pay" to explore London and one knows that it would pay. . . . But one never does it. After I had written my classic about the soul of London I discovered that I had never been in the Tower or St. Paul's. . . . Americans will not under-stand that. Every Londoner will.

Nevertheless the fascination of London is that it can be explored. You could not explore New York: you go from place to place. You can know all the ar-rondissements of Paris sufficiently well to have in your mind a bird's-eye view of the city. But who ever car-ried about with him at the back of his brain a bird's-eye view of London? . . . No one. I know my London—the four miles from Hammersmith Broadway to Piccadilly Circus and I have been the mile or so eastward from the Fountain to the Mansion House. . . . But London is ninety miles across. What happens in Battersea Park? Where is Norwood? I have not the ghost of an idea. Perhaps in the one they practice voodoo or play *pelota*; the other may be somewhere near Bogota or Ispahan and have hanging gardens. . . .

So it can be explored. It ought to be explored. Sitting here in Paris I find myself filled with an itch to spend a hundred years strolling between St. Paul's Cray and the Monument—with an English descended American of course to keep my interest alive and tell me all about it. . . . I was not telling the strict truth when I said I had not seen the Tower before I wrote my classic about Dick Whittington's city. I went there once when I was nineteen. But I went with a young lady from Richmond, Va., long, long since dead, and of such a charm, vivacity and accent! So of course I did see the Tower, but not to notice! . . .

It was in that way that I should still have written of this city of my birth until I stood on that kerb in Campden Hill, say on the 1st March, 1919. . . . But as I extended my foot to make that crossing something snapped. It was the iron band around my heart that had hitherto made it London's own. "London only! London only! This train London only!" say the porters beside the trains in Ashford or Darlington or Exeter. . . . That could never again be said of me. When I went to

London after that it would never be *"back* to London."
I should be visiting a town where I had no place and
that knew not me! I was perfectly aware of that. The
motto of the citizens and city of London is *"Domine
dirige nos. . . ."*—"Lord guide us." The arms of Paris
show a ship and beneath it: *"Fluctuat nec mergitur.
. . . "*—"It goes up and down and is not sunk. . . ."
That was thenceforth to be my device and condition.
But now one may be sinking. With all the world and
the dollar.

And I knew then that that was to be my fate. I had
known it, probably, in my deep sub-consciousness perhaps a year before. The conviction had reached the surface of my mind only that afternoon.

That afternoon I had driven in an open taxi with a
lady novelist of position and activity to a garden party
at the house of another lady novelist of extraordinary
position and activity. It may have been the lady who
wrote the *Rosary*, or it may have been Mrs. Annie S.
Swan and the place may have been Ashford, Middlesex,
or it may have been Uxbridge. I suffered from complete
failure of memory for a period after the first battle of
the Somme and my memory of events for some twelve
months after the war is still extremely uncertain. But
I do remember that drive with a queer distinctness as to
one episode. . . . I said, as it were out of the blue:

"I shall leave London now, for good!"

We were passing through some horror of a suburb
with wide streets and a railed-in Green. It comes back
to me now as resembling any raw assemblage of filling

stations and new villas in the Albany Post Road. I do not think that I had ever been in an outer suburb of London before and the squalor of that sight completed my depression.

So because of some mental trick of connection I had said to my companion:

"I shall leave London for good."

The announcement did not much move her but she was polite enough to ask why.

I said—and I didn't in the least mean to say it:

"Because there is no one here I can talk to." I added: "No one understands what I say."

Then I got, I assure you, what at school we used to call a wigging! I was upbraided for my conceit until, if I had cared about the matter, my ears would have tingled. I was told that London was full of the most brilliant men and women imaginable. On account of the sparkle of its society, London was the most exciting place in the world. How then dare I say what I had said? . . . Besides, whilst I had been absent on my nonsensical job a whole crop of lady novelists had sprung up and taken the amazed world by storm. . . . There were Dash and Dashdash and Blank . . . a rush of feminine names that were entirely unknown to me.

My head bowed humbly before the storm. I have not the slightest objection to being called conceited but I do not think that conceit had had anything to do with what had slipped from me at that moment. I hadn't meant to say what I had said. I was unconscious that I had even thought of leaving London for more than a country visit. And I don't think I had even meant to high hat anybody on that occasion though I am perfectly ready to high hat people when I am in the mood. What I think I had really in the back of my mind was the feeling that for my friends—as opposed to my acquaintances—London had become a terribly sad place. The people I had known and liked before the war seemed to have fallen all alike under a curse. Several had died in their beds, many had been killed in the war, some had aged disproportionately; all were terribly impoverished and shabby. Some had been militantly pro-German and I didn't want to see them; some were actually German and still interned so that I could not see them.

My acquaintances on the other hand, when they had not been killed or promoted to incredible elevations, had prospered unbelievably. Except those who had been rich already, they had all become war-rich, whilst those who had been rich now exuded gold from every pore. They provided the brilliant society of which the lady novelist had spoken but it was a society in which, for financial reasons, I could hardly hope to share. My British upbringing had seen to it that I was—as indeed I remain—a determined chop-for-chop man.

Less expensive brilliance was provided by the semi-militantly pro-Germans who had done themselves well in government jobs and by conscientious objectors who emerged from various obscurities and proved themselves heroes indeed to the sound of the gramophone and beer bottles, tankards and pails. I have never seen such hilarious and noisy assemblies, not even in Greenwich Village during Holy Week. I didn't like them much.

And, in the meantime, my late comrades were a prey to every kind of disaster and persecution. I would not like to say how many of the ex-officers of one regiment with whose mess I was intimately acquainted went to prison and God knows how many of its other Ranks were a prey to the vengeance of the Law. And all for small crimes, disturbances of the peace and trivial misdemeanours that, had they been committed by non-combatants would have received the benefit of the First Offenders Act. It was not right and it was driving me mad.

I was talking yesterday to a French comrade of the war. He said: Yes . . . for the year after 1919 they were all mad—all those who had fought. And they were allowed to dissipate their energies and get themselves back to a normal frame of mind. In his riverine *pays* they would get themselves up as Red Indians, get barges, go into town in them, paint shop fronts in astonishing colours, play the wildest practical jokes. All the while the police would go round corners or, with their hands behind their backs, gaze up at the weathercocks on the church steeples. The more sober elders and employers of labour grumbled about the *génération perdue*—the lost generation that would not labour soberly in their workshops. But at the end of the year authority gradually reasserted itself and the young men got tired of playing pranks that grew dull because they were met with no resentment. So that generation became inspired with hope and with ideas of reconstruction. It *conspuéd* Anatole France on his deathbed, eschewed all negational writers . . . and was found again. . . .

But our martyred generation was lost for good—for sheer want of imagination. . . .

The lady novelist in the open taxi was continuing to belabour me for my conceit. We were passing old manor houses, mangled and martyrised, and old roadside oaks, felled. It did not raise my spirits. She was upbraiding me for saying that I found no one to talk to. She supposed that was because I considered myself an "artist." Did I consider that the brilliant Miss Bullock-White, the adorably witty Miss Mary Gordon Prince, the admirable Miss Gwillyson Jones, Miss Brandon Churchill, the poetess, and innumerable other women-writers of whom the crop had blossomed since the war . . .

I interrupted her to say that I hadn't based my allegation that I was not understood on the fact that I considered myself an artist. I was not an artist; I was a broken officer. I expected no quarter on that account. But I claimed the right to have my view of the universe. . . .

She was not of course listening to me. She was asking me to consider how inconsistent I was. I had always been a supporter of Woman's Suffrage. That was what had made her tolerate me in spite of my conceit. Did I then consider that I was subtler than . . . and she reeled off all those names again? Was I so subtle that I could not be understood by *them*?

I continued my own speculations. I said I supposed I was misunderstood by most people I talked to because I took as the basis of all my conversation two axioms: the first was that the artist—the man who added to the thought and emotions of mankind, and he alone—had any divine right to existence. The rest of humanity was merely the stuff to fill graveyards. . . .

At that my companion screamed: really as if she had found herself alone in a taxi with a satyr. She delivered herself of names of the Great. . . . Her friend Lord X—— who owned a thousand papers; her dearest friend's husband, Lord Y—— who had revolutionized cobalt for accumulators, nickel, salt, glass-making; Lord Z—— who had invented x-rays; or even the splendid athlete, Sir Archibald MacGregor, who could go round the tennis court in sixty-eight. . . . Did I consider myself immortal whilst all those were merely common clay? . . .

I said that my second axiom was that it was only by its arts that a nation could be saved—even commercially.

A loud, dull explosion made her scream again. . . . It was only the blowing out of the stump of a cedar in a nearby field that had once been a lawn. She apologised for having—involuntarily—clung to me for protection. Her nerves were still on edge from the late air-raids. . . .

I said that it wasn't to be expected that anyone who took those as his axiomatic facts of life could be understood by people whose axioms were different. If I said that someone was a good man, I meant one who had evolved a new technique in painting or had a keen brain that let him demolish accepted ideas. If the infinite and the sane majority of the inhabitants of London called someone a good man they meant one who subscribed freely to charity for the well-behaved poor, or who read and acted on the work of Mr. Samuel Smiles or did not sleep with his housemaids. . . . So I differed from most Londoners as to the mere meaning of words.

She was saying that it was like my snobbishness to be contemptuous of housemaids. Surely one of the elementary teachings of the Suffragette movement had been that domestic service was as worthy an occupation as any other! Besides there were no housemaids. They had all gone into Armaments. If you could find as much as a tweeny you were lucky. Even house-parlourmaids were unattainable.

. . . So you see it was difficult for me to find comprehension. Even the most *spirituelle* of lady novelists found me incomprehensible—and unpleasant at that. If you are *spirituelle* the incomprehensible must be unpleasant to you. And one may take it that lady novelists are the most comprehending of the sex that claims to be the more subtle.

And I am not sure that it was not the lady novelists of that day—the new crop—that really drove me out of London. I do not know how I got to any literary teas. I was no longer a literary figure and I was battered and mournful. I suppose I had nothing to do and drifting, drifted into old places. And there I had the unpleasant experience that was once R. L. Stevenson's. You remember—I must have told the story several times

86

for I had it from my father who had it from the author of "Treasure Island"—Stevenson in search of colour once dressed up as a working man and so walked the streets. I do not know that he found any adventures but he came upon one definite and mortifying side of life. He found that women completely ignored him. As if he had been invisible! Normally, when he went his way women passing him would at least show a sense of his existence. It might not go as far as what was called a glad eye. But in every woman—as in every man— there is hidden something of the goose-girl who dreams of fairy princes. . . . Dressed as a working man he found none of this and he was mortified. He could only attribute his normal attractions to his clothes!

Well, it was like that with me and the lady novelists. At the literary teas I must have been as a ghost. Occasionally a man—presumably a writer—would address a word to me. They would even ask me if I hadn't once written something. One young fellow—thirtyish and dark—told me he had once read a hunting scene of mine and thought it rather good. I had never written a hunting scene and his breath was very bad. So I did not pursue the conversation. . . .

But for the ladies I did not exist. Not one of them addressed a remark to me. They sat, awfully gazing into the distance. Occasionally they spoke one to the other. If I said anything they stopped talking as if a disagreeable sound were interrupting them. Then they went on with their conversation. It was of course a matter of dress. I was still in uniform. . . .

However, I went to one reception—at Lady Ottilie Murrell's I should think. I knew no one there and was sitting on a scarlet divan beside an unknown man. The gracious hostess with an attendant band was going by. She stopped and pointed one finger at the two of us.

"Those two," she said, "are the only men in the world who can write English."

She passed on. I do not think I had ever seen her before. My divan-mate and I inspected each other with curiosity and suspicion. I mentioned my name and he said that he had never heard of me. Then he said that he was Mr. Ben Hecht. I said I admired his work very much.

I do not want to be taken as denying all lady novelists. It was only the 1919-20 crop that, as far as I know, displayed these characteristics. . . . And why shouldn't they? They were very conscious that their tender hands had preserved for the world the arts and amenities that, the world-over, barbarians like myself had been violating. And they had just come into their own and women had the vote. Why should they not take themselves seriously?

There was however one woman writer whose acquaintance I was privileged to make about this time who took her work more seriously than herself. That was Miss Braddon, the authoress of "East Lynne." . . . I had always had the greatest possible respect for this literary figure. Few novelists of her day had her workmanlike knowledge or could write such sound English —like Cobbett's. And I had a great liking for her son,

Mr.. W. B. Maxwell whose novels had the qualities of hers. . . . Conrad, by the by, used to say that he had learned English from "East Lynne."

She lived, down Richmond way if my memory is not playing me tricks, in one of those old manor houses that are gradually being crowded out by the raw villas that disfigure all the approaches to London. The legend of her youth was that her husband—Maxwell, the publisher—used to take away her riding habit and lock her in her room every day until she had turned out her quota of writing. She preferred hunting in those days.

At eighty-two or thereabouts she naturally no longer rode to hounds but her mind chased thoughts with astonishing nimbleness. In dress and appearance she equally naturally resembled the late Queen Victoria but at eighty she had set herself to learn Greek in order to read Homer "in the original." She was then reading the "Iliad." I hope she finished the "Odyssey" too before she died.

At any rate there she sat, with her family, W. B. Maxwell and his wife, who had once been carried off by a Khan of Afghanistan and held for ransom, and another Mr. Maxwell, who, I think, was a publisher, and with vicars and maids of honour and vaguely theatrical early lights of the stage of the tradition of Mrs. Kendal. There she sat with her court and the Greek words running round in her mind. And her room even was perfection.

There were long, black velvet curtains with gold-edged scallopings a-top, and embroidered fire-shields like the pennants of knights and a great Turkey carpet with a pile into which the feet sank as if into a Scotch lawn. And there was the great ormolu drawing-room table. Upon it was a great album of Views of Venice; on that a slightly smaller Views of Rome; a still slightly smaller Views of Heidelberg, and so, on the top of the pyramid, an ivory model of the Taj Mahal. When Miss Braddon did not talk of the "Iliad" she talked of the Indian mutiny and the first London appearance of Sir Henry Irving. Her voice was low, soft and, as it were, inexorable, as if some of the intolerant youth of the young woman who had ridden to hounds remained at the back of that acute brain. The good sea coal fire shone on gleaming steel and gilt accoutrements. So there you had the clean fire, the clean hearth, and the vigour of the Victorian game.

You might have had worse. I think that in those days I might have read even the essays of Elia. . . .

Regent Street was coming down. . . . I think that that was the final reason for leaving London that I gave to that Lady Novelist in the taxicab—that Regent Street was coming down. . . . As who should say: "Oh, Troy town, tall Troy's on fire!"

She said:

"Why not? Surely Swan and Edgar's have a right to enlarge their premises. Not that I ever got anything there. But you must move with the times."

I think sometimes you shouldn't!

For the young of my days, Swan and Edgar's corner was the throbbing heart of the Kingdom, of the Empire, of the Universe. . . . The sub-lieutenants and second mates keeping their lonely dog-watches whilst reading Miss Braddon beneath the blazing tropical stars, the subaltern in the parched ghârts, the shadeless veldt, the trooper of the N. W. Mounted police—all Mr. Kipling's caboodle that gave us dominion; all these in dreams beheld, not the Hebrides, but that blunt-nosed, three-storied redan that, in all but height, is most resembled by the Flatiron itself. And if, when I was young and far away—and so long ago!—we wanted to show what devils of fellows we were, we would begin our stories: "As I was looking into Swan and Edgar's window. . . . " Why, once in Cornwall, which is as far as you can get from the Circus without falling off into the Atlantic—and it was at the time when King Edward's coronation was put off because of his illness, I heard in a third-class smoker an enormous blue-jacket thus address a trembling and pallid little Cockney clerk. . . . The unfortunate small being had been uttering some small Socialist twitterings. The blue-jacket held a black-haired fist as large as a leg of lamb under the other's nose and said:

"Don't you dare say a word against 'Is Gracious Majesty! Don't you dare!" He turned to the rest of us and said: "Don't we all know what a boiling good sport 'e is? . . . Ain't we all seen 'is brougham waiting on the kerb at Swan and Edgar's corner? . . . Ain't we? . . ."

It was things like that that—under the tremendous hand on far-flung dunes and pines—set in the hearts

of an adoring people the features of an almost wor-
shipped good sport! . . .

And I had heard that they were to tear down and
re-edify Swan and Edgar's, and hideously restore the
Quadrant and convert the Palladian curve of Soane's
Regent Street, with its broad and gracious sweep, into
a congregation of reinforced-concrete mud-pies, so
many-storied that they would make the broad street
look narrow and squalid—and yet so low that they
would have none of the soaring dignity that great
heights will give to roads till they look like cañons
at the foot of great crags! . . . And what made it the
more bitter was that the land of Regent Street belongs
to the Crown. . . . For a little paltry gold that which
should preserve not only the liberties but the beauties
of its lieges was ruthlessly to destroy the most beautiful street in the Empire. . . .

And what made it the more bitter still for me was
this. . . . One evening of a great air-raid I had been
on leave and in pitch black silence had wandered out
of the jetty darkness of Glasshouse Street into the dimness of London's Great White Way beneath the stars.
. . . The white, Greek houses loomed against the
celestial pin-points, like temples, like forums. And it
was as if, awfully, they listened, awaiting doom. . . .

The minute was majestic; it had been as if I were
alone in a vast cave, the heart of a city that had paused
in its beat. . . . And the houses all listening. . . .

PART ONE

CHAPTER THREE

IN THAT SCENE I HAD STOOD LOOKING WITH A sense of awe—as if I had stumbled into unsuspected mysteries. For me houses always seem to be alive, listeners, watching the ways of men with sardonic eyes. . . . And then they had appeared to be afraid. . . . Listening, watching with fear the blaze of the Milky Way. . . .

As Charles Masterman had predicted in 1913, London had indeed once more, after 250 years, heard the roar of foreign guns. Nay, more, she had undergone her baptism of fire.

And it had been no trifling one. At that moment the German plane squadron had disappeared to the Southwest and those houses were listening for its return. It had already smashed many houses and killed a great many people in their cellars. It would smash and kill yet more that night. . . .

In the line we were used to consider that air-raids over London must be trifling enough. But I know I found that one sufficiently frightful and disagreeable, and hilarious and a nuisance and an occasion for prayer. With all the range of emotions of the line enhanced.

. . . It provided even Blighties—the thing we all prayed for. . . . I met next day a colonel of my own regiment who had come home to receive the Victoria Cross and who was so badly shell-shocked by a bomb falling on his house in Belgravia that he was rendered unfit for further service. I met also a young man who had insisted, to the distraction of his female friends, on emerging from the sofas and champagne of a bomb-proof cellar under a Piccadilly Club in order to walk around the parapet of the fountain-basin whilst all sorts of things fell from the sky, and the deserted ladies accompanied him.

It was the raid when the *John Bull* office was destroyed with God knows how many poor people in what was supposed to be a bomb-proof shelter beneath the building. For myself I had been dining the wife of another of my colonels at Kettner's which had been quite close enough to the *John Bull* affair. I had got her safely home to the *Berkeley*— These names of a former London come savorously off a foreign pen!— and though the All Clear had not sounded I had gone for a stroll in the soft black air. So I had come into Regent Street. I was seeing it for the last time in that state! And even then I had a sense of it in my bones.

I was home and nearly in bed by the time they came back. But when the noise began again I thought I had better go and see how my mother was. She lived on Brook Green and I can assure you that walking along High Street Kensington was a sufficiently frightful experience so that I prayed I might be back in places where you would be hit by a nice clean piece of shell casing. In there the air seemed to be filled with bits of flying chimney pots and coping stones and our own shrapnel, whilst the guns in Holland Park past whose wall I had to go made a noise which seemed to make memories of the first battle of the Somme very pale affairs.

I found my mother sitting in her bedroom window —which she should not have been!—reading "Lorna Doone" in between the shrapnel flashes in the sky. She was a lady of romantic temperament and complete absence of physical fear—except when it was a matter of cows. . . . For her everything with horns was a mad bull . . . a portent of malignant destiny's. But shrapnel, shells, airbombs, and the rest were merely the toys of the silly children that her menfolk were and, wrapped in a good shawl, she ignored them.

She held her book to her candle flame and said: "Fordie, isn't this a beautiful poem:

" 'Love and if there be one, come my love to be,
    My love is for the one, loving unto me
    Not for me the show, love, of a gilded bliss
    O only thou shalt know, love, what my value is!' "

I agreed that it was a beautiful poem—Lorna's song. And indeed I am proud still to be able to write it—as, as a boy I could have written the whole of "Lorna Doone"—by heart. . . . So we had a little pre-Raphaelite conversation—about Rossetti and Lizzie Rossetti and the pictures of my aunt Lucy Rossetti and all their tantrums and alarums. Then, the All Clear having gone, I borrowed the tin hat of my brother who had lately been wounded and in hospital, and precious glad I was to have it. I had started out that day in a top hat and morning suit and was still in them because when one was home on leave one did not waste much time changing one's clothes. . . . So I left the top hat with my mother. And that was the last time I saw it or wore one. And in tin hat and morning coat—which would have got me sent back to my unit if there had been a provost marshal in High Street—I started back home up the completely empty street in the dead silence.

Then I met a friend and we walked up and down for a long time in the quiet, talking of old times. When we were just in front of Holland House it all began all over again—the whole jamboree. I suppose the Germans must have got as far as Windsor, say, and that they had been chased back again. We continued to walk up and down and to talk of old times. . . . I just hated it. . . . But we were Londoners of the old school and Londoners of the old school do not acknowledge that anything can happen to their city because the London police, the County Council, the Home Secretary, and the other incorruptibles will see to it that she does not put on corruption. The skies must first fall.

This may seem a ridiculous situation to the unreflecting— But I am reminded of an incident of a year ago in New York state. It was a Fifth of July and it was nine o'clock in the morning. Fourths may or may not be agreeable but Fifths are almost always Blue Mondays. I was returning from Paterson, N. J., being driven in a car noted for its speed. I was not so much somnolent as temporarily unobserving. When we got to the White Plains highroad we seemed to be travelling rather fast. I looked at the speedometer. It showed seventy-eight. I am used to speedometers that register kilometers and seventy-eight in kilometers is not much. . . . Then suddenly I understood that they were miles and flashing telegraph poles seemed objects of horror.

I said nothing. New Yorkers with cars noted for speed have for the credit of New York to speed. Visitors to New York who wish to preserve even their reputation must appear phlegmatic in the face of danger. . . . But perhaps mankind progresses. For my companion and driver said suddenly:

"I just hate this!"

And with thankfulness I exclaimed from my heart:

"I positively loathe it."

We drove after that at humdrum thirty until we reached White Plains station where I took the train. . . .

I tell this tale of a London air raid not for what it is worth in itself but in order to emphasise my point that London really had undergone a baptism of fire. To me—and I daresay to others—it takes fire, pestilence, sieges and sackings to put the final seal on a city's dig-

nity. Until then London had lacked that. It had had
its Fire, its Plague and it had heard the roar of foreign guns, all within a decade, but in the reign of
Charles II. But it had to wait a quarter of a thousand
years for final consecration. It had found it. . . .

I suppose that cities that have known misfortune
gain dignity because of the stamp conferred on the
citizens. . . . A Parisian of before the siege of 1870-71
was frivolous and aimless compared with the grim-
ish Parisians of the period up to 1914 and the quite
grim inhabitants of the post-war city. So the pre-war
Londoner was carefree—and even reckless.

It is the misfortune of the place that the very meas-
ures necessitated by that increased dignity should have
robbed the city of all her former characteristics. Her
former characteristics had been an easy freedom, a
vastness, an absence of all official interference. One
came and went; anyone came and went. One lived
one's whole life long without passport, paper, means
of identity. One never saw an official. One knew they
existed: They were your servants. If one got born,
married or died, you saw a Registrar. He called you:
"Sir." Not merely you, but the shoeblack at the corner. You might possibly meet a tax collector delivering
his papers. He called you: "Sir." Not merely you but
the poorest taxpayer.

Two days after the war started—as I have elsewhere
recorded—I was coming home late along the wall of
the Campden Hill waterworks. A fellow in scarlet with

a long steel affair jumped out of a shadow and exclaimed:

"Halt! Who goes there?"

I said:

"God da——n and bl—st you! What the —— do you mean by leaping about and startling me?"

He said:

"Beg your pardon, sir, I didn't see you were a gentleman."

A policeman approached. I have not recorded this and this is the point. I said:

"Officer, tell this jack in the box not to jump about and startle people," and he gave the fellow a proper telling off! . . . Our servants, that was what these fellows were. . . . But before I had reached my front door I had realised what had happened. And it was never, as it were, to un-happen.

The unlovely Dora was London's answer to the raids—the Defence of the Realm Act. Even during the war she was offensive and stupid in patches but one bore with her because it was then expedient and necessary to support authority, however stupid Authority might be.

But after the war Authority itself became an offence to the Realm. Even during the Armistice Dora meddled imbecilely with the sales of cigarettes, candies, new bread, liquors. . . . Life became a perpetual round of petty annoyances and the once faithful servants of the public a horde of petty spies in the hands of contemptible dictators.

If you had asked me the day before what I thought of freedom or of the rights of man I should probably have replied that I never gave freedom a thought and that men had no rights—only duties. But on that Campden Hill kerb that day many things were opened to me—as to what went on inside me. . . .

I had never found the Army irksome. I do not think that I have any desire for personal liberty. In the Army I had been ordered about and had found it agreeable because, having no personal responsibilities to ponder over, my mind was free. I asked really nothing better— and I ask nothing better now when nine-tenths of my mind has to be given to pondering on the destinies of my family, my dependents, my starving friends and the foundering world. No . . . I would rather be a galley slave than have my freedom and nothing but my pen and spade with which to keep back the waves.

Nevertheless my blood boils at the thought of interference with the freedom of others by the oafs called politicians and publicists. I remember that at Whitehall when I had gone to get my orders for joining my regiment a rather superior staff officer of about my own age mildly dissuaded me. He said he imagined I should find it disagreeable to be ordered about by dirty little squits of boys who might be my superior officers. He said he would find it intolerable himself. . . . But I had not found it in the least intolerable. . . .

On the other hand, there at the end of the war, I found it utterly detestable that infinitely dirty little squits of civilians should have the power to interfere with the movements of either civilians or the military. Yet it was for that that our labours had been given. In any Army there must be giving and receiving of orders since these are necessary for the mere existence of an Army. But that an accidental clerk in a political office should have the power to forbid my going where I wanted, I found intolerable. And those fellows could interfere not only with me but with infinite millions. . . .

And I suddenly realised what had been my proudest consideration of that part of me that was English. For whilst I had worn His Majesty's uniform I had been, not merely politically but to the mental backbone as English as it was possible to be. My most glorious memory of England had been that in the 'nineties I had seen hundreds of Jewish refugees from the pogroms in Russia land at Tilbury dock. And as each unit of these hundreds stepped on the dock he or she fell on their knees and kissed the ground—the sacred soil of Liberty. It was not of course because they were Jews or were martyrs. And I daresay it was not merely because England was my country. It was pride in humanity. If one body of men confined in one island could evolve that tradition that for centuries had given glory to England—then there had been hope for mankind. . . . What a hope!

No political fugitives, no martyrs for whatever faith were ever any more to land on those shores—because of an order in Council—an Order in Council evolved by some unknown member of the most suspect govern-

ment the realm had ever suffered from! What then was
to become of England of the glorious traditions? It
had been political fugitives and martyrs that had given
England her place among the nations. It had been the
Flemish weavers, the Anabaptists, the Huguenots, the
ceaseless tide of the discontented from every nation that
had given England not alone her tradition of freedom
but her crafts, her system of merchanting, her sense of
probity, her very security. . . . This then was the last
of England, the last of London. . . .

Easy, free, vast! . . . Why, even the very illusion
of vastness had gone with that taxi-ride into the suburbs! . . . Why had I taken it? . . . The lady novelist had singled me out for the honour of paying for
that vehicle on a journey that I had not in the least
wanted to take. It had been at a party of other lady
novelists and being of a pre-war crop she had been
less unapproachable than the others. I suppose she had
taken me to be wealthy-ish, safe, sound. But I must
have shocked her terribly on that journey for she went
back with another party, leaving me to return by third-
class underground.

I do not think I had ever before visited an outer suburb. I must have been once in Sydenham or Balham and
it had appeared to be a grey region of brooding brick.
At any rate I had hitherto thought that the suburbs
prolonged the grey graveness of the metropolis, pro-
longing its vastness in the same spirit. But in that ride
I had seen merely innumerable horrors of pink and
white cheerfulnesses. In the outer suburbs of New York

—on the Albany Post Road, in Westchester County or round Mount Kisco they would have been inoffensive or even agreeable. . . . But cheerfulness and London! It was a profanation. One had been accustomed to think of London as the vastest city in the world . . . as being, precisely, London, the bloody world! One had imagined her as covering the space of a continent with its grey, brooding. But if these outer regions were really white and pink and bright with almond blossom and filling stations and picture palaces, that outer ring was no longer London. For all one knew London—real London!—might be but a very small affair, extending merely from Campden Hill to Mile End . . . merely as broad as Paris and as long as Manhattan. And with Regent Street torn down!

Ease then was gone; freedom was no more; the great proportions were diminished; cigarettes were not to be had after eight o'clock; foreigners must register with the police; passports were to be had before you could leave the land; government spies accompanied your every step.

Why, the great fascination of London and her great security had been that when you stepped out of a London terminus you sank out of human sight. Now authority was imitating the imbecile police authorities of Paris and Berlin. In the old days in London to be "unknown to the police" had been your highest credential whilst in Paris or Berlin it had meant you were a hobo. Now "papers" had come to London—with the corollary that every decent citizen or foreigner would be hampered by them and every criminal having the skill to obtain false "papers" would be secure against police unless taken in the act of a crime. . . . The fact is that if you have a place like London which by its very atmosphere conduces to the observation of laws it is worse than folly to plaster it with papers that make the peaceful citizen and the racketeer all one in the eyes of a suspicious police. It is merely to manufacture racketeers! And that is what London has done so that today the most peaceful city of the pre-war world has become almost on a par with Chicago for crimes of violence. . . .

. . . At any rate I saw, standing on that Campden Hill kerb, that as far as London was concerned there was nothing to do but to get out or go under!

I wish to guard the reader from thinking that I felt any personal despair. I have been in many tight places in my life but, except for the period of nervous breakdown the particulars of which I have recorded in a former book, I do not think I have ever failed to show composure in the face of adversity or the treachery of friends. I have been accustomed to regard myself as of the family of the dung-beetle. This stoical creature I came across on the mountain that is topped by the Genoese castle above Gatti di Vivario in South Corsica. I was stopping with a retired bandit whose wife had once been engaged to Ruskin. Their baked earth hut—for it was little more—was therefore adorned with products of the firm of Morris & Co. and relics of my pre-Raphaelite past whilst it stood deep in the *macchia* —the trackless forest of white heather that is the resort of bandits.

On the first day—at my first meal of kid and white haricots—I committed an unpardonable offence. I was a great salt-lover and, before even tasting the ragout, I sprinkled a great deal of salt on it. . . . I have never repeated that offence. The ex-fiancée of Ruskin behaved as if I had questioned her virtue. One must *never* add condiments to hospitable dishes in France, Italy or the Isles of the Mediterranean. It is to suggest that the lady of the house does not know how her meats should be prepared. . . . Even the aged brigand with his one eye and black skull cap became almost as agitated as Mr. Ruskin when he discovered traces of immorality in the brushwork of Millais. . . . And that septuagenarian was said still to be very handy with his knife!

To escape from the thunder-clouded atmosphere I went to take my siesta on a goat path of the mountain. And there, reclining on one elbow, I looked down and saw the dung-beetle.

Henry James used to say that the best goods are not done up in the most fashionable looking parcels and certainly for a paladin of industry and benefactor to the world, the dung-beetle wore no very shining armour. He was an obfusc, brownish, bullet-shaped mortal and he pushed before him up the mountain another bullet of obfusc, brownish matter—dung rolled and patted into form and pushed so far up what sundried precipices and grasses beaten to steel by the hoofs of the goats! Even as I looked at him—and perhaps but for that my eye would not have been attracted to him —gripping his load of dung he rolled backwards and over and over until he was level with my foot, say. . . . Without as much pause as would have given him time to spit on his hands or say: "What a hope!", he was at his dung-bullet again. He pushed and strained and the bullet wavered and jolted upwards until he was on a level with my forehead. Then with the suddenness of catastrophe, so that one started, he slipped again and rolled and rolled till he was a foot below my shoes. And then . . . at it again at once.

I do not suppose that Providence who had prescribed adaptation, or the survival of the fittest for all mortal beings, was here at fault. The normal dung-beetle lives on level ground: a rounded fragment of dung is there more easily pushed. But this beetle had chosen the mountain top for his abode and thus the normal packing of his material told heavily against him. It is not enough to choose exalted mansions:—I am addressing this apologue to poets!—you must then adapt your material to your situation. . . .

I watched that poor beast for the whole of a dreamy afternoon, on the baked hill-side, looking over the Mediterranean whose liquid cord of horizon was indistinguishable from the vivid edge of the sky, and in the soft odours of white heather, of rosemary, of lavender . . . oh, intoxicating land! And, at the end of my siesta and the afternoon that poor beast was not more than a foot above the level of my head.

A certain Puritanism—inculcated into me, I suppose, by Mr. W. H. Hudson—prevented my taking up that beetle and setting him down some yards further up the hill. I fancy I have always had an instinctive dislike for playing Providence. I have never taken ants out of spiders' webs though contests between ants and spiders must be more cruel than anything since there were combats between *hastiarii* and *retiarii* in the Roman arenas. I fancy that without the influence of Hudson I should have tried to bring up orphaned wild rabbits— or fledglings that had fallen from nests. But, with his Spanish gravity and power of making me feel like a worm when it was a question of thoughtfulness to dumb animals, Huddie had long since proved to me that nothing was less desirable than an interfering providence in the realm of feather, fur and claw. A fledgling fallen from the nest is the weakest of its batch: to handrear with chosen food a young animal with an inherent weakness was to give to a world of fear and cruelty a being that, after a short span of dreads and pains, must incur a fearful death in the talons of a hawk or the jaws of a fox, whereas young animals die quietly and with-out fear passing gently back into the First Principle that supplied their feeble lives.

I daresay he was right. All the same on my first eve-ning in Red Ford, leaning on my elbow on my camp bed and watching the death of my first fire of twigs and driftwood in a completely empty house I wished that I had played providence to that beetle. I wished it very intensely indeed. I could not see how, without the

intervention of an immense and august finger and
thumb that should take me up and transport me through
the dark air—how, without that, I should ever reach
the top of . . . say, Parnassus! Or even effect a lodg-
ment in a kitchen garden on the slopes of the little Alps
above the *Plateau des Antiquités* by St. Rémy in
Provence.

I don't mean to say that I was unaware of the
romance of the situation . . . but I wanted to get to
Provence. Not to Italy where the lemons glare in dark
foliage; nor to the Hesperides where you may find ap-
ples of gold. Not even to the land of Cockaigne where
little roasted pigs run about and beg to be eaten. . . .
Just to Provence, with the arid hillsides and the tufts
of aromatic herbs and the skeleton-white castles and
the great Rhone and, beyond the sky-line, the Mediterranean! . . .

There I lay, the ruined author in a bare room that
shadows were beginning to invade from every corner. The fire was a mere glimmer that just gleamed in
the jet irregularities of the small, leaded window panes.
I lay on one elbow in my old bed of fitted rods with
for sole furniture a canvas bucket with a rope handle
and a green canvas table with a defective leg that was
propped against the bare plaster of the wall. . . . The
floor of tiles was covered with dead leaves that must
last autumn have drifted in through spaces in the windows from which the panes had fallen. With the last
light of day I had raked out of an outhouse a cast iron
crock that I had washed and filled at the spring under

the oak tree and there, near the fire, from a pot-rack it hung and was half filled with a stew.

The rest of the stew was giving me courage . . . I had said to myself: "I will never look back. . . . From now on I will never look back . . ." and I do not believe that I have!

I have related in a former book of reminiscences something of what I am about to relate. The book concerned itself a little with the war and much more with the Armistice. It is long since out of print and according to the publisher's figures few more than a hundred people can have read it. So I need not scruple to repeat myself.

I have always been, not so much a believer in, as subject to omens. Indeed, as I have already said, I think any man who is impervious to them is either a fool or something more than a man. I had, then, that night come through Pulborough in a farm-waggon and had brought some haphazard eatables—a leg of mutton, some shallots, bread, salt, and a bottle of port. I had had to lug these along with my impedimenta—the green canvas army sacks—across a stretch of ploughed field in the dusk, the waggoner not having dared to take me and my load further than his master's farm. The farmer—who was also my landlord, was a tartar!

I had come round the corner, heavy with my swag, upon Red Ford in its hollow and I had felt dismay. I like old, moldering houses and I like solitude. But Red Ford was almost too old and too moldering and its solitude—between dog and wolf—had a peculiar quality. I had never seen the house before. It had been taken for me by a friend who knew my tastes—and my means. I had no knowledge of the countryside: West Sussex to a Kentminded man is as foreign in speech and habits as is China. I knew not a soul for miles and miles and I was even ignorant of how far away the nearest house might be. I had never been so alone and with my heavy sack to represent his burden I was indeed the dung beetle. I had rolled clean down to the bottom of the hill.

I have said that the word despair is not to be found in my vocabulary. . . . The immense rusty key grated in the lock of the door of an unknown room. It was a space filled with shadows. The house had been unoccupied for many years: If one had spoken one would have whispered. The floor was ankle deep in dry leaves; on the hearth were bushels of twigs dropped by the starlings who had nested in the chimney. I lit a candle and used the last daylight outside in, as I have said, finding more wood and the cast-iron crock. Fortunately the house was bone dry.

I had my bed and my canvas table up very quickly and then had to face my mutton-neck and shallots. Here there came in the ridiculous omen. It was when I confronted my shallots. A shallot is perhaps the best of all the onion tribe: but shallots are very small things: scores of them lay under my nose. I touched the frontiers of dismay where it borders on the slough of despair. I was at the lowest ebb of my life. It would take me hours and the last of my strength to skin those bulbs. I could not tackle that job.

That really shamed me. One may be poor, friendless, fallen in estate, infinitely alone. But if one goes back on one's arts one loses self respect and once one loses that—so I have been told—one is lost indeed. And I knew I should never skin those dwarf onions. I sat on the edge of my bed and faced facts and the fire.

On it, in the crock, the neck of mutton was already browning in butter. Cooking is an art the first of whose canons is that all stewed meats must first be braised in butter or olive oil according as your cooking is *au buerre* or *à l'huile*. (The French call the process *rissoler*.) The second canon is that a portion at least of your onion matter—onions, garlic, shallots, chives even —must be browned too.

I said to destiny:

"Look here, I will skin and brown nine shallots. . . . But not a single other one."

So far I had not lost self-respect. The shallots browned. But then I did a thing that I have never done before or since. When the mutton and the rest were nicely *rissoléd* and I had added the quota of water and the water had come to the boil, I closed my eyes so that I might not see the deed and tipped all the rest of the shallots into that crock—skins and all (I *had* washed them).

I said to destiny:

"Now I have lost my self-respect!" . . . The crock began again to boil.

I added that, nevertheless I would make a pact with myself. I would try once more to push that dung up the long hill if those onions came unstuck in the course of boiling. I was not of course trying to tempt providence. The pact I made was simply with myself. I had no reason to believe that destiny cared whether I made further efforts or not. It seemed reasonable to imagine that that august force took no interest in the matter. . . . So I sat on my bed and gazed at the viands.

But the hour and the nature of the place made it impossible not to think of the supernatural. The half-ruined cottage creaked unceasingly. There was no wind. The fire had ceased fluttering. There was no sound save the creak of the old stairs and the ancient rafters working in their sockets in the walls. Whilst there had been anything to do I had had no need to think. Now there was nothing. I am one of those fortunate—or unfortunate—beings who can think of only one thing at once. Whilst I am building a fire I cannot think out a letter I want to write nor, whilst tree-felling can I make myself think about the development of the plot of a novel. I live in my moment.

That type of temperament is fortunate in that, if you have worries you have only to, say, set to work to clean your shoes or rearrange your books to be immune from depressions. Perhaps, too, if you are of the single-minded type you do your material jobs better. Possibly even you think better. . . .

But it is unfortunate in that, if you are of that type, whilst you are doing anything concrete your powers of observation desert you. I found that to be eminently the case when I was in the line or in support. As long as I had any job to do—and Heaven knows I did three men's jobs and sometimes five—from the 14th August 1914 to the 11th November 1918—as long then as I had any duty to perform I would be almost completely dead to my surroundings. I remember very distinctly having to go from our headquarters behind Bécourt Bécourdel wood—to give some instructions to an officer in charge of a detachment by an artillery observation post on the ridge facing Martinpuich. The orders were rather intricate, their being properly carried out depended on careful synchronisation and observation of a trench map. I had had the orders from Battalion Headquarters by telephone and had committed them to writing myself. But I was not satisfied that my wording was plain: that was why I went myself instead of merely sending an orderly.

All the way I was thinking of how I could have worded these orders to make them plainer. Finally I satisfied myself and, over the ridge saw the valley of the Somme beneath the August sun—for all the world like the downlands behind the Pent. And when I had done my job and chatted a little with the gunners I remembered I had nothing at all to do till dinner. I needed exercise, for the battalion had just come out, so I gave my horse to my orderly and told him to take it back to camp while I walked.

I found myself on an extraordinarily bright, thistle-covered hillside without the least idea of where I was or how to get back to camp. . . . In coming up I had had the orderly to guide me and I had noticed nothing

—not the brilliant sunlight, not the thistles, not the bul-let-stripped trees nor even the contours of the land-scape. So perhaps the engrossed temperament is un-fortunate. I might otherwise have written better about the war.

But now, in Red Ford, there was nothing to do and there would not have been light enough to do anything. I had in my bag the adaptation of one of my books to French that I had begun on the Somme and was minded to finish there. But, on account of paper shortage it had been written in a hand so minute that in the light of my one candle I could not read it. . . . The crock went on boiling and fatalistically its contents swayed my destiny. . . .

A single candle, some pot-herbs, a neck of mutton, the shallots, a meat chopper, a tin plate, a washing-up bowl, a loaf of bread, a bottle of port. . . . In a store in the market town I had grabbed these things hastily —and it is characteristic that after the candle the first thing I had thought of had been the pot-herbs. . . Thyme, sage, bay leaves, chives, and garlic. For light is your first necessity and then flavour for whatever food you have. . . . I might have bought more than one candle. But when one is in a hurry the mind works queerly. They say there is no knowing what you will not snatch up when escaping from a house on fire. . . . And whilst I had been buying those things the wag-goner with the farm-cart outside was all on edge to be going. He went in dread of his master the farmer. He was a tartar. So I had only a single candle and could not read. And the crock was boiling. A good stew takes hours and hours to make—three, four, seven, simmering slowly. I had decided to give it an hour . . . and as much longer as I could stick it!

It is in such circumstances that the supernatural becomes clamant for your thoughts. . . .

I had given little thought to the supernatural but I have a sense of it as usually accompanying me in the shape of luck at cards, or in finance and the little imps of doubts and fears. I suppose most men have that sense. . . . When I was a boy I had an orthodox Roman Catholic training. But when I was between seventeen and eighteen I went to my Confessor and said:

"Father, I find it very difficult to believe in—to conceive of—the Third Person of the Trinity. The rest of the Creed does not trouble me but that is too difficult."

He was a very old, old Passionist who had been on a mission in Australia and, a native having speared him through the lattice of the Confessional, he had been sent to Paris to recover from the effects of his wound in the monastery attached to the American Church in the Avenue Hoche. He said:

"Calm yourself, my son; that is a matter for theologians. Believe as much as you can and be a good boy." And I do not believe I have ever given a thought to what may be called the supernatural-major from that day to this. Prayer for personal ends I have almost never permitted myself. One's personal ends usually imply that what one desires will have to be taken from someone else and one can hardly contemplate asking the

Heavenly powers' arbitraments in one's favour against others.—These I take it are the sentiments of most proper men.—During the worst phase of the first battle of the Somme—on the 13th July 1916—at night, when one had a long period of waiting, with nothing to do, in pitch blackness, in the midst of gunfire that shook the earth I did once pray to the major Heavenly powers that my reason might be preserved. In the end, if one is a writer one is a writer and if one was in that hell it was a major motive that one should be able to write of it, if only for the benefit—to the extent of the light vouchsafed one!—of one's fellow men. So what reason I had was preserved to me, and I eventually placed my candle in front of the image of Our Lady of Good Help to the left of the entrance door in Notre Dame.

That apart, I do not think that I have much troubled the major powers with supplications. . . . But in Red Ford, whilst the crock boiled over the sinking fire the cottage was filled with a horde of minor malices and doubts. The stairs creaked; the rafters stirred; in the chimney the starlings, distressed by my fire, kept up a continuous rustling. The rest of that empty house I had only dimly seen by the light of one candle. It was unknown ground. I had a sense that the shadows were alive with winged malices and maladies and that the dark, gleaming panes of the windows hid other, whispering beings that jeered behind my back, hanging from the rose stems in the outer night. And the crock went on boiling out destiny. If the skins came off the shallots I was to make a further effort. If not I was to let go.

To where? . . . To where the dung beetle finally slid? I don't know. But by that time I was already in the peasant frame of mind. All over that countryside and all over the world; on the Alpilles of Provence as in Kent; on the Roman Campagna as in the islands of the South Seas and the lands flooded by the Yellow River the peasant has the final gift of the really Happy Dispatch. Perhaps Providence who prescribes for him a life of endless monotonies, unending toils, exposures, heats, frosts, blights, murrains and pestilences, gives to him a means of departure from life more merciful than the sword of the daimio. He can say: "Enough" and fade—and fade further, and lie down in the shadow of a rick, under a date palm or in his bed and so pass away.

My mind ran on tired people. . . . There had been an old butler in Albert in 1916. The shells were falling on the town desultorily; one here one there. He sat asleep in the sunlight, with his black alpaca béret, his striped waistcoat and his green baize apron and his horn-rimmed spectacles. The *Matin* was on the table before him: above his head the canary spattered from its cage the seed over his skull cap. . . . He was worn out with the effort of keeping the officers and orderlies of Headquarters from walking with muddy boots on the bright, waxed tiles of the *salon* of his absent master —and worn out with all the obscure toil that had gone before.

And my thoughts went back to my grandfather who had slaved all his life with his brush and then laid it down and went up to bed and died in the night. And to my father who had slaved with his pen and died worn out and to my mother who at the end of her life was so tired that she would not even go to see the exhibition of her own work that someone had got together—and to poor Stephen Crane in his porch-room on Brede Place, covering with his tiny handwriting, laboriously, the immense sheets of white paper. . . . Alas, in my valise I had sheets of faded paper covered with minute handwriting. . . .

Do you know the epitaph in Beaulieu Churchyard? As far as I remember it it runs:

Here lies an old woman who always was tired.
She lived in a house where no help was hired.
Her last words on earth were: "Dear friends, I am going
"Where since there's no clothes there's no need of my
   sewing.
"Loud anthems in chorus continual are ringing,
"But since I've no voice there's no need of my singing.
"And ev'rything there is complete to my wishes
"For since there's no meat there's no washing of dishes.
"Don't mourn for me now, don't mourn for me never.
"I'm going to do nothing for ever and ever!"

And with these memories and the thought of all the fatigue that would be entailed by keeping, as old Meary used to say, all on gooing, I was ready to be contented if the skins did not come off those shallots. For all the maladies that flitted in the empty shadows of the house and all the doubts that peered in at the windows and creaked in the stairs and rafters—all these would accompany me to a dreaded end.

I wonder if any one remembers poor Edwin Waugh's story of the Boggart of Boggart's Ho' Clough?

There was a family of Rachda' in Lancashire. They were plagued with a Boggart—a malicious ghost—and they called in a Wise Woman to drive it out, and parsons to lay it, and priests to exorcise it and gipsies to work magic on it. But always it stayed. Then they knew that they must flit. They piled all their goods and gear on a great ol' waggon and drove away saying: "Now we're well shet o' that ol' Boggart." But the Boggart put his head out of a mattress at the tail of the waggon and shouted: "Hoots, mon, a gradely fine flittin' we're ha'ein'."

But the skins came off those shallots and floated in the bubbling on the top of the crock. So, after an hour and three quarters of waiting I skimmed them off and ate a fair to middling stew and drank half a bottle of port.

PART ONE

CHAPTER FOUR

Before next nightfall i had a dog and a
man-servant. This caused amusement to my friends, I
do not know why. They said it was typical of me. I
can't again see why. The dog was just dog, of no particular race and no particular intelligence—white with
black patches. The man-servant was a nasty boy of fourteen of no particular gifts and of no apparent intelligence
though in later years it grew evident that he possessed
extraordinary gifts of foul language and had most of the
human vices in a marked degree. . . . For the moment
I employed him in drawing water from the spring, clear-
ing roots, doing a little digging and looking after the
dog. I had acquired the dog from a wandering man by
the roadside—for half a crown, say sixty cents. In consequence he had little homing sense and a great part of the
man-servant's time was taken up in running after the dog
and retrieving him from other cottages or farms. The
dog's name was Beau, that of the boy, Jo. . . . Later I
acquired a goat, called Penny because it had a certain
facial resemblance to Mr. Pound and a drake that someone called Fordie because it lived at Red Ford and was
good to look at. These beasts had a great dislike of being

left alone so that when I went out I was followed by dog, drake and goat—sometimes for great distances. A little later I acquired a black pig. This animal was also companionate but I thought my procession would look too noticeable if she were added to it. I built her a sty in part of a sort of natural cave in the bank at the back of the house. So she died.

The veterinary surgeon before her death diagnosed it as a case of swine-fever. He advised me to kill the animal at once and dispose of it as pork. In that way, he said, I should not lose money and should be saved the considerable inconvenience of having to notify the case. I said that I was not going to poison my neighbours. He offered to dispose of the pork himself on commission. He said that, if the pig died and the case came out, it would cause him considerable inconvenience. He would have to be disinfected, or quarantined and no one would call him in for some time. Swine-fever is a dread and horribly infectious disease. . . .

The pig died while we were arguing about it. The doctor immediately performed a post-mortem examination and declared that the pig had died of inflammation of the lungs. He insisted nevertheless that it should be buried under a great quantity of quicklime so I suppose it may really have been swine-fever. . . . I mention this case as being one more instance—if such were necessary—of the desirability that no meat should be sold for human consumption—or even for consumption by hounds—unless the animal from which it comes has been slaughtered under state-inspection. . . .

In those halcyon days—just before peace was declared —everyone was filled with public spirit. That was the era of reconstruction and each human being had his own plan for the salvation of humanity. My own contributions were to be two. Leaning on my spade handle I would dream long dreams about them.

The sun, as I look back upon it, seemed always to shine—though I remember coming out of my cottage door one morning and seeing all my beautiful beans cut down and blackened—by frost. But sunshine and stillness seemed to brood over the land, awaiting the sound of the guns from Portsmouth. And in that stillness I dreamed—of evolving a disease-proof potato! The second dream was so audacious that I hardly dared acknowledge it to myself.

The final arcanum—the philosopher's stone—of agriculture is to discover a method of wastelessly administering nutriment to plants. An incredible dream. For, as manure is at present employed an immense percentage of it is wasted in the ground or on the nourishment of weeds—and a vast amount of labour is wasted in the distribution. If then a method could be discovered by which each plant planted—or each seed sown—could be directly supplied with the nutriment it is to require the addition to human wealth would be almost unmeasurable. As against that the transmutation of base metals into gold would be a mere flea-bite. . . . And then, presumably, you would throw men out of work. . . .

I have had these dreams ever since I can remember—

certainly ever since the 'nineties when in Paris I studied
kitchen-gardening. I tried to introduce wine—and to-
bacco-growing—into Kent, but was stopped by the Ex-
cise authorities: I experimented along the lines of the
discoveries of the great Professor Bottomley, but stopped
them in order to write a book. Literature kept creeping in.

Now literature seemed to be done for as far as I
was concerned and I began with enthusiasm and inde-
fatigable industry on the evolution of my potato. I had
scraped together somehow a little furniture. The first
thing I bought was a brass candle-snuffer tray, an eighteenth century gadget which my friends declared to be
a characteristic extravagance. But it looked consoling,
lying with a goose-quill pen in it on my broken-legged
green canvas table, and round it I could conjure up
a whole *décor* of XVIIIth century rooms. Then Mr.
Clifford Bax lent me a chest of drawers and a bedstead
—an act of kindness from a poet who must have
cordially disliked my work if he had ever heard of it!
. . . Then I bought five knives and some spoons and
forks at the sale of a lieutenant of the East Sussex Regiment. He had committed suicide.

Growing potatoes from seed is quite different from
the usual propagation. Instead of cutting a potato in
half and committing the halves to the ground you have
to take the seeds that are contained in the green, apple-
like fruits of the plant in the autumn. These you sow in
pots from which finally arise tiny potato plants. You

then set out these plants and in due course obtain a few tubers. These will be your future seed-potatoes. Theoretically each separate plant should differ from every other one. Each should be the progenitor of a new race, and, the race being new, should for a time be immune from disease. . . . Actually a great proportion—say six out of ten—seem to inherit ancestral diseases. But three out of ten will be markedly different from their ancestor and from each other, and the tenth will be a sport—with black, scarlet or five-fingered tubers or with blossoms of unusual blues and pinks.

Of, say, fifty different plants by the end of 1922 I had succeeded in selecting nine that seemed to be reasonably new varieties and two that apparently resisted all the diseases they were likely to meet. They were not however very attractive in appearance and, presumably on that account, received no commendation at the Pulborough Flower Show. I daresay I could have bred them to be smooth and oblong. I had planted them, on purpose to test them, in very bad ground so that, though very large and heavy-cropping, they were lumpy, one quite white and the other peculiarly purple. If, next year, I had planted them in fine, friable, carefully sifted soil they might have turned out to be smooth enough to please the market gardeners and to have established a race as famous as the Beauties of Hebron or the great Scottish varieties. Then I might have known fame as a benefactor to my kind—and near-wealth. . . . Alas! America, as you shall hear, came creeping in, and the fear of the effects of another win-

ter on my poor lungs, or the mirage of Provence . . .
and the illusion that I might, by then, be able to write
a book!

So Mary Butts and Samuel Johnson remain unhonoured, unplanted and unrowed and my buttonhole lacks
the green ribbon of the Order of Agricultural Merit
that otherwise might have adorned it. . . .

I have tried in various departments of life to be a
benefactor to my species. In the South, long ago, I
thought out a method of conveying moisture to the
roots of sweet corn which needs a wet bottom and a
scorching top. And I have by that means obtained, both
in America and in various places in Europe, corn that I
don't believe could be easily beaten. Indeed to-day—
on the 9th April 1933—when I lay down my pen I am
going to sow corn by that method. It is a Sunday—and
the better the day, the better the deed. It is the 9th of
the month and just before the full of the moon. So,
under Providence, I may hope to raise the best of
Golden Bantam that will be grown between here and
Memphis, Tenn.

I communicated that method to several Southern
papers, and tried to get it into the pages of the New
York *Herald* Sunday Supplement—which wasn't, however, taking any. But I have never received any thanks
from grateful sweet-corn growers. . . . Shortly afterward I invented a collar stud with a bayonet attachment. This I gave to Mr. Fred Karno as against a trifling
poker debt, on board the Minnetonka in 1906. I don't

know whether that amazing impresario who had at the time sixteen companies running in the United States and I don't know how many in England and who—without benefit of clergy—managed them all from what had once been a barn in St. Helen's, Lancashire—I don't know whether the genial and amazing Mr. Karno, with his magnificent Lancashire brogue, ever patented that engaging device. I hope he did and made a fortune, since brass, very properly, addles brass. But I do know hundreds and hundreds of thousands of agonised dressers for dinner and hurriers to catch suburban trains have had cause, down the years of a quarter of a century or more, to bless whoever did put that stud on the market. . . .

Then too I invented a method of nicely adjusting the flavour of garlic in dishes to the taste of the individual diner. . . . Ah that!

But the guns announcing Peace had not yet sounded. . . . You are to imagine me, in halcyon weather, leaning on my spade, in the garden in front of crumbling Red Ford under its great oak. . . . It was an admirable, loamy soil, all the better for having rested for the duration of the war. My first crop of white haricots never came up and I rocked most of the beds round and raised them; thus I got better drainage and after that, none of my crops failed. Even the beans that the frost had touched came round all right.

So my thoughts found larger horizons. . . . I dreamt of the Sussex Large Black Pig—the largest Hog in the

World. . . . I had been to a conference, in Storrington, presided over by the seductive Mr. S. F. Edge who is famous in the automobile world—and irresistible when it comes to pigs. His address on the Large Black—of which he possessed all the champions—would have fired brute beasts with imagination. . . . And I dreamt of vast territories over which my Large Blacks of the size and compactness of the rhinoceros should rove and prodigiously increase. . . . And also, I sighed: "If I only had capital. . . . A windfall or two and my Large Black beauties shall have their photographs in all the porcine fashion papers. . . ." And they did. The windfalls came. . . .

I have always had luck when gardening. I imagine it is because I observe the rules of the game of gardening life. I propitiate the little winged devils of doubt and destiny. I always seed whilst the moon is waxing; I never begin a planting on a Friday or a 13th but always on a 9th, an 18th, or a 27th. I attach superstitious reverence to certain favourite plants or beds. If there is a wishing well in the neighbourhood I fetch a bottleful of it to start my first watering of the spring. . . . So I attached names of friends to each of my potato plants.

In consequence Joseph, when he woke me in the mornings, would dash in with startling pieces of literary information:

"Mr. 'Enry James have picked up proper in the night, but Mr. Conrad do peek and pine and is yallowin'. Mr. Galsworthy's beetles 'ave spread all over Miss Austin. . . ."

He was exceedingly enthusiastic about those plants. . . .

Those little imbecilities of a jocular kind are maybe necessary to the proper conduct of an innocent and agricultural existence. They cause a little merriment by the juxtaposition of the improbable; they enhance the zeal of one's finds; perhaps they are palliatives against the imps and little devils of doubts; perhaps they induce the contemplative and bovine frame of mind that is conducive to good gardening. . . . Perhaps too that is why Mr. Lucas's favourite periodical is a necessity for the Briton. . . .

I had at Red Ford a rook called: "O Sapientia!" We found him with a broken wing, in the paddock on the 17th December. . . . The collects of the octave of Christmas are the collects of the Great O's. . . . They begin: "O Sapientia . . . ," "O Innocentia" and so on. . . . My birthday happens to fall on the 17th, so my collect begins: "Oh Sapience. . . ." That should make me be listened to with more respect.

Certainly: "O Sapientia" was remarkably propitious to one's boots. He hung in a wicker cage by the kitchen door and showed a prodigious appetite for cheese. If Joseph was allowed to give that rook a couple of chunks of cheese he would clean and grease, not only one's boots, but the donkey's hooves, dreamily whilst he gazed at O Sapientia, but in the most masterly fashion. . . . And there are ways and ways of greasing boots and hooves. . . . I cannot remember the donkey's name but

Joseph never looked after his hooves properly till he could do it looking up from time to time at that wicker cage. . . .

Mr. Galsworthy—the novelist, not the potato—once nearly jumped over my verandah at Winchelsea because I said:

"Here's Hall Caine coming."

I always thought that Poor Jack suspected me of keeping queer literary company and on that occasion he ejaculated:

"My God!", though usually the least profane of mortals.

But the Hall Caine who was walking with a disdainful nonchalance down the middle of Winchelsea High Street was only the Blue Angora cat of the House.

That cat was the most contemptuous being that I have ever even imagined. Once Conrad threw the match from his cigarette at the fire place. It fell short, onto the magnificent tail of Hall Caine who was gazing at the coals. The tail caught fire. But did that cat move? No. . . . It simply gazed contemptuously down and the master of adorned English had to spring like a lamp lighter to extinguish the flames. . . .

And the hilarity that cat's expression caused in Conrad was so great that—this is the point of the story— he immediately wrote three pages of the "End of the Tether" right off the reel. . . . And I see that it has got me through eighteen lines of minute writing and writer's cramp at a time when I am just longing to be out, sowing my corn in the gorgeous Mediterranean day. . . .

All this domestic-pet stuff is very English and, I suppose, beneath the notice of the philosopher. But if one is in England where there is no intellectual life and, in the English countryside where there is not even any intelligent occupation save gardening—which is an Art—these things, by the tyranny of environment, force themselves on your attention. . . . In Provence it is different. The cat-dog-wild-bird-wild-flower obsession needs heavy green, dampish backgrounds. Under limpid skies and amongst the sun-baked rocks it will no more live than will Brussels Sprouts. For the Provençal every wild flower is *"quelque giroflée"*—"some sort of wallflower" and every wild bird: *"Quelque moineau"*—"some sort of sparrow": unless of course it is large enough to be called a *"grive,"* and eaten. . . . It is wonderful how refreshing that is. In England, if you don't wish to be ostracised you must know—or pretend to know—the difference between a bearded tit and a crested grebe, and between the nest of a golden plover and that of a wood pigeon and your conversation must be perpetually larded with the names of all the wearisome tits and trying finches and with anecdotes of foxes and spaniels and pointers and hares. . . . If you want to talk about international politics you must from time to time tell an anecdote about a badger or bring in the local, West Riding name of the dandelion—to shew that you are really "sound." . . . But the first walk I took after my enlargement, in Provence, I took in the neighbourhood of Antibes with the son of a French Prime Minister who was also Professor of Colonial History at the Sorbonne and with an heiress of Judith Gautier who talked of Wagner and of Stendhal . . . and Hindu Spiritualism.

We descended a valley towards the Mediterranean. The Professor talked of the laws of inheritance in Annam and the lady about the silk that Wagner used for his dressing gowns. . . . And there under a hedge was *The First Primrose!* . . . I got ready all the quotations one pants out on such occasions and then from amongst the blossom of a cherry tree burst out the notes of *The First Nightingale. I* burst out:

"*Regardez. . . . La première primevère. . . . Vous savez:* 'A primrose on a river's brim . . .' and . . . *Ecoutez. . . . Le premier rossignol. . . . Vous savez:* 'Infiniment musical, infiniment mélancolique. . . .' "

The Professor looked over his pince-nez at the pale yellow nestling tuft.

"*En effet,*" he said, "*c'est quelque giroflée,*" and went on talking about the rice laws of Siam.

The lady glanced up at the cherry tree. She said:

"*En effet. . . . C'est quelque moineau . . .*" and went on talking about l'Amour as treated by Henri Beyle, incidentally giving an account of an apparition she had seen in the garden of a Yoghi in Suresnes.

I heaved an immense sigh as the burden of nature-quotation fell forever from my aching back and plunged like a huge rock into the laughing waves. . . . I need never say again

"Before the swallow dares and take . . ."

Not even ever:

"The darling buds of May
"With a hey, the doxy over the dale" . . .

But the day of my enlargement was, in June 1919, still far distant and I dreamt of a miraculous tuber and a Largest Black Sow to the accompaniment of work, drake, donkey, old mare, goat, stable-boy, with a background of heavy green June grass laced with the streak of scarlet of a rivulet.

And then. . . . All my planting was finished. In a day or two the guns from Portsmouth would sound, the halcyon days were over. Life would begin. . . . If I could scrape together the capital, in spite of all the devils, little and, big, I would have some Large Black Sussex pedigree sows of Mr. Edge's famous herd—my name should be in all the agricultural papers. . . . But where was capital to come from? . . . It seemed almost an occasion for prayer! . . .

I went up to London, partly to try to get capital, partly in order to sign a petition to the Throne asking to be allowed to change my surname. Because peace would soon be declared. . . .

I signed the petition easily and then drifted about the Strand. The streets of London are paved with gold. . . . I doubted if I could afford even a sherry and bitters at Short's. . . . I was homeless in the familiar streets. So I took a cheerless room in the Cecil which cost me £2.17.6.

I drifted, more desultorily than ever, in on Pinker whose office was just around the corner. It was always cheering to tease Pinker. I would pretend to make a joke about Henry James and he would jam his glasses onto his intelligent eyes, spring out of his chair declaiming the dreadful things he would do to me if I dared to speak disrespectfully about the man who of all his clients was his Grand Panjandrum . . . and mine!

Poor dear Pinker. . . . When, a year later, I heard, as I have already narrated, that he had died of pneumonia in New York, I remember I thought that New York could be no place for me . . . if it could kill anyone so granite-hard as that Scotsman. . . . It seemed as if an unbelievable nut-cracker had smashed a corundum walnut! How little I foresaw!

He received me, then, with the words:

"You've just got ten minutes!" He was panting with excitement. He said: "The option expires today and the American Embassy closes at four . . . in ten minutes. . . . Hell, get a move on. . . ."

Mr. Pinker had been searching for me all over the habitable globe for some time. . . .

So I had my large Blacks—the two largest sows in the world, and others!—and thousands of acres of common land over which they could roam; and land of my own for the potatoes; and a spring above the house from which the water could be piped; and a house that had been old before Columbus committed his indiscretion, and orchards and a copse and oaks of great girth and a proper bailiff to pull Joseph's ear . . . and an immense view. They said locally that it looked over twelve counties and I daresay we really could see three from the west window.

It was, I need not say Hollywood, under Destiny, that had intervened. Not the gorgeous Hollywood of a few years later but one sufficiently bounteous and just craving for plots in a world getting ready for boom years. . . .

This is of course the romance of *Un Jeune Homme Pauvre* . . . and observe how, in it, virtue is rewarded and how nicely, with Hollywood for its machine, Destiny arranges its effects. For, if I had gone into Short's and had spent ten minutes over that sherry and bitters—for which I really craved—I should have been too late to sign Pinker's contract at the Embassy and the contract would have expired. But I had resisted temptation—at the dictates of Economy. For the first and last time in my life!

And other virtues had come into it. . . . For, if I had not come up to town on that day I should not, equally, have come upon Mr. Pinker in the nick of time. And I had come up to town on that day because I wanted my change of name to take effect exactly on the day when the peace terms were signed and the world was to begin again. I had long wanted, for quite private family and material reasons, to adopt the name of a distant relative of my mother's, and the temptation to do so whilst the war was still on was considerable. To have a foreign-looking name in those days had been very inconvenient and to have adopted my present surname during the life of my mother's relative might have been profitable for he was childless and eccentric, with considerable property in Sussex and in Kent, in the neighbourhood of the Crays where I had come across him a little before the war, though I only saw him once. The property he had inherited from the Madoxes, Welsh people who, as the rich Welsh so often did, had emigrated to Kent and bought land in the 17th century. It lay mostly in the Crays which has since become part of London so that the wealth I might possibly have inherited would have been very great.

But I had said to myself the moment war broke out that it would ill befit me to go back at that juncture on the name of my father though actually he himself had begun the process. Properly speaking—and during his first years in England—his name was Huffer, which in Ruthenian or some Polish dialect signifies a plover. . . . The legend was that, during one of the Crusades, one of his ancestors was asleep in the desert and lapwings awakened him just in time to save him from the approaching Paynims. I should have thought myself that, plovers liking marshy places would have avoided deserts. Be that as it may three plovers natural and courant figured in the first and third quarters of my father's coat of arms and his crest was, equally, a lapwing natural and courant. With the romantic feeling of one who was a master of the poetry and language of the troubadours

135

—a fact which may account for my passion for Provence and all that is in it—he used to say that those lapwings were doves—but doves natural do not have little crests, neither do they run

> "But look how Beatrice like a lapwing runs,
> Close to the ground . . ."

In any case, on his arrival in England, a man of immense erudition who had run musical journals in Paris and in Rome, he looked naturally into a dictionary and found that Huffer = (a) "An Ass." (b) "An idle and boasting fellow." He therefore incontinently inserted an "e" into Huffer which became Hueffer—a name so suspect and unpronounceable that anyone bearing it might well expect without trial to be shot as a queer enemy spy. Out of filial piety I chanced that, though in June 1915 I made some change in my Christian names, getting rid of a bushel of saints' and other scriptural names which caused singular emotions in Orderly Room when I had to sign my full name to military documents. . . .

Observe again then with what a just observance of the novelist's necessities Destiny conducts its coincidences. For, once more, if I had changed my troublesome patronymic in 1915 I should not have gone up to town in 1919 and again should not have found Pinker nor have raced to the American Embassy to sign the Hollywood agreement. . . .

I may make the note that I had intended to keep the change of name as a strictly private matter and to con-

tinue to write, if I ever wrote again, as Hueffer. . . .
But one day Mr. Gerald Duckworth said to me:

"If only you'd sign your books 'Ford' I might be able
to sell the beastly things." He said that nothing so puts
people off buying books as any difficulty in pronouncing
an author's name. A book-buyer hates to feel like a fool
or as one unacquainted with proper pronunciations.
"And how *should* one pronounce your beastly name?"
he asked, "Hoo-effer? Hweffer? Hoifer? Hyoofer? It's
impossible to know." He added that his traveller had
implored him to ask me to make the change. . . . That
is why nowadays a great number of readers hesitate to
buy my books, thinking that they must be about auto-
mobiles, or Detroit—or against bankers. . . .

So that amount of filial piety I shewed! . . . I never
knew my father well. He died whilst I was still a child
and, as I was sent to a boarding school at the age of
eight and he, during the summer holidays, was usually
at Bayreuth, I have hardly any memories of him. I
remember a few stories that he used to tell me in rare
moments when he must have felt the urge to shape my
infant mind. They were mostly about travelling afoot
in the forests of Silesia, with bears and robbers or of
his grandfather's adventures in Russia during 1813
which I have narrated elsewhere. . . . But even of
these stories my memory is now very vague. There was
one of a robber who said to his wife: "We must kill
them both" when my father and a friend were sleeping
in his loft. . . . And another that comes back to me as
rather amusing about a party of survivors of the war

of 1870 who had each lost something—a leg, a hand, an eye in battle. They were dining together in a restaurant and each in turn at the end of the meal said to the waiter, whilst taking off a leg or an eye:

"Waiter, you may remove the fish. . . . And while you are about it you may as well take away my leg . . ." or "You may as well take away my eye . . ." or "my hair . . ." or "my hand . . ." until, when it came to a gentleman who had lost both feet and a nose the waiter fled and was only found hours afterward in a wine cellar. . . .

My father, however, represents for me the Just Man! . . . *In memoriam aeternam erit justus* and I do not believe he can ever have faltered before any judgment seat. He was enormous in stature, had a great red beard and rather a high voice. He comes back to me most frequently as standing back on his heels and visibly growing larger and larger. . . . My mother who was incurably romantic and unreasonable with the unreason that was proper to the femininity of pre-Suffrage days comes back to me as saying:

"Frank: isn't it just that Fordie should give his rabbit to his brother?" My brother having accidentally stepped on his own rabbit and killed it, my mother considered that I as the eldest should shew an example of magnanimity by giving him mine.

So my father, as large as Rhadamanthus and much more terrible says: "No, my dear, it is not *just* that Fordie should give his rabbit to his brother but if you wish it he must obey your orders as a matter of filial

piety. . . ." And then the dread, slow: "Fordie . . .
give your . . . rabbit . . . to your . . . brother. . . .
Et plus vite que ça!" He was fond of throwing in a
French phrase.

I don't know who was more dissatisfied with that
judgment, I or my mother. But that is no doubt what
justice is for.

Analysing, as I sometimes do, my heredity I suppose
I got from my mother—who got it from her father—
my faculty for running up against oddnesses . . . and
for taking geese for swans. From my father I must have
acquired my passion for Provence, for good cooking—
and possibly for New York. He was never in New
York but he was forever sighing for the country of
Guillem de Cabestanh and a little before his death he
was tremendously excited over the revival of an old
project. . . . Just before his marriage to my mother,
whilst he was still most passionately a student of the
Provençal poets, he was offered, through the poet Mistral, a professorial post in, I think, Arles. It is actually
more probable that it was in the University of Montpellier but it comes back to me as having been Arles.
The project fell through but in 1885 or so he again, in
Paris, met Mistral—who comes back to me as having exactly resembled my childhood's hero, Buffalo Bill. . . .
My father, who was worn out with his labours on the
Times, again expressed his longing to settle down for
good in the country of the troubadours and Mistral
again promised to find him something. In the meantime
he had him elected a member of the Félibrige, the

Provence Academy for the promulgation of the Langue
d'Oc. . . . My father, however, died before that came
to anything. . . . But to this day it thrills me to think
that I might have been born in Arles. . . . Or at least
in Montpellier! . . . Alas: *dis aliter visum!*

On my culinary and American predestinations that
my father's heredity inflicted on me I will descant when
the time comes to consider, here, these matters.[1]

Let us return to the Hollywood incident, which I
dwell upon for the benefit of poor, good novelists. The
moral is that one should never cut one's throat—if one
is a novelist. For there is always Hollywood. Literature is said to be a good stick but a bad crutch. Sometimes it's a pretty poor stick. Nevertheless the life of
the writer—of any artist—is the best life if only because
he alone never "retires." His philosopher's stone—the
technical discovery that will at last content him with his
own work—is always just around the corner.

There was Hokusai—the Old Man Mad about painting. The following version of his life was given me by

[1] Note. My father amongst his other activities wrote several libretti
for operas and translated a great many more. His verse was often
excruciating to the poet's mind but apparently it suited opera singers
for it was in great demand. Singers ask more for open vowel sounds
and for the absence of sibilants than for good verse. Major Suther-
land Edwardes, who was my father's most intimate friend once,
in a jocular article accused him of having written the worst line of
verse in the English language. The verse however was not my father's,
whose memory I am glad here to rehabilitate. It was quoted by him
as an instance of bad libretto writing in an article urging librettists to
study the needs of the voices of singers. The line was this . . . In a
translation of *Don Giovanni* the Don, approaching Zerlina is made to
exclaim:
"Can that eye a cottage hide?"
I leave the reader to divine what it means.

Mr. A. E. Coppard, sitting on the trunk of a felled beech above the great common where my Large Blacks roamed. . . . There are of course many versions of the sayings of Hokusai but this one pleased me most because of the dark gipsy earnestness of the narrator who was such a great artist in words—and who so admirably lived the only life worth living.

Hokusai, then, when he was seventy, said: "Now at last I begin to divine faintly what painting may be." At eighty he said: "Now I really think that after ten more years of research I shall know how to paint." At ninety he said: "Now it is coming. A little more research and thought! . . ." On attaining the age of a hundred years, he said: "Tomorrow I am going to begin my Work of Works. . . ." And so died. . . .

It is that that makes the following of an Art such a blessed thing. Muscles may go back on you; your head is frosted; your eyes grow a little dim; the sense of taste palls; and the soul must pause to breathe and love itself have rest. . . . But always, just around the corner, you know there is your secret. . . . For myself I know that, next Autumn, I shall begin on a novel. . . . Ah! . . . Well, at least it shall begin to do what I have wanted all my life to do!

So one supports with equanimity what would make a banker commit suicide. There are times when one seems to have to do without anything. In moments of bitterness one says: "Why is it that I alone must for ever make bricks without straw?" For myself, though I love luxuries, I despise—and dislike—comfort. The domestic apparatus, the armchairs, the heating arrangements, the hair oils, the boot-trees, the shaving glasses, the golf gadgets, the first editions, the orchid houses, . . . all the things that are the necessities of the most ordinary banker would make me, if I had them, think that I was doomed to go to hell. . . . Yet upon occasion one thinks that, for the dignity of one's art one ought to possess say—at least a really handsome blotter! . . .

I was once coming back from New York to Marseilles on a not particularly smart boat and there was on board a Banker! Not much of a banker, as was denoted by the vessel he had chosen to travel on. He had a little bank in some Southern small town—it might have been Clarksville, Tennessee. . . . And just because he was called banker, the whole of that vessel navigated only for him. He was a fat fool yet every man hung on his lips, every woman fought with every other for the privilege of walking beside him, every sailor holystoning the deck got out of his way and the sacred bridge of the captain himself was just an annex of the smoking room for that banker and his lady of the moment. I sat in a corner, neglected.

And I said to myself:

"This is wrong. . . . I am the only person on this boat who, for what it is worth, am of any distinction, the only one whose name is known, not to a few score small people in Clarksville, Tenn., or Stanton, Va., but to several thousand keen intellects on each of three continents. I perform work of beneficence to humanity.

Never did I obtain money from my fellows in order
to speculate in dubious undertakings and so get myself
the air of a prince whilst being the meanest kind of
chevalier of industry. . . ."

In short, I said then in the height of the boom years
what the President of the United States has just discovered. . . .

And then, black at heart, looking over the bulwarks,
at the Azores which I could not afford to visit in style
whilst that fellow had had sent for him the launch of
His Excellency the Governor, a sudden lightness came
upon me. I bought a bunch of the tiny Azores bananas
from a bumboat under the side—a sheer extravagance
since we should have them at dinner. And I addressed
to the back of that fellow, speeding over the harbour
in his gilded barge the once popular lines:

"The bells of Hell go ting a ling a ling for you but not
　　for me.
　For me the angels sing a ling a ling: they've got the goods
　　for me."

That came true enough for him on the 7th March,
1933. . . . Even at that there were not *too* many goods
for me. I had to get on for a week on fifty borrowed
francs in Paris. . . .

But it is in windfalls from places like Hollywood that,
materially, the writer who is mad about writing gets
his reward. In windfalls: in buckshee! And, if he has
been mad enough about his writings they will come
just frequently enough and just sufficiently in the nick
of time to make him keep all on going.

I am not of course talking to the novelist of commerce—the admirable fellow who by the study of the market is enabled to hold up the banner of our Craft on the very battlefield of the banker. He is able to look after himself. Of him there are perhaps a dozen within a dozen miles of the plot of Mediterranean hillside that I cultivate. When I enter—though I am seldom given the privilege!—his sumptuously restored Provencal house, his be-bathroomed palazzo, his English-flower-gardened, tennis-courted Mexican adobe villa I am humbly grateful that Providence should vouchsafe so much to practitioners of the Arts in the practice of which my ancestors for generations have died in reduced circumstances. . . . But it is not for them that I write nor will they ever read me.

No, I am concerned for a queer, not easily defined fellow. To him writing has the aspects of an art. One's art is a small enclosed garden within whose high walls one moves administering certain manures and certain treatments in order to get certain effects. One thinks that people ought to like these effects, say of saxifrages against granite. If the public does not like the effect and will not pay to see it. . . . Well, it is unfortunate. But one has got one's effect. . . . Or one has come somewhere near it: or one has failed because of the *puceron noir*. . . . The cuckoo pint is in one's brain. Next year one will try again. Maybe people will come to see that. In ten years' time: or in seventeen. . . . Or maybe someone from Hollywood—as happened in my case—may walk into one of your twenty-year-old and forgotten gardens. He is overwhelmed by the beauties and, to the sound of his shawms and halalis, people rush in. . . . Very likely they will be rendered better men and women by the sight of the beauties you produced in your forgotten past. . . .

I don't imagine anyone was rendered any better by the relic of my forgotten past that, thus saving my life, Hollywood came upon in June 1919. . . . Years after, outside Loew's theatre at the corner of Sheridan Square and Sixth Avenue, I came upon the photographs of what Hollywood had made of my forgotten work with Mr. Rudolph Valentino going strong in the part of the hero. . . . Or it may have been Mr. Ramon Novarro! . . . The effect upon me was to make me run as fast as I could to the nearest speakeasy which fortunately was no further than the back parlour of a drug store in Greenwich Avenue. There, combating an almost irresistible desire to dive under the counter, I asked the clerk for a dose of the strongest alcohol he had, mixed with sal volatile which encourages the heart. . . . And, in those fumes as, gradually I grew calmer, I saw poor Mr. Pinker and his sanguine spectacles in his office and the garden of Red Ford when that day I got back to it . . . and the rook and the duck and the stable boy and the donkey and the dog . . . and some less pleasant objects. . . . For a week or so I avoided lower Sixth Avenue. I might have been tempted to go in and look at that monstrosity. I never did. But I heard enough about it from my friends!

I had better make the chronological note that the

Loew's theatre episode occurred in the Fall of either 1923 or 1924 whereas the date with which this chapter is in the main concerned was the 4th June 1919. . . .

Before however returning to Red Ford I will answer the question of whether, if one desires to be an artist one can write for money. I answer without hesitation that one cannot. The bluff Englishman—and the Anglo Saxon of other breeds when he desires to appear bluff—will say that you are a fool or worse if you do not. He will say that the business of a proper man is to make a living complete with bathrooms, Buicks and the receipts of tax collectors. But perhaps an artist is not a proper man. At any rate he will be a fool if he write, or paint, or compose or make statues—for money. He will be a fool because his work will go to pieces. And the last thing he will make will be money in any quantity.

No: his only chance in life is to try to get his effects with saxifrages, or pigments, or words . . . and only then hope that someone will come into his garden. He may even then try to get publicity—all the publicity that is going. But whilst writing and still more whilst he is thinking out what he is going to write he must consider only the work itself. . . .

There is a personal devil. . . . He is a man with a husky voice—a Literary Agent. When for years you have cultivated the Muses on a little thin oatmeal you may have conquered the esteem of a certain body of your fellowmen. Then the Agent will approach you and whisper in your ear:

"Why not give up writing novels and write a spiced biography of the Queen Jezebel whom Joshua slew or of the Queen of Sheba who was black but comely? Or of Napoleon? Or General Grant? . . . There is a fortune in it."

You should shew him the door. Politely if possible for Satan has great powers of evil when offended. But shew him the door. . . .

And yet you may be pleased. For if the devil thinks you a person that it is worth his while to corrupt you may be assured that you have a certain value. It may one day become even commercial value sufficient at least to bring you windfalls that make life delightful. . . .

There is a useful word—buckshee—which is current in the British Army, all of whose units in turn spend long years in India and pick up and transmute terms from the native vernacular. Buckshee = *Backshish*, the universal Oriental word for "a tip." Buckshee is more than backshish. It is a gift from Providence whereas the other is a mere coin blackmailed by force of whining from a Sahib—a white man. . . . But say your regiment which is detailed to march at seven a.m. does not make off till nine because the Colonel—who was out overnight—has mislaid his false teeth. The two hours extra you get for poker or "house" are "buckshee" rest. Or your company cook finds he has two pounds or so of stew over when all the other tables are served. He dumps the whole lot into the mess can for your table. That is buckshee grub. . . . So Providence will act towards you, the poor, good writer. And buckshee rest and buckshee grub are the best of all. They come to no banker . . . or at any rate to no pre-1933 banker.

And the Destiny that looks after some potato-growers and pig-raisers is kind, too! . . . It can be kind in the way it arranges events. . . . For shortly after I got back to Red Ford serene in the consciousness that I had at least a year or two of respite I was struck by two of the disasters that are the worst a man can know. Had they overwhelmed me before I called in on Pinker these lines would never have been written to the long rhythm of the Mediterranean wave. Or never written at all.

I had a secret . . . a dark secret that I concealed even to myself as horticulturist. There are things done by the right hand that one's left does not even think of. I had, then, translated the *Alcestis* of Euripides.

I had done this as it were underground, at odd moments, almost anywhere and, really, as if in fear. On the very day after I had left the army Mr. —— now I think Sir —— Nigel Playfair had commissioned me to make an acting version of that masterpiece. He was then, deservedly, making a fortune by the production of the *Beggar's Opera* at the King's Theatre. It was natural that he should contemplate the exquisite masterpieces of the past.

If I had not known that the *Alcestis* was perfectly fitted for the stage without any adaptation—and, still more, if I had not known that Mr. Playfair was an extremely intelligent producer and one with reverence for masterpieces—I should not have undertaken the really formidable task. As it was all I did in order to produce an acting version was to make an exact translation from the original into quite modern English.

I am no sort of Greek scholar in the modern sense and I can no longer do more than make a guess at the meaning of any Greek text outside Xenophon and the *Bacchae* and *Alcestis*. Those two were drummed into me at school and until 1914 I used to read the *Bacchae* and at least Alcestis' address to her bed once, and possibly more often, every year. So making a rough rendering was not very difficult, but to find modern words that one could put into the mouth of Hercules and that would not jar was labour enough.

I worked on it in the little studio I had taken on Campden Hill and over the Red Ford fire. . . . Mr. Playfair came and heard me read it. He made some suggestions for alterations but, as I had expected, I was able to argue him out of them. The only departure from the original production that was contemplated was that, after the departure of Hercules in search of Alcestis, the curtain was to come down for five minutes.

Mr. Playfair took the manuscript away. . . . That would be in March 1919. The understanding was that it was to be the penultimate production at the King's Theatre. . . .

I had about £120 in the Bank then—all that remained of my blood money. I had had the vague hope that when the *Alcestis* was produced I might earn more by other productions and so—though my left hand was not to know it—I might remain at least the poor miserable sort of a literary man that a translator is. That I should myself build up a book I knew to be still impossible. In the process of work on the *Alcestis* I had however recovered some shadow of power over words. But not much.

I still regarded the possible production of that work as it were with averted eyes. . . . I have always sworn that I would never write a play and hope for any kind of gain from the theatre. . . . I had seen Henry James and Conrad—and even Mr. H. G. Wells—all going through the agonies of hope and despair before the theatrical mirage. As compared with the earnings of even a successful novelist those of a half successful playwright are vast. One of my poor dear friends would hear Mr. George Bernard Shaw say that, even before Mr. Granville Barker took him in hand and made his fortune, his dramatic earnings were £75 a week—£3,900 a year! . . . And poor James or the wretched Conrad would snatch at pen and paper and scheme at play after play. And there would be miserable ecstasies at the merest shade of a chance of production and insupportable despair when the shade died away. And the perpetual restlessness of alchemists in search of the Philosopher's Stone! . . . So I had steeled myself against indulging in any dreams at all. I was convinced that Mr. Playfair would never produce the play or if he did that it would not survive the first night. I forced and forced myself to think that.

In May Mr. Playfair wrote to say that the run of the

Beggar's Opera—or perhaps of its successor—looked like being so prolonged that he had decided to put the *Alcestis* on at Mr. Drinkwater's Repertory Theatre in Birmingham. It was to go into rehearsal at once. In a month he would be writing to ask me to go up and attend rehearsals. . . .

I had then £72 in the bank. I might just do it. . . . I had got through three months and installed myself in Red Ford on £48. The £72 might keep me going the six months that the *Alcestis* would certainly be delayed. . . . I began trying to make a version of the *Elektra* of Sophocles. . . .

Just after returning from calling on Pinker—Just after, you observe! . . . I drew two small cheques on my account. They were dishonoured. For a man of English public school training there is nothing left when faced by such discreditable bits of paper—nothing left but to leave the world.

By the next post I had a letter from Mr. Playfair. He asked me to send Mr. Drinkwater another copy of the *Alcestis*. Mr. Drinkwater had lost my manuscript. The play was to go into rehearsal at once.

There was no copy of the *Alcestis*. For economy's sake I had not had a duplicate copy typed and I had thrown away my manuscript. . . .

A friend had drawn out the whole of my £72 on two forged cheques! . . . Think of what my position would have been if Destiny had made me put off my call on Mr. Pinker!

PART TWO

"FLUCTUAT NEC MERGITUR"

PART TWO

CHAPTER ONE

On the 11th November 1922 Authority granted me a passport that permitted me to proceed to France. There was, as I passed through Trafalgar Square, a dense fog and the results of a general election coming in . . . an immense shouting mob in a muffled and vast obscurity. The roars made the fog sway in vast curtains over the baffled light-standard. That for me was the last of England.

It was perhaps November that had done it: or perhaps America, or perhaps an election agent. . . . I don't think I could have lived, with damaged lungs, through a third English winter. It had seemed to rise up before me like a black wall that I could never cross. . . . And America had come creeping in.

I had by then written a book—indeed I had written four . . . in the winters when one could not get out on the land. . . . And indeed, with my immense bailiff, Standing, and various other helpers I had more leisure. . . . So one book had been published—a sort of survey of letters and thought in England of the day. . . . I should imagine it was not a very good book. It was mostly propaganda for Ezra and his various schools of

Imagistes, Vorticistes and *vers libretistes* and, it must have been written in some bitterness. . . . No doubt it was even a little mad. I was still bitter about the treatment of my ex-comrades in arms. Those years come back to me as a sort of fog in which people moved about dimly, forging one's cheques, losing one's manuscripts, sewing tares amongst one's potatoes, and doing what they could to suppress one. In it one was completely isolated and forgotten.

Indeed I do not think I had many contacts with the outer world, being hidden in a green—a far too green —corner of England, on a hilltop that was almost inaccessible to motor traffic, under an immense screen of giant beeches. But I must have had some contacts. Fabians, as has always been the case on hilltops, drifted about and seemed to regard me as a brand to be snatched from the fires of militarism and Teutophobia and to be turned into a whitened fingerpost on the road towards Guild Socialism. . . . And Mr. Pound appeared, aloft on the seat of my immensely high dogcart, like a bewildered Stewart pretender visiting a repellent portion of his realms. For Mr. Pound hated the country, though I will put it on record that he can carve a sucking pig as few others can. With him I quarrelled about *vers libres* and he shortly afterwards left England and acquired his mastery of the more resounding rhythms. About the same time I had a visit from Mr. F. S. Flint, the beautiful imagiste poet who, unfortunately, had had a difference with Mr. Pound about French poetry and declared that he had given up writing poetry of his own. . . . That gang, which had given London its chance to become an Art Centre of the world had, to my great mournfulness, disappeared as the Rhine separates at its mouth and sinks into Dutch sands. Gaudier Brzeska had been killed; I had lost touch with H. D. and Mr. Percy Wyndham Lewis. . . . Conrad wrote to say that he had not earned a penny for over two years. . . . And we had ninety days of drought!

Then my book was published. . . . It met with no attention whatever. The gentleman who had approached me at the French Embassy wrote that it appeared to have been written in my dressing gown and slippers. A gentleman on the *Times*—which was still the property of Lord Northcliffe and on which I was blacklisted—declared that I seemed to think myself a literary personage, but I wasn't. Both statements were true. I nearly always write in my dressing gown and slippers. I am doing it at this moment—in a room that looks over the Mediterranean. . . . I tumble out of bed soon after it is dawn, put on those offending garments and start to write. I do my thinking for the day, in bed, looking at the sea as it dimly appears and, with my thoughts fresh in my mind, go straight to my writing. In that way I have finished work by ten or thereabouts, for the rest of the day I can garden. It seems as good a way as any other. I can not understand why that gentleman was so offended. . . . Mr. H. G. Wells used to write in that way: I daresay he still does. . . .

And then America came creeping in. *Poetry*, under

the editorship of Miss Harriet Monroe, suddenly, out of the blue awarded me a prize for the best poem of the year. I was making a stake and binder hedge on the top of the twelve-acre field with the glorious view when the letter was brought me. . . . My gigantic sows were forever breaking out. Their gentleman friend lived at Fittleworth, two miles down the hill, and they were a great nuisance for nothing in the world could stop them. Normally, when you live on a common, you have to fence out, not fence in. My beasts had grazing rights and if the neighbours' fences did not keep them out I had no responsibility for any damage they did. But that dread plague, the foot-and-mouth disease, appeared in that part of Sussex and there was a penalty of £50 for every beast of yours that was found on a road. That did not apply as far as the Common was concerned. Unfortunately Fittleworth was off the Common and that attractive boar lived next to the rose-covered, thatched cottage that was the police station.

And it was really agony to two stout gentlemen like myself and Mr. Standing to have to chase those enamoured and monstrous quadrupeds up and down those roof-like, beech-grown declivities, assisted by the red-headed hind and Joseph, the stable-boy, and the kitchen maid and the carpenter and his wife all yelling and beating tins—and all to almost no purpose. That county was Sussex and the emblem of Sussex is a hog and its motto: "Wunt be druv," and those were Sussex sows, impervious to blows, deaf to objurgations, indifferent, when love filled their bosoms, to the choicest porcine condiments. . . . Yet there was one thing they feared!

On one dreadful afternoon we had been completely worsted. We wiped our dripping brows and lumbered, Standing and I, to the shed where the cider barrels were. The red-headed Irishman went back to his digging of the potatoes, Joseph to his more uncongenial boots, the kitchen maid who dearly loved scampering over the hillside to her novelette in the scullery; Hunt, the carpenter, to his boards, and his wife to her washing, and their son who was in the Royal Artillery to his damnable bugle. And the great sow, Anna, was over the hills and away down to her beau.

And Standing interspersed his reminiscences of the hard old cider that the local earl used to give his workmen with the rueful words:

"Fifty pounds. It do seem a lot of money to lose over a sow. . . . It do seem a lot of money to lose over a sow. . . . Fifty pounds. . . ."

And I was, equally ruefully, thinking about overdrafts and interviews with a sympathetic but obdurate bank manager. . . .

A voice called from above the hedge—a lady's voice: "Hullo, Standing: Hi, Standing. . . . Here's your pig. . . . Here's the sow, Anna . . ." and there she was, trembling with eagerness to be let into her sty. . . .

That heroic lady, wheeling a perambulator with a baby in it had been coming up Fittleworth hill. She had met Anna and had driven the perambulator right against that monstrosity. . . . That had been too much for the sow, who dreaded perambulators as she feared no fiends. The sow had tried to make a break through, a turnip field but everywhere she went she met the perambulator, the lady occupying a strategic position on the road. So the sow had given in. . . . And we locked and bolted her in her sty, and we went to make up the gap in the hedge the sow had made . . . and Miss Monroe's amazing cheque came from the Middle West—from Porcopolis itself. . . .

The first queer thought that came into my head was: "Now I will get a *chien de berger alsacien*, a police dog. And call him Chicago! . . ."

I don't know why that came to me. I had never been conscious of wanting a police dog. I do not like dogs much unless they can be made to be useful and I don't believe you could train a police dog to herd pigs. . . .

In any case, it must have been an odd piece of double or triple cerebration. For whilst I was feeling thankful that someone—anyone in the world had noticed my poor poem, and meditating purchasing the dog, and thanking God that Anna, by a miracle, was in her sty, Standing said:

"I do hear it be a wonderful country. . . ."

I said:

"What country? . . . Where? . . ."

He said:

"This here South of France. . . . They do say it is a wonderful country."

I said:

"Yes: it's a wonderful country. But who's been talking about it?"

He said:

"You, Cahpt'n! You did say that if you had a few more windfalls you could get away to the South of France. . . . I hear it do be a wonderful country. They say the bees do work there all the year round. Here in the winter they has to creep to their haims and dorm till the spring. . . ."

Queer cerebration—for I had been quite unconscious of having mentioned the South of France. . . .

The New York *Times* said the other day that I am a master of the time-shift and duplicate cerebration in the novel. I daresay I am: at any rate I try to be . . . and if I have that ambition it is—it amuses me to think —the product, born that moment, of Miss Monroe, walking in the shadow of the water tower in the city of hogs—and of queer, heavy, badgerlike Standing, with his old dialect that was just half Anglo-Saxon and half forgotten French words—in the country whose emblem is also a hog. . . .

These things came together. . . . I should otherwise show more respect for the home of *Poetry* than to call it Porcopolis—a forgotten name.

Next day Standing had gone to Pulborough market to sell the eggs and I was feeding Anna in her sty. I was covered with mud to the eyes, in old khakis, shorts and an old khaki army shirt. . . .

A voice said over the hedge:

"Didn't I once meet you at Henry James's?"

Standing above me on the bank was the comfortable and distinguished figure of Sir Edward Elgar. I did not remember having met him at Henry James's but I knew him for the local great man—and of course as the composer of the *Dream of Gerontius*—and *Land of Hope and Glory*. . . .

There came into my mind suddenly the words:

"The band will play: '*Land of Hope and Glory*' . . .
The adjutant will say: 'There will be no more parades . . .' "

It worried me slightly that I could no longer be certain of all the phrases of that ceremonial for the disbanding of a battalion. . . . Nothing in the world was further from my thoughts than writing about the late war. But I suppose the idea was somewhere in my own sub-consciousness, for I said to myself:

"If I do not do something about it soon it is possible I shall forget about the details. . . ." And I wondered how the common friend of myself and Sir Edward would have treated that intractable subject. I imagined the tortuous mind getting to work, the New England scrupulousness, the terrific involutions . . . and for the rest of the day and for several days more I lost myself in working out an imaginary war-novel on the lines of "What Maisie Knew."

Then after a period of immense rains when it had dried a little and I was going to carry a pail of corn down to the bottom of the twelve-acre an immense shining automobile stopped outside the top-hedge. Two ladies like apparitions from a fashion paper descended and asked me the way to Mrs. Higgins's. Mrs. Higgins's was a thatched cottage just outside the hedge at the bottom of my land. They were going to see about Miss Higgins who had advertised herself as being a professed cook. . . .

I told them they had better not go down. They wore what appeared to be dancing pumps and the most elegant stockings, and woodmen had been hauling timber up the path which in the best of times was like a small watercourse. But they chanced it. Either they must have been good, plucked ones or they needed a cook very badly.

It had been long since I had met such creatures. It appeared that they had been at a garden party at Sir Edward's. They sank in mud to the knee over and over again, but they persisted and talked to me as if I were a bâtman of their husbands' regiment, saying once or twice: "My good man. . . ."

They came out of Mrs. Higgins' cottage. I waited for them outside to show them back over a dry path in my own copse. Mrs. Higgins must have primed them, for I had become for them the poor wounded and broken officer fellow. . . . It was: "Captain F——" this, and Captain F——" that in the best style of ladies bountiful visiting a sick camp.

Then they found that to be a terribly lonely place. What did I do in the long winter nights? . . . I was ready to be the poor wounded and broken footlogger if it pleased them. . . . I said:

"Oh you know . . . I . . . er . . . smoke a pipe, don't you know. . . ."

One of them announced herself as Mrs. Major So and So of somewhere away to the East on the chalk downs. The other was Miss So and So, the major's sister.

Miss So and So said:

"Don't you ever read a book?"

I said:

"Er . . . yes . . . I don't mind takin' a read in a book. . . . Now and then, you know. . . ."

The Mrs. Major said:

"Oh, but you ought to read books. . . . It's a good thing to do. . . . It broadens the mind. . . . You'll go rusty if you never read books. . . ."

Two or three days afterwards there arrived in my porch an immense parcel of books. I took it that some paper had had the impertinence to send me books for review and I did not open the parcel. Someone else did however and found a singular assortment of novels. There were works by Mr. Edgar Wallace and Mr. E. Phillips Oppenheim, and works of Mr. Archibald Marshall, and Conrad's "Chance" and Galsworthy's "Island Pharisees." . . . And they were accompanied by a card of Mrs. Major So and So bearing the words:

"In memory of your kindness. . . . Do read some of these books. There is something here for every taste. You appear to be quite an intelligent man. It is a pity to let yourself rust. . . ." But what most pleased me was that the parcel contained two novels by Major So and So himself.

They were productions of an almost incredible youth and innocence. You would have thought that Major—who had gone through the war in all its horror—had lived all his life in a rose-covered vicarage and the society of blameless milkmaids. . . . But there was a certain literary gift, and as far as they went, the subjects were rather ingenious.

So, being in the mood, I sat down and wrote an immensely long letter to Mrs. Major So and So—about her husband's books. I gave him counsel as I have so often given counsel to the innumerable beginners who send me manuscripts or first books. Only I took more trouble. I took those books to pieces and turned them inside out, I suggested alterations, analysed phrases and pointed out where it would have been a good thing to use the device of the time-shift. . . . Yes, I took some trouble with that letter. . . .

Two days later I got a post-card signed with the initials of the Major's wife and containing the two words:

"You *beast!*" and a quotation from one of my books.

But, once started working on the idea of the construction of novels, my mind went on and on. . . . And communications from America went on dropping in. They came from the East and they came from the West and they came from in between. They were mostly about my verse. I had thought no one knew that I wrote verse. Then they began to be about my lately published book which had sold a hundred copies in England and had not appeared at all in the United States.

One Western University announced that its English class was using that work as a textbook of 19th century literature.

That is not as astonishing as it sounds. I think my book was the only *au fond* study of Vorticism and Imagism and 1913 *vers Libre* that at the time existed. Those activities of Mr. Pound and his young friends had died in London. But during the war they had sown seeds in New York about West 8th Street between Fifth and Sixth Avenues and in the North Western University in Chicago and in places like Iowa or Berkeley, Cal. . . . I fancy those seeds have not yet died there. . . .

As I have elsewhere recounted, then there came a letter and an article about my work from a real Professor in a great Western University. That Don had pursued me through life with the persistency of a sleuth in a moving picture. No word of mine had he left unread: there seemed to be no phase of my life to which he had not applied the microscope. He provided me moreover with a full-fledged philosophy, religious views and a disbelief in the Infallibility of the Pope. It appeared that, years before, he had gone up the Rhine as far as Heidelberg on the same boat as myself. "But," he wrote modestly, "although I have read over a thousand anecdotes by this writer in not one of them does he mention myself. So I can only imagine that my personality made no impression at all upon him."

Next came—not by letter but in person—an intense and very energetic journalist from one of Mr. Hearst's papers. He professed a knowledge of my work and career, at least equal to those of the Professor of English, but I think he must have acquired it not by hard reading but, as it were, by the grace of God. He stayed with me for some time but if I ever, as must be the case with even quite retiring writers, mentioned one of my books it always happened to be one that, by accident, he had not read. I was none the less flattered that one with such varied attainments should even give himself the trouble to imagine he had read me.

There was nothing that fellow had not done. He had fought and farmed and camped in virgin forests and shot grizzlies and tracked down murderers and felled giant oaks and fought desperadoes. Unfortunately my tools did not suit him. He volunteered to drive the mare to the mill for middlings. He came back leading that amiable beast, having overturned the cart into a stream and broken off one of the wheels whilst the middlings melted in the water. I should have thought it impossible to make that mare do anything wrong. You could let off a firecracker under her tail and she would do no more than wag her ears. My friend however said he was unused to that sort of harness. In the far West they drive with the reins crossed. . . . He professed to share my passion for garlic and pulled up and devoured a large part of my plantation—raw. He told the doctor who administered the stomach pump that the garlic you bought in Avenue A. was different. . . .

But his great achievement was in felling trees. He described with enormous animation to Standing—who regarded him as a fabulous monster!—how he had cut down a hundred of the giant California redwood pines in—I think, an afternoon. Standing said:

" 'Is Lordship would pay him a pretty penny to be 'is wood-reeve!" and we went to cut some of my oak saplings, about as big as my thigh. Standing and I, when we used an axe, would take it near the end of the helve with the left hand and then, sliding our rights up to the axehead would use the left for strength in the down stroke and the right for guidance and weight. In that way we usually with little fatigue could go on for most of an afternoon. They must have used different axes in California. . . . My young friend grasped his firmly with both hands at the lowest extremity of the helve. He whirled it round and round his head as if he were giving a display with Indian clubs. Then he let go at the tree. The axehead glanced off and cut off the heel of his shoe.

Standing screamed! . . . That elderly, tough, bristling giant of a man gave a high scream like a horse that has broken its back. He went chalk-pale under his week's bristles and said:

"I could do with a gill of 'is Lordship's brandy!"

Then he turned on that young man like one of the grizzly bears he had shot. He described how Jim Selby had cut his leg clean through at the shin and how Jack Wilmot had killed his little daughter standing near him.

"I've seen fools!" he said. "But never a fool like you! Do you think a haxe is the teaspoon your mother fed pap to you with. . . ." And on and on and on. . . .

When it came to carrying these logs up the hill he selected—he was the master of the team—the heaviest and longest of all for that hero to stagger under.

"No, Cahpt'n," he said, when I remonstrated, "Yon one's felled in Caliyifornyer. . . . Let'm carry in Old England. . . ."

So Mr. Hearst's star provided infinite amazement in Sussex. In the end he took down by shorthand my best story and sold it to a London magazine for £16 that I could well have done with myself. . . . I don't know why people do things like that to me. I suppose they think I don't notice. . . .

There came afterwards through the summer a number of, as it were, paler Americans, most of them asking for no more than autographs. And I began to feel as if I must have a large American public. . . . Years ago, as I have elsewhere related, S. S. McClure had told me that my books would never sell in America because Americans could not tell whether I was or was not in earnest whilst they would not sell in England because the English knew that I was too damn in earnest.

I began to think that some quality of earnestness must have gotten into my work. It perhaps transcended in that quality what had disturbed hitherto my compatriots. . . . And I contemplated at last a novel. . . .

It was however the coming of the Middle West that gave me the final tilt towards Literature and away, alas apparently forever from hogs! . . . I will here interpose a note on the marketing of hogs. For it was hogs that made Chicago what she was and it was in the end

Chicago with its North Western University that tipped my scale away from them. The wise student of agricultural markets will tell you—as you could very well tell him!—that to make money by hogs you must buy when the market is low and market when it is high. . . . That is easy, but, alas, I have never had money to buy with when the market was low, only when, as in this case, it was at its very apex! Though my hogs increased in girth and progeny, in exactly the same progression the market fell. Thus when at last I sold I broke exactly even, my considerable herd of swine fetching almost to a penny what my original two or three pedigree beasts had cost in 1919. So that, if we put the pork and hams that we ate and sold against what we bought in the way of food for the hogs, I had lost only my time and labour. This, though it might have disappointed another man was eminently satisfactory to me since it was the money brought in by those beasts and other stock that let me eventually make my break away to Provence. So Anna and her sisters and descendants proved to be money pigs. But for them I should have frittered away both my time and my money. Moreover the labour spent on them in the open air had enormously improved my health, and robust health is a necessity for any very large literary undertaking!

Letters then, had for some time been coming to me from the North Western University. I guessed it to be—as indeed it was!—a regular nest of singing birds. And there was about those letters from the unknown

a certain freshness at once of outlook and expression.
. . . My old bones stirred. . . .

Then came several agreeable young men and then
a letter from Mr. Cunninghame Graham introducing
other young men from the Middle West. That immense
region appeared to hear of that incomparable writer of
English and noble horseman at about the same moment
as it heard of myself. The letter giving the name and
address of one of these young men I immediately lost
and although I remembered the young man's name I
could not for the life of me remember the address except that it was near either Earl's Court or Gloucester
Road station on the underground. Mr. Graham's letter
had been so generous in praise of the young poet that
I addressed two letters to him in that neighbourhood,
the one being addressed simply: "Near Earl's Court Station" and the other "near Gloucester Road." His
Majesty's intelligent Postoffice promptly delivered the
first into the hands of Mr. Glenway Wescott and returned the second to me.

So destiny and the mail service conspired to make
me write. For if Mr. Wescott had not paid me a visit
of some duration I do not think that I should have
taken seriously again to writing. He was himself charming, intelligent in the extreme and a delicious poet just
having his first affair with the muse. That in itself was
good enough. But, in addition, he gave me an idea of a
great background of youth, intelligence and energy in
æsthetic pursuits. It was as if a sort of French Romantic
movement that in its æsthetic aims alone was not spe-

cifically romantic—as if a great stirring of æsthetic life were taking place on the shores of those Lakes. I saw indeed, even then, that it must be from there that an initial spurt towards new literary life must come—if it was to come from anywhere. Here was a vast country of new and hitherto unknown intelligences. And it was the one great tract in the Western World that had remained at once unstirred and unwearied by the late War. It was virgin soil indeed.

I must make the confession of selfishness that it was rather in the light of a possible audience than as a ground to produce masterpieces that I viewed that new public. If one is to write one must have at least the mirage of an audience and I could not see anywhere else in the world any body of men that could, by the light of the wildest optimism, be expected to give me any kind of suffrage. These young men seemed already to have accepted my ideas.

That in England I should ever have any hearers I knew to be impossible. More or less consciously for me to be in touch with youth is a necessity if I am to write, so that I have gone on writing until my hair is as white as it ever will be and still it is usual for critics to write of me—usually with distaste—as belonging to the Younger School. But in England at that date there appeared to be no youth—outside the workhouse or the gaol. The young men that I saw were charming and well mannered but the charming and well mannered are no audience for me. Indeed there seems to be about me something repellent to the well-bred English mind. I presume I am too much in earnest!

And the few contacts I had with literary London were not such as to inspirit me. Conrad wrote, as I have said, that for two years he had not earned a penny by his pen. Mr. Cunninghame Graham wrote that he had no readers at all. My own work had not sold a hundred copies in England. . . . And there was Mr. Coppard. . . .

I don't know what made Mr. Coppard come and stay with me. . . . Or perhaps I do. My old friend the *Saturday Review* under a new editorship was pursuing the very admirable policy of preserving in what it published a reasonable balance between creative and what is called "serious" writing. I bought it one day at a book stall and came upon a piece of work that made me at once see that a new force existed in England. It was a story by Mr. Coppard relating how when he was nearly starving he had bought some bananas. I had never till then heard of Mr. Coppard. . . . Then I saw other stories by that writer and I became convinced that England possessed a short-story writer as great as any there ever had been. Of that opinion I remain. . . .

I happened to have tried my own hand at a short story. I was never any good at that form. I need length —and as often as not quite preposterous length—to get an effect. But as I was convinced I could not then write anything competent I thought I might as well try that form as any other. I did not feel proud of that story— but if one is to live one must have some illusions as to work one has just finished and I sent it to the *Saturday Review*. I added to my accompanying letter some sentences of admiration for Mr. Coppard's stories and said that I should be obliged if the Editor would get someone in his office to send me Mr. Coppard's address.

That story came back with astonishing promptitude. By the post mark on the stamp I could see that it could not have been in the office of that journal for more than ten minutes. . . . It had been time enough for someone to write on the printed slip of rejection a message to the effect that the writer would have imagined that I could have told from inspection of the columns of the *Saturday* that that journal demanded at least a glimmering of technical ability in the short stories that it printed. He added that they never gave the addresses of their contributors to outsiders.

I understood that whoever wrote that could not have liked me much. I fancy—but indeed I know—that he talked about what he had written to one or other of the amiable young men about Fleet Street who had been down to see me. At any rate a day or two later the young man in question wrote to me to say that Mr. Coppard would consent to honour me with a visit if I would write and invite him.

Then Mr. Coppard came. I have said that he produced on me the impression of a gipsy. I had taken him, from his writings, to be Irish or Welsh but he was neither and, with his exquisite perception of form he could not be English. So I found in my mind the conviction that he must be a gipsy and that conviction gained immensely when I met him, dark, lean, hard in physique as in intellect and with piercing dark eyes under a deep hat brim, sitting on beech-logs and giving out all the wisdom of an ancient and cruel world. From what he chose to relate of his biography—of how, from being employed as a little boy by a kindly sweating tailor, he came at last to be secretary of the local branch of the Fabian Society in Oxford and met the more intelligent of the undergraduates, all the while working in an electric light bulb factory and reading unceasingly Conrad and other writers in that day unknown—I gathered that this real prophet had met with very little honour in the country he had honoured by his birth. It was not merely that for an extended space of time he had had practically nothing but raw grated carrots to eat in a lost cottage in a damp corner. I had lately—and at times frequent enough before and since I have—been through sufficient experiences of lost, damp cottages and little to eat to know that such vicissitudes do the writer himself little but good. I am not one of those who believe that the writer should have knowledge of millionaire yachting on the Aegean or Palace Hotels on the Côte d'Azur. I would rather pass my life in the dampest of damp hovels and nothing is more deleterious for a writer than to devote serious attention to the fixings of a Blue Train. If in short he cannot imagine for himself what happens in yachts, palaces and drawing rooms he may as well not start out on the career of writer. . . . But it is bitter bad for a country that it should have a writer of the genius of Mr. Cop-

175

pard and let him live in lost cottages on a diet of grated carrots. It proves itself to be a country that no writer will love and that all will leave as soon as they can. I care, in fact, very little about the personal vicissitudes of artists. Hardships will kill some but make men of more. But I will if I can live in a country where the arts are at least enough honoured to get their practitioners, again at least, lip service. . . . Here when I am writing, when I am finishing a book, the grocer and the butcher and the laundress and the proprietor of the bureau de tabac all learn of the fact through no volition of mine and, if members of my family go through the village they will at every step be stopped by inquirers asking how the work progresses, whether I am bearing up under the strain and how long it will take. My landlord will travel to distant forests to get me a root of asphodel because all poets must have asphodel! . . . Why, only yesterday, there was living in that village a poet—American, not even French. Because of the fall of the dollar he left precipitately. His landlady was at a loss to understand his departure and when told that the reason had in fact been nothing but pennilessness:

"My God!" she exclaimed, "If I had known that. . . . The great poet! . . . He could have had my house for nothing, and I would have found food for him and his family. . . . For good, if necessary. . . ."

I was lying this morning before dawn, looking at the Mediterranean framed in a tall oblong by the pillars of the terrace. The lights of the Island of St. M——

were still burning; the light-house at the entry of the harbour flashed hurriedly and without ceasing. As abruptly as if a conductor had raised his bâton the chorus of small birds began. There was no visible greyness. Nevertheless that was the salute to the saffron finger of the dawn. Ulysses, it is said, once put in for shelter in the cave beneath the garden.

The bird chorus is an unceasing, silver pizzicato. There are none of the great woodwind performers that you get in the immense uproar of the London dawn. Here they eat all the thrushes and blackbirds and larger warblers. They call them, as I have said, all *grives*, and in consequence the vines are devoured by Eudernes, Pyrales, Grisettes, Erinoses, Cochineal beetles, wasps, hornets. . . . But the little voices fuse into one volume. It drowns the courtship of the frogs and the silver bell-note of the toad that have sounded all night.

A greyness is there and a single, agonising note infinitely prolonged. Instantly the chorus of small ones ceases—as picadors, banderilleros, and all the rest of the *corrida* fall to mere spectators when the great shining one advances solitary over the sand. The lights of St. M— die; the sea is like listening, grey satin. The lighthouse turns more slowly so as to miss no note. It is the nightingale:

In April
Come he will:
In May
He sings all day:
In June

He changes his tune:
In July
He prepares to fly:
In August
Go he must. . . .   the bird from Africa that
broods there across the sea.

The first beam of the sun struck on the white foot
atip of the mountainous island. The flash of the light-
house was no more there. That soloist concluded his
rhapsody. It was the silence of dawn.

I went down into the garden to see how the pimentos
we had pricked out last evening had got through the
night. The nights are still too cool—cold even!—to let
things make the progress they should when the sun
is down. . . . But the first beams of the sun are as
warm as in a New England July. . . .

I went back to lie down and think. . . . I went back
to London in September 1922. . . . Someone had asked
me to a dinner at the Kettner's to meet Mr. Sinclair
Lewis and his wife. . . . Mrs. Lewis had a golden
sheath-gown and her golden hair coiled over her ears.
I sat between her and Miss May Sinclair and opposite
to Mr. H. G. Wells and an American lady journalist—
Mrs. Ryan I think—and various of the English great. I
should not have gone there if I had known they would
be there. I felt like a toad in a dréss waistcoat
pocket. . . .

The dinner was—of course!—given by Mr. Harry
Forman, the editor of *Collier's Weekly* who sent me
to report the Cardinals' Consistory at Rome. He had

a great admiration for my style—years ago. I know it was real because, not only did he ask me from amongst my hogs to that dinner, but, years after, he asked me to his house on Reading Ridge. It looks over to the distant, romantic gleam of the Sound as, from *Le Revest des Eaux* here, you look over a more Southern Sea. And he opened his last bottle of Perrier-Jouet which he had kept against my chance coming ever since the descent of the 18th Amendment on those climes. You *must* sincerely admire a man's style if you do that for him. Why: it is to treat you like Apollo, the very god of stylists!

I wonder if he still admires my style! For it is one of the tragedies of the long literary round that they drop out one by one, your admirers! You mark, as it were, a day of praise with a red mile-stone. . . . Then, years afterward, you get a letter saying—or they say to you . . . as Mr. Watts Dunton said to Mr. —— afterwards Sir Ralph—Ralph—Hall Caine:

"H——, you left us long ago. And since then we have seen from the public prints that you have written some books. . . ."

Years ago—I should say in 1913—I was on the top of a bus in front of the Bon Marché. I saw Miss Gertrude Stein driving with a snail-like precision her Ford car. It was a vehicle of the original model of my namesake and with its great height above the roadway gave to Miss Stein, driving, the air of awfulness of Pope or Pharaoh, borne aloft and swaying on their golden thrones. I sprang down from my bus in order to pursue that phenomenon, for I had been going to call on her. I wanted to speak to her. I was leaving Paris that afternoon and should have no opportunity for a long time.

I do not remember what it was exactly that I wanted to talk to her about. I have had so many and such long arguments with that old friend—or enemy—that they seem to fuse, the one into the other in an unbroken chain of battle. It must however have been about the sculpture of either Mr. Joseph Epstein or poor Gaudier Brzeska. She had written—or more probably she was reported to me as having said—something caustic and contemptuous, probably about Gaudier. And at that date Miss Stein was both Pope and Pharaoh of the picture-buying world.

At any rate I was determined to have it out with her about something and I trotted on keeping that procession in sight for quite a number of blocks. She outdistanced me in a stretch of roadway that was quite clear of traffic whereas the sidewalks were blocked. It occurred to me that she must be going to Picasso's: I took a taxi. But she was not at Picasso's. A number of people were and they were all disliking the new stage in which that cubist found himself, all having been enthusiastic patrons of his earlier representational work. Upon one of them—I think it was that prominent dilettante, the Comte de Beaumont—the painter turned and said:

"You used in the old days to say that I drew better than Raphael and painted better than Velasquez. You said it, not I. I never said it." How then was it that they—being nobodies—dared to question him—the divine master, by their own accounts!—if in his wisdom he saw fit to take other directions? Did they imagine that he could no longer draw better than Raphael or was it to be imagined that they thought that they, the nobodies of the audience, made the masterpieces of the divine draughtsman? That was probably what they did think. . . . Then let them go away and find other divine artists to paint, under their directions, works which were better than those of Raphael.

I am not Picasso. My sympathies are altogether with revolutionary work and with no other. I would rather read work of Miss Stein or Mr. Joyce or look at the work of Picasso himself than consider the work of a gentleman who wrote like Thackeray or drew like Apelles. They may write or draw better than either master: I can do without them. But I cannot see that my own work is in the least revolutionary. I go on my way like a nice old gentleman at a tea-party. Occasionally it strikes me that if I change a little my method of sequence in presenting scenes, or shorten my sentences and occasionally put in instead of chasing out all assonances I may feel a little better. But all over the world there are, I am aware, gentlemen and ladies lamenting that I don't write as I wrote when I was eighteen or twenty-seven or thirty-six or forty-five. Or even fifty-four.

There is a German Professor, in Hamburg, I think, who castigates me for no longer imitating the verse of the Minnesingers; a critic in New York asks each time

I produce a book, why don't I continue the adventures of the hero of a book I was sick and tired of ten years ago; painters upbraid me for no longer writing about Art as I used to do in 1913; Mr. Gordon Craig burst in on me the other day and said, from 9 p.m. to 4 a.m. that I never should be any good again unless I once more dabbled in theatrical managing and propaganda as I did in the early days of the Irish Theatre. My most cherished disciple banged me over the head the other day because I try nowadays to break up my sentences a little. Hemingway, I was told, had done that until he was quite written out. Was I to gain immortality imitating Hemingway? Let me pull myself together.

I didn't know that I was imitating Mr. Hemingway. I may have been. I am not above taking anything from anybody if it will help me not to be bored by my own rhythms. I sometimes get a shock as if in a nightmare at hearing my own voice going on and on. And on. Little, short sentences are conversations. Wave answers wave. It is no longer monologue that flows and flows and how can you stop it? . . . But if you do stop it you lose disciples and patrons. You can only hope to pick up others.

Sometimes you do not. . . . Berkeley, Cal., used to be a regular centre for the dissemination of my writings. That was because of the efforts of the Professor of English. I have mentioned him several times out of gratitude because the article in which he provided me with a philosophy and said I disbelieved in the infallibility of the Pope gave me my initial shove back into literature.

I have, it must be apparent, no philosophy and subscribe to the doctrine of Papal Infallibility. Why shouldn't I? It does not seem to matter much. All the same it was Professor Marsden Price who made me again suffer from writer's cramp.

One should not meet one's life heroes. The poor professor came to stay with me on that farm and he was dismayed. He was on his way to Strasburg for his Sabbatical year and he expected to find me looking like a poet. I looked like a tramp dressed in military clothes that I had rescued from a scarecrow and talking of hogs. And after dinner—it was midsummer and the days very long—we made him ted hay—in evening dress.—I have always dressed for dinner when I was farming.—And it was warm and American evening dress is not made for tedding hay!—And my house having been built before the discovery of the United States contained nothing in the way of what the French call *conforts modernes*. . . . I have said that I am indifferent to comfort! . . . And after a long summer day of farming I am usually indifferent to literary conversation. . . .

So in his first lecture on his return from Strasburg to Berkeley the Professor took it out of me by saying that I was inarticulate and—this was what was bitter—that I did not talk German as well as I thought I did. . . . I daresay I am inarticulate. At tea-parties I find it difficult to know what to talk about and frequently wish that I had made notes for conversational openings on my shirt-cuffs. . . . But I had never thought about how I talked German any more than I think about how I wind up

the clock. I just talk—as I talk half a dozen languages.
. . . So how could the professor measure my own estimate of my powers over the tongue of Mr. Hitler? . . .

That rankled for years. At last I found myself in
Strasburg. The day of my revenge had come. I positively seized a postcard and wrote upon it that I did not
wonder the Professor thought my German faulty—if
that was where he learnt the language! . . . The language of Strasburg, like everything else in Alsace since
the war, is admirable. It is better than German German
—but it is not the German of Goethe. Or even of President Hindenburg!

It was a regrettable incident. I should not have written that postcard. I never indulged in any other contro-
versy in my life. So to punish me no one from Berkeley,
Cal., ever now asks me for autographs. . . .

It all came really from dressing for dinner. I don't
quite know why I do dress for dinner. My grandfather
always did it. He said that, after a hard day's work when
you were covered with paint you had to change your
clothes and you might just as well put on a boiled rag
and what goes with it as anything else. Marwood also
used to dress always. He said it was economical. It gives
your day clothes a longer life and evening things last
for ever. Certainly that dress suit in which I entertained
Professor Price and tedded hay bore Marwood out for
I had had it—in 1922—since 1898 and most of my other
clothes must have been nearly as old. . . . But I think
I do it because I like the feel of broadcloth and silk on
my hands after I have been all day in the open and the

dreadful mud. . . . America in any case went on clos-
ing in on me.

At Mrs. Forman's dinner the brilliant and noisy conversation turned on nothing but boxing. Kid Lewis was
fighting someone—it may have been Carpentier trying
to stage a return. Everyone of the great at that table
except Miss May Sinclair bet a little on one or the other.
I myself have never made a bet on a sporting event in
my life. Mr. Sinclair Lewis took bets with the gay
désinvolture of a bookie at the Derby. He backed his
namesake and I didn't know whether to be more concerned at the amount he stood to lose or impressed by
the fact that a mere novelist could even contemplate
such high finance. . . . And the talk about boxing
went on and on and on. . . .

I myself might have talked. It was a little my subject.
The Welsh Regiment was famous for its boxers. We had
produced Bombardier Wells, the incomparable Jimmy
Wilde, the famous Ted Driscoll. I had refereed at innumerable boxing matches and had of course put on
the gloves a little. But I held my tongue in face of my
literary betters.

It was unfortunate. Miss May Sinclair alone had no
opinions on boxing—the world was boxing-mad in
those days: I suppose it was the last reverberation of
militarism. But Miss Sinclair—all praise to her—had no
opinions about it. She therefore fixed upon me and demanded fifty pounds—for a poet at Oxford. The poet,
she said was a very good poet. He had, during the war,
contracted tuberculosis of the brain whilst serving in

his father's khaki clothing-store. In return for those war services he was given two free years at Oxford. But these were coming to an end; the tuberculosis of the brain was no better and it was imperative that the poor fellow should be sent to Palermo and kept there for two years more. Miss Sinclair said she thought that rich writers like herself and a celebrity at the other end of the table and I . . .

I said: "I beg your pardon. . . ."

Miss Sinclair said that if the writers who had grown rich by writing, like myself, herself, and the other celebrity . . .

The celebrity at the other end of the table was the gentleman who had said in the *Times* that I thought I was a personage but I wasn't. He was saying that boxing had nothing to do with thews or sinews. It was a matter of relative brain convolutions. A man with short brain convolutions . . .

From the other side of the table Mr. Wells cried:

"What's Fordie whispering to May? . . . Fordie move your chair away from May's. . . . We all want to hear. . . ."

Miss Sinclair said:

"It is certainly your duty to subscribe to this fund. . . . You've done well by writing. . . . You've come into this large fortune. . . ."

The celebrity at the other end of the table exclaimed:

"Give me the training of the smallest guttersnipe

against the largest brute and if he's got the right convolutions . . ."

I couldn't help it: I said:

"Did you ever *see* a fight . . ."

He went on:

"When Bombardier Wells fought Carpentier . . ."

I had been all through the training of Bombardier
Wells. He had been Sergeant-Instructor in my battalion
and I had been all through the fight over and over again
with him in the last four years. He had rotten legs.

I was in the worst of moods. I have made it a practice
all my life to give anyone anything they asked for—
supposing I had it. . . . I had not at the moment fifty
pounds but I had my capital in hogs. . . . I wondered
if it was my duty to sell my hogs. . . . I was even then
harassed beyond bearing by starving ex-soldiers. If Miss
Sinclair's protegé had served in anything else than a
shoddy store I would have sold my hogs. . . . On the
other hand he was a poet. Miss Sinclair said he was a
good poet. It is one's duty to help poets. . . .

Mr. H. G. Wells exclaimed from the other side of the
table:

"Fordie, move your chair away from May's. . . .
We want to hear. . . ."

All the while Kid Lewis was fighting at the Albert
Hall. I could see the firm flesh of those boxers though I
was looking at Mrs. Sinclair Lewis who was in a golden
sheath gown and had her hair in bandeaux over her ears.

The celebrity said:

"The brain convolutions of Carpentier . . ."

Miss Sinclair said:

"Come now, Fordie, it's your duty. I am surprised at you. You pass for being generous. . . ."

I exclaimed as loud as I could:

"Damn it all, Wells has got rotten legs! No man in spite of his excellent foot work . . . Wells's foot work is the best there is. But no man with legs like Wells's can stand up in the limelight without his knees knocking together. . . . Wells can't stand the limelight. . . . But look at Lewis. . . . There are legs for you. . . ."

A lady said: "But we can't *see* their legs! Couldn't they stand up,"

Mr. Wells said to Mr. Forman:

"Look here: you make Fordie move his chair away from May's."

Miss Sinclair said hotly:

"What does he mean? . . . What's the horrid little man? . . ."

The celebrity was looking disgusted at being interrupted by a nobody. He was wiping his lips with his handkerchief. I wondered why he used his handkerchief instead of his napkin.

Mr. Wells said:

"Fordie knows everything. . . . He knows which man's been doped or which is fighting on the cross. . . . He ought to share his information and not give it to a desperate gambler like May who will doublecross us all."

Miss Sinclair said:

188

"Don't pay any attention to him. . . . I am trying to make you see that unless we writers stick together. . . ."

The celebrity called from the other end of the table:

"Haw. . . . H. G. who's your omniscient friend?"

Mr. Wells at that time had a little joke about my omniscience just as he liked to tease Miss Sinclair about her sporting proclivities. He exclaimed:

"That's . . ." and he declaimed my name and titles.

It was as if the celebrity felt something disagreeing violently with him.

He said:

"Good God! Disgraceful! They told me that that fellow . . ."

I did not hear the end of his sentence because at the moment there came the news of the result of the fight. . . . But I fancy "they" had told that fellow that, like everyone else who had served in the War, Mr. Well's omniscient friend was in either the workhouse or the gaol. Otherwise he would hardly have written what he had written in the *Times*. For to the Londoner it is incredible that you could leave London—even though it is to earn your living on a hogfarm or to idle by the Mediterranean—to the real ingrained Londoner it is incredible that you should leave London except under the stress of poverty or *force majeure*. . . .

The only results of the great fight that I can remember was that Mr. Sinclair Lewis raked in an incredible number of banknotes. He garnered them from the table-cloth and stuffed them into his hat. Then he inverted the hatful over the hands of one of the waiters! It was an impressive gesture and gave one to dream of what, in America, may await the novelist who unites as Henry James would have said, considerable technical ability to an enviable gift of popularity.

PART TWO

CHAPTER TWO

IT IS TO BE TRANQUILLY OVERWHELMED TO
see the Mediterranean just before dawn, stretching out
beneath your windows. There will be the grey satin of
the sea, the mountains behind, the absolutely convincing
outline of Reinach's Greek villa at the end of Beaulieu
Point. And the memory of Greek Gods.

As I have said, I do not suppose I retain more than
the merest crumbs of classical scholarship. . . . A
couple of hundred lines of the Æneid; a few score
couplets of Ovid; the usual tags of Horace, a little
Catullus; even less of the Greek Anthology; a few sentences of Xenophon! But my passion for the classics remains. It is one of the greatest pleasures of my life that
a legend avers that Ulysses once sheltered in the sea-
cave below my garden. If I close my eyes I can see
Pallas Athene with shield and spear stand in the sky
and brood above her sea. Or if you quote to me: "*Saepe
te in somnis vidi* . . ." or merely mention to me the
name of Catullus you will have me in such a state that I
must leave my writing and walk from end to end of the
terrace for some minutes. . . .

But I do not think it is that that has given me my life-long passion for the shores of this inland sea . . . nor even the glamour of the poets of Provence in the land that lies behind these coasts. . . . It is perhaps almost more the tradition of the wonderful country where the bees do work all the year round—the land where the lemon flower blooms. . . . Or perhaps it is the absolute conviction that the weariness and griefs of humanity came when they put these shores behind them. . . . Mankind ought never to have left these islands. . . .

I reached Harold Munro's villa at St. Jean Cap Ferrat on one of the last days of 1922. It was six years since I had seen the Mediterranean, going back to the line from the Red Cross hospital at Mentone. . . . The Red Cross train had stopped for an hour, at midnight, at Tarascon, and, from the high railway platform I had seen the whole of the Camargue and half Provence under snow. That is a thing you will see only once every forty or fifty years. . . . And I was to see the whole of France under snow—white from Marseilles to Hazebrouck. There a reddish coloration seemed to add itself to the dark landscape.

That would be in February 1916. . . . I desperately disliked going back to the line. My lungs were in a terrible condition still and I knew that I had been sent up because of the mistake of a Category Clerk. The depot authorities who wanted to retain my services had told me as much—but in those days you did not claim exemptions merely on the score of a lung or so. . . . It was nevertheless hard. . . .

It was then I think that I had really taken my farewell

of literature. Under the shrouded lamps of the railway bookstall at Hazebrouck I had seen one of my own books. That had filled me with intense melancholy—with overpowering sadness. . . . The ambition to write dies hard and till then, either through the French publication of my propaganda works or because, even during the first battle of the Somme, I received orders to write this or that, I had retained at any rate some contact with the world of letters. . . . In that ghostly station it was as if the silver cord had snapped.

But I was no sooner installed on those heights from which one could throw a biscuit on to the decks of the men of war in Villefranche bay—and see the octopus and mullet swim beneath those keels . . . than at once, to invert the words of M. Herriot, this English poet, no longer so very young, threw away the sword and grasped the goose quill. . . . I wrote the first words of an immense novel. . . .

That climax had begun on the Feast of St. Katherine —the 25th of November 1922, as I was crossing the square in front of Notre Dame de Paris. It was perhaps not quite the 25th but I like to think that most phases of my career have begun on or about that feast of a saint for whom I have the greatest admiration. I met, under the shadow of the statue of Charlemagne a man called Evans. He had been in my regiment and we stopped to talk for a minute or two. Then we went into Notre Dame and looked at the little bright tablet that commemorates the death of over a million men.

I said:

"Do you remember that 17th September?"

He said:

"Surely to gootness, ton't I!" He was of course Welsh—one of the little, dark persistent race. . . .

In September 1916 we had both been rejoining the battalion after sick leave. He came from England where he had been recovering after a wound in the thigh; I from a place called Corbie where nothing more romantic had happened than having my teeth fixed after having been blown into the air by something and falling on my face.

It had been from some date in August till about the 17th September that I had completely lost my memory so that, as I have said, three weeks of my life are completely dead to me though I seem to have gone about my duties as usual. But, by the first of September I had managed to remember at least my own name and, by the 17th, when Evans and I rejoined the battalion, which had come out of the line and gone in again to the G trenches in front of Kemmal Hill, facing Wyndschaete, I could remember most Army matters fairly well.

We had gone down hill in clear sunlight over an atrocious field road. We were sitting on the driver's seat of a G. S. limbered waggon that held our luggage, going down sharply and barbarously jolted. . . . Evans said—in Notre Dame:

"Surely to gootness, whateffer, I thocht my powels would drop out when I saw our shells pursting on Wyhtschaete!"

194

I felt like that too, as I could assure him. We had commanded a tremendous view of the Salient from our box seats where we jolted down between broad fields covered with wheat in shooks and tobacco plants yellowing beneath the sun. And there, on the dark line, under the remaining roofs of the martyred village, in the light of the same sun, came the little white bursts—like cotton pods. It was all going on just as it had always gone on —and as if it had always gone on like that, all our lives. . . . Yes, I had felt as if my heart were dropping through my bowels.

The wagon had jolted more abominably than ever and I could, in Notre Dame, remember that I had felt beside my right thigh, for the brake. The beginnings of panic came over me. I had forgotten whether I found the brake!

I said urgently:

"Evans, do you remember what sort of brake a limbered wagon has?" Was it a little wheel that you turned round and round? or an iron lever that operated the shoe on the wheel?

Evans could not say whether limbered waggons had any brakes at all.

My panic became worse. It seemed a catastrophe that I could not remember what those brakes had been like. The memory that had chosen to return after Corbie must be forsaking me again. . . . I could remember that the Germans had dropped bombs on the hospital and that a nun had been killed. . . . But it was a catastrophe to forget about the brakes. . . . There were perhaps no brakes. . . .

I exclaimed hurriedly:

"Evans. . . . Let's go and have some . . . oysters!" They were the only things I could think of. Drink would only increase my panic and I wanted to keep my head clear.

We sat for a long time outside the café, on the right of the Place St. Michel, where you look towards the Seine. They used to have very good oysters there and towards the end of November when the sea grows really cold they are at their best. . . .

I thought Evans had been killed the day after we had got back to the line—but he obviously hadn't. He had been farming in Canada after a very bad wound. He had had a hard time and that, as much as the war, had made him prematurely bald. Bald men are usually fat but he was thin as it was possible to be, and small, with ecclesiastical features and a rather mournful manner. He was not really mournful for he had done well in Alberta and had come to Paris to have some fun and to buy agricultural machinery. He went on talking and talking in his mournful voice—about putting in rail posts, I think, with the frost at 30 below zero. . . . He fortunately didn't want to do anything but talk and my panic grew and grew. . . . I sat there, watching the crowds of students that go ceaselessly by after the classes of the Sorbonne are over. I sat thinking and thinking till long after Evans had gone—trying to pluck up courage. It would not come.

At last I went to a cocktail party, given by a French writer with an American wife. That party was like death. People sat about with panic-stricken faces, silent. You would have thought that everyone there had lost all his relations and all their fortunes and a war. . . . Proust was dead. He had died that afternoon. My taxi-driver had said to me as I paid him:

"*Paraît qu'il est mort! C'était bien inattendu!*" I had thought he had been speaking of Clémenceau who was sick at the time.

Paris was a stricken city. In every house, in every café, on all the sidewalks people said continually: "It seems that he is dead. It was very unexpected." They knew that Proust had complained of his health for many years. The whole city knew that. He had adopted fantastic modes of life on account of his health. . . . But that had been taken to be merely hypochondria expressed in the terms of a great, exotic novelist. . . . Now—it seemed that he was dead and Paris was a stricken city.

I had seen something like it in London—when Marie Lloyd died. London traffic stopped for half a minute whilst the paper boys ran down the streets shouting: "Ma-*rie* dies! Ma-*rie*'s dead!" But Paris was hushed for three days—and not for a music hall singer. . . . At that time if you said to a waiter: "Where's the funeral?" he told you or if, being in deep black you hailed a taxi, the man, without orders, drove you straight to where Proust lay in state. . . . At the same time Paris was preparing the paroxysm of hatred that attended the

hideously stage-managed last hours of Anatole France.
. . . On the boulevards they hissed: "Ten thousand
men of letters are starving whilst they walk the pavements of the city yet that irreverend dotard who betrayed France has spent upon his prolonged death-rattle
a fortune drawn from the pockets of a world that hates
France!" . . . For indeed the fortunes spent on cabling
the old man's last babblings to innumerable papers of a
gaping world came from German and Anglo-Saxon
coffers. Paris would have let him drift out of life quietly
enough but for that.

Proust represented France of that day with a singular
intimacy that is not easy for the poor world-at-large to
understand. He was the culmination of a school of
writers that had been long in coming and, still more, he
was the Unknown Soldier of the literature of that
decade. Literature enters with an unparalleled intimacy
into French life and the country had a sense of the
subterranean and ignored strivings of that steadfast personality—as if indeed he had been the personification of
the obscure beings who, working subterraneously with
small spades in hidden tunnels, had saved France for the
world.

I shared the feeling to the full. The death of Proust
came to me like the dull blow of a softened club. That
statement, I am aware, will read like hypocrisy when
I go on to say that I had not read a word he had written.
But it is not hypocrisy. I had not read him for a very
definite professional reason but I had heard with avidity
all that was to be heard of him. Thus for a long time I

had had an extremely vivid sense of his personality and of his activities. . . . And indeed it added to the blow that I was to have met Proust himself on the very evening of his death.

Nevertheless it was his death that made it certain that I should again take up a serious pen. I think those that know my record will acquit me of the implication that might be read into that statement. I had no idea of occupying Proust's place and even at that date I still dreaded the weaknesses in myself that I knew I should find if I now made my prolonged effort. I was still tired and I have always been lazy.

I think I am incapable of any thoughts of rivalry. There is certain literary work to be done. As long as it is done I don't care who does it. The work that at that time—and now—I wanted to see done was something on an immense scale, a little cloudy in immediate attack but with the salient points and the final impression extraordinarily clear. I wanted the Novelist in fact to appear in his really proud position as historian of his own time. Proust being dead I could see no one who was doing that. . . .

I was at the time merely passing through darkly tumultuous and crowded Paris. I wanted to get to my Mediterranean shores and their sunlight and solitary peace. I wanted to hear on the dry rocks the baked wind sift through the tufts of lavender and thyme amongst which the bees do work the year round. . . . They really do!

But I stayed in Paris long enough to get a fair view

of the literary situation. . . . One cannot, of course, if one is a working novelist, ever afford to get completely out of touch with the Paris literary situation. I certainly never have. One buys a book here and there. Someone mentions a French name and you store it in the memory. And, during my obscuration, Flint and Pound had kept me terrifically aware of at least the verse situation in Paris. When they were together they quarrelled like giants fighting with the arms of windmills. When they were apart they bombarded me with letters accusing each other of the worst of crimes. But the crimes were all obscurely connected with the merits of Paul Fort and Spire and Claudel and Paul Valéry and Francis Jammes so that I got a fair view of those poets. Occasionally they would fight about the Dada movement which was then going strong or I would learn about Piccabia and Philippe Soupault and Tristan Tsara and would rejoice to think that at last in the post-war world there existed a noisy and ferocious movement. . . . I wish a little that one's friends wouldn't be so quarrelsome. But they will be at each other's throats and when they fight are at least illuminative. . . . And occasionally Ezra—who has his jealousies—would, on the side, batter me with abuse of Proust. . . . And I had my view of foreign literary life in Paris through Miss Sylvia Beach. That untiring lady battered me without ceasing. She demanded that I should write innumerable articles about "Ulysses" and, with lance in rest, slaughter all his English detractors. I did! So I had a view of Joyce enthroned with adorers complete somewhere on the slopes of Mount Parnassus which is one of the Seven Hills of Paris. And I was brought into contact with Mr. Valéry Larbaud, Joyce's chief Continental champion. . . .

So I was not completely unaware of Paris's literary geography. I was indeed almost too keenly aware of the activities of the *Nouvelle Révue Française* and M. Gide who was not content to be the mere *Prince de la Prose* of that day.

And I had not been ten minutes in Paris before I was invited to a *lunch d'honneur* at the Paris branch of the Pen Club. Such functions are always desolate. You sit rigidly at attention between two French eminences. And French eminences never believe that a foreign writer can speak French. So each will have a little paper of notes and once every quarter of an hour, each will address to you in English a remark about the writings of Dickens, Thackeray, Sir Ralph Hall Caine and Mr. Galsworthy. For the rest of the time they denounce to their neighbours the *Nouvelle Révue Française* if they do not belong to M. Gide's group. If they do belong to M. Gide's group they denounce with even greater vehemence every one who is not published by the *Nouvelle Révue Française*. . . . It has been my good luck to be guest of honour at many such occasions. . . . I suppose that is because of the million sale of my "Entre St. Denis et St. Georges" during the war. When the French decide to be grateful they are grateful. . . . Indeed, before I left Paris for the South I had received a contract to write six novels in French. The publisher was not the *Nouvelle Révue Française*. . . . I speak French with a bad accent but write it more easily than I write English.

And, but for the interview with Evans in Notre Dame and the death of Proust I imagine that I might then have become a French writer. I ask nothing better. . . . French publishers pay almost nothing. On the other hand French novels are very short. I should have to contend with the enmity of M. Gide's group; on the other hand I could count on the powerful backing of M. Edmond Jaloux and M. Benjamin Crémieux who had been my sponsors at that lunch and of M. Philippe Soupault, the Dadaists and the other *jeunes* of that day.

On leaving England I had made up my mind that if I was to earn a living it must be by writing. And indeed before that event I had written and sold a poor, slight novel. Mr. Lucas's favourite journal had declared it the most amusing novel of that era and it had been largely on its proceeds that I had been able to come South-wards. I thought that I could with ease turn out similar slight novels for the Paris publisher and, even if I found that impracticable, I had a very pleasant contract with Mr. Duckworth for a further series of novels. So that, if I became a commercial writer I might consider myself safe—as safety goes!

It was however not to be. I had never liked Paris much. But I always find that to be there makes me excited—and ambitious. I had not at that date any idea of leaving England for good. I had given up any idea of farming there. The three years after the war had been pretty good for farming but I knew enough of markets to see that, as had been the case in the past, the farmer was about once more to be sacrificed to the industrialist. That of course is in England a necessity. In the rest of the world it is only a taste, except in France where the peasant rules the roost. So I took my bearings in Paris.

Affairs in French literature were as I have adumbrated. There was however at that date a great colony of Anglo-Saxon *littérateurs* and practitioners of other arts. The two centres for writers were Ezra Pound and James Joyce. The sun about which the plastic artists revolved more or less wistfully was, as I have equally adumbrated, Miss Gertrude Stein who at that time had more essentially the aspect of a patroness of painters than an imaginative writer. Miss Nathalie Barney, the protectress of Rémy de Gourmont, was a social centre for men of letters and Academicians of several countries, writing herself admirably distracted volumes of stray thoughts.

Mr. Joyce seemed to take little share in the rough and tumble of the several vortices. As befitted the English writer of distinction, he sat as if wrapped in sacred shawls, a high priest on an altar at which one was instructed to offer homage. It was a good thing. It was salutary that the most distinguished Anglo-Saxon writer in Paris should observe an attitude of dignity. Some one there must be to preserve the cult of the sacred flame.

It was of course Mr. Pound who stirred up all the wasps' nests. I wonder if the Latin Grammar from which we learnt when I was a boy is still used in schools. But perhaps no Latin Grammar is now used in any schools. Our first exercise began:

1. Balbus was building a wall. 2. The boy will lose some time. 3. He came to irritate wasps. 4. The boy dances: Balbus is laughing at the boy.

I always think when, after an absence, I come on Mr. Pound in one of his new incarnations, that I must be Balbus. I am always building walls, sometimes without mortar, not unusually even without stones. And Mr. Pound is always irritating wasps. And dancing! After a time he leaves that place. . . .

The story goes—and it is too good not to be true —that, to add to the harmony of the war years, Mr. Pound left London because he sent seconds to a harmless poet of the type that writes articles on Milton on the front page of the *Times Literary Supplement*. The poet asked for police protection. So Ezra went. To issue a challenge to a duel to a British subject is, by British law, to conspire to commit murder. And the British police model themselves on Milton. There is the same majesty about their approach.

Anyhow it is always good to come upon Mr. Pound in a new city. I never could discover that he had any sympathy for my writing. He wrote to me last week to say that eighty per cent of my work is rubbish— because I am an English gentleman. Patriotism is a fine thing!

All the same if Mr. Pound is established in Capharnaum and I go there Mr. Pound leads me in procession incontinently to the sound of shawms round the city walls. You would think I was the infinitely aged mummy of a Pharaoh, nodding in senility on the box seat of Miss Stein's first automobile. And before the car Mr. Pound dances the slow, ceremonial dance that William Penn danced before the Sachems. Then when I have told the elders and the scribes that Ezra is the greatest poet in the world Ezra goes and whispers to the loud speakers that, beneath the bedizened shawls I have asses' ears. The drone is thus killed.

It was like that for three weeks or so in Paris. I learnt of the existence of several thousand literary scandals of the basest complexion and of perhaps seven and a half shining cygnets. I had the glimpse of an idea that something could be done if one could succeed in uniting all those hornets—with the exception always of the supporters of the *Nouvelle Révue Française*—in some sort of common activity it might be a good thing. But towards the 12th December rain fell for three days. It became cold with the cold that Paris alone knows as winter sets in. And, sighing, I departed to the South to write an immense big novel. Poor dung-beetle!

I have related elsewhere how, under St. Anthony, I found in a secret drawer of Harold Munro's grandfather's secretaire a number of golden guineas. A guinea is a satisfactory coin to find. A pound is good, but a guinea is handsomer and the extra shilling makes the difference between a fee or payment and an honorarium. It was as if the Saint regarded me as a member of a learned profession. A good omen!

From that dimly candle-lit Provençal room I went out into the garden that sloped, stage by stage precipitously down to the water. Nothing was missing. The moon was in its second quarter; growing therefore. I had not been in the place ten minutes before I had sowed some vegetable seeds. And there was even the great chorus of frogs. It was early days for frogs to go wooing. But there it was, rising and falling. The frogs, like the bees, do their work all the year round. The lights of Villefranche were reflected right across the absolutely motionless water of the bay. Again halcyon days! The night was as warm as new milk.

I stood there for a long time, taking stock. Like Robinson Crusoe. Things had piled up. By that time I had both my "subject" and my principal characters. My subject was the public events of a decade. My principal character I had compounded in the railway carriage between Calais—where my grandfather had been born—and Paris. It was as if my mind had not felt free to work until I was safe on this side of the sentry at Calais harbour mouth.

It was curious how it came. In the train at Calais there had been a young Coyli officer—of the King's Own Yorkshire Light Infantry. He was in mufti. He was going to Marseilles to sail from there to Egypt to join his regiment. A persistent douanier insisted on searching him and he protested violently. He said:

"Oh: it wasn't in this way you received us when we last landed in France." And indeed it hadn't been!

I intervened with the Douanier but the fellow insisted on searching that officer. He found nothing dutiable and went away grumbling. The young man followed him with his eyes. He said:

"If that's the only way he has of addling his brass his country would be well shut on him!"

He had paid his own fare overland when he might have gone free on a transport. He had wanted, full of enthusiasm and friendship, to see in peace a country he had last seen when more than a million of his comrades were getting ready there to leave their corpses.

I said:

"Hard luck, old bean. You hit on a wrong un. Let's wet it!"

It was whilst we were running through the Pas de Calais, wetting it, that my idea came. It was because the young man had used the Yorkshire dialect phrase, "addling his brass"—and a little because I had said: "Hard luck!"

The Yorkshire phrase had reminded me of Marwood. In familiar conversation he would constantly use it. It is more forcible than to say "earning his money." It is more forcible even than "gold-getting"! He used to say: "In Yorkshire they say about money: It takes three generations: 'one to addle, one to hold, one to spend. . . .'"

And, when that young fellow had used that phrase I suddenly saw Marwood—the heavy Yorkshire squire with his dark hair startlingly silver in places, his keen blue eyes, his florid complexion, his immense, expressive hands and his great shapelessness. He used to say of himself beside Conrad's vibrating small figure:

"We're the two ends of human creation: he's like a quivering ant and I'm an elephant built out of meal sacks!"

So the last words of my trilogy are:

"On an elephant. A dear, meal sack elephant. She was setting out. . . ."

He was a man of infinite benevolence, comprehensions and knowledges. He actually, as I have related, went through the whole of the Ninth Edition of the Encyclopaedia Britannica wagering that, out of his own head, he would find seven times as many errors and misstatements as there were pages in that compilation. And he did. . . . I repeat these characterisations which I have already made in several other places partly because it is pleasant to me to dwell upon the thought of Marwood but partly too because they here accent the synchronisation. . . .

I thought then of Marwood, whilst escaping past the fields and farms and Normandy poplars, over the last "small Guinness" that I was to drink for perhaps ten years and across the table from the last young English soldierman that I was to speak to for who knows how many! . . . I like young English army officers. I think they are the best breed the country produces and do their jobs as well as any set of men in the world. . . .

I was nevertheless not thinking of him. . . . For the large work that I might write—the word was still only "might"—I needed someone, some character, in lasting tribulation—with a permanent shackle and ball on his leg. . . . A physical defect it could not be, for if I wrote about that character he would have to go into the trenches. It must be something of a moral order and something inscrutable. . . .

Human tribulations are the only things worth writing about. You can write about Napoleon at St. Helena or even at Elba. No one could present him as he was in his triumphs. I needed then a hard-luck story. The hardest human luck! . . .

I was in a railway carriage—not in a French one running down through France but in a first-class carriage running from Ashford in Kent to Winchelsea in Sussex. We were going back to our cottages after a hard week over manuscripts in the office of the *English Review*. I said to Marwood:

"What really became of Waring?"

He said:

"The poor devil, he picked up a bitch on a train between Calais and Paris. She persuaded him that he had got her with child. . . . He felt he had to marry her. . . . Then he found out that the child might be another man's, just as well as his. . . . There was no real knowing. . . . It was the hardest luck I ever heard of. . . . She was as unfaithful to him as a street walker. . . ."

I said:

"Couldn't he divorce?"

—But he couldn't divorce. He held that a decent man could never divorce a woman. The woman on the other hand would not divorce him because she was a Roman Catholic.

Marwood added:

"Her people were pretty good people and she looked as straight as a die . . . straighter. . . . But her mother was one of the bad Hennessys. . . . There are good Hennessys and bad. . . . You should never marry a bad Hennessy. . . . Poor Dash did. . . . And look what has happened to him. . . ."

Dash was a writer of the most admirable gifts for whom both Marwood and I had the greatest possible admiration. He had a dreadful history of despair behind him. The name of the famous family who are legendary in Europe was not Hennessy, by the bye. . . .

So, coming back to the other carriage somewhere near Amiens, I had the tribulations for my central character. He was to go through the public affairs of distracted Europe with that private cannonball all the time dragging at his ankle! . . .

And I had my two central female characters. One I had long ago thought of. She was, as I have already narrated, Miss Dorothy Minto who had played in the *Silver Box* of Galsworthy's and was also one of the principal actresses in a play about Suffragettes . . . and admirable at that. . . . She would have to be a militant if my book ever came to anything. She was small and blonde and light on her feet. . . . I do not think I ever spoke more than two or three words to her but she seemed extremely familiar to me because I had seen her so very often on the stage of the Court Theatre under Mr. Granville Barker's admirable régime. . . .

And suddenly, in Amiens station, I had my other. . . . She stood before me in the shadows above the luggage barrack and the waiting passengers as the train ran into the station. She was in a golden sheath-gown and her golden hair was done in bandeaux, extraordinarily brilliant in the dimness. Like a goddess come in from the forest of Amiens!

I exclaimed:

"Sylvia!" So I didn't have to cast about for a name.

I hasten to add that the lady I have mentioned in a former chapter was guiltless of any of the vagaries of the character that ultimately resulted from that image. . . . She met me, like the lady in "Epipsychidion," that once, on life's dull way and charmed me towards enormous labours. I do not know that I ever even spoke to her. But I remember her discoursing with infinite wisdom . . . about Higher Education.

I may make the note that I never in my life, as far as I can remember, used a character from actual life for purposes of fiction—or never without concealing their attributes very carefully. This is not so much because I wish to avoid hurting people's characters as because it is, artistically, a very dangerous practice. It is even fatal.

The first thing that you have to consider when writing a novel is your story, and then your story—and then your story! If you wish to feel more dignified you may call it your "subject." Once started it must go on and on to its appointed end. Any digression will make a *longueur*, a patch over which the mind will progress heavily. You may have the most wonderful scene from real life that you might introduce into your book. But if it does not make your subject progress it will divert the attention of the reader. A good novel needs all the attention the reader can give it. And then some more.

Of course you must appear to digress. That is the art which conceals your Art. The reader, you should premise, will always dislike you and your book. He thinks it an insult that you should dare to claim his attention, and if lunch is announced or there is a ring at the bell he will welcome the digression. So you will provide him with what he thinks are digressions—with occasions on which he thinks he may let his attention relax. . . . But really not one single thread must ever escape your purpose.

I am—I may hazard the digression!—using that principle of technique in writing this book. You may think it slipshod and discursive. It will appear to drag in all sorts of subjects just to make up the requisite length. Actually it contains nothing that has not been selected to carry forward the story or the mood.

There is nothing really startling in the method. It is that of every writer of workmanlike detective stories. My friend on the New York *Times* calls me a master of the time-shift. He adds that a great many people dislike my books because I use that device. But he is mistaken. It is me they dislike, not the time-shift which is a thing that delights everybody. It is in fact indispensable to the detective writer. He begins his story with the words: "He is dead," she said. Then he gives some details of the past of him and her. He returns to the present to introduce the sleuths and the district attorney. The chief sleuth delves for pages into the past of him or her, going back thirty years to "his" past in Muddy Creek and Pekin. He returns to lunch with the District Attorney who is trying to doublecross him and then back and back and back. . . . And back once more to the "15th March 19—". Eventually the final clue is given, by something that happened in 1922 and you return to the present for half a page to dispose of the sleuth and the dashing young lady.

I mean nothing derogatory to the detective story and am delighted that it should be immensely read. It is far more educational and of benefit to society than all the most pompous "serious" works that have been written in the last decade. I will thankfully give up my own work if someone will come in with the latest book by the authors of the "Maze" or of the "Glass Key" and will pass the rest of the day in a deck chair in the sunlight, thankful and filled with admiration for the technique of the writers. But that technique is identical with that of all modern novelists, or of myself. . . . Or Proust.

And, when you get added to projections of that technique the *saeva indignatio*—the icy indignation with life of Mr. Oliver Onions in "According to the Evidence" and the "Story of Louie"; or the genuine sympathy and poetry that M. Georges Simenon gets into "Le Chien

Jaune" or "Le Charretier de la Providence," then you get mystery stories that are real literature. The authors will be too neglected as is the case with Mr. Oliver Onions to whom I am glad to introduce this tiny tribute. Or they will be adored by a whole nation as is deservedly the case with M. Simenon. . . .

It was along such lines that I proposed to conduct my ponderous novel. . . . I was walking up and down, you will remember, in the moonlight, under the olive trees of Mr. Munro's garden on a still night of the winter of 1922-23. . . . I had imagined an audience to which I could address myself—in the Middle West that had given birth to Mr. Glenway Wescott. I do not mean that I was confident that the Middle West would do me the honour to read me. But to write with any composure you must invent and cherish for yourself the illusion that you will find *some* readers in sympathy with you. I had then my illusion!

I had two of my principal characters. Proust was dead and I did not see anyone else who was carrying on the ponderous work that seemed to be needed by the world. As a matter of fact there was M. René Béhaine whom I find to be the greatest writer of complexities now in the world. But it was to be some years before, through M. Léon Daudet, I was to make acquaintance with M. Béhaine's work.

I still, however, needed my central character . . . in, as it were, the flesh. His tribulations I had.

The "subject" was the world as it culminated in the war. You—or at least I—cannot make the world your central character. Perhaps it ought to be done. Perhaps that may prove to be the culmination of the novel. I at any rate did not feel that I had the strength to do without the attraction of human nature. For mankind in the bulk seems to lose the character of humanity and to become mere statistics. I sit frequently and dream of writing an immense novel in which all the characters should be great masses of people—or interests. You would have Interest A, remorselessly and under the stress of blind necessities, slowly or cataclysmically overwhelming Interest Z. Without the attraction of sympathy for a picturesque or upright individual. It ought, I have felt for years, to be done. But I doubt if I shall ever get to it. More power, then, to the elbow of the man who eventually tackles the job.

In the garden of the Villa des Moulins at St. Jean Cap Ferrat I knew that I should have to fall back on the old device of a world seen through the eyes of a central observer. The tribulations of the central observer must be sufficient to carry the reader through his observations of the crumbling world. For the tribulations of the central figure to be sympathetic it would be better if they were supported with composure. That is not essential. It is possible and is sometimes even desirable that your central character should excite sympathy by his weakness. How otherwise could you have Dostoevski? or even Turgenev? or indeed any serious writer?

But the very nature of my subject called for a character of some strength of mind and composure. No one else could have supported at once the tremendous pressure of the war and private troubles of a very dire description. He must have lost the power of cool observation. And my scheme called, before everything, for the power of cool observation in tremendous crises.

My own observation of active warfare had led me to a singular conclusion. . . . What preyed most on the mind of the majority of not professionally military men who went through it was what was happening at home. Wounds, rain, fear, and other horrors are terrible but relatively simple matters; you either endure them or you do not. But you have no way by which, by taking thought, you may avoid them. There are no alternatives. And, when they are not immediately probable, it is singular, in the majority of mankind, how easily they can be put out of the mind. . . . But what is happening at home, within the four walls, and the immediate little circle of the individual—that is the unceasing strain! . . . You are tied by the leg: your children may be sick, your business going to rack and ruin; any of the disasters that beset humanity may be happening there. . . . And you are not even powerless to do anything.

You would think that, out there, in a French dugout, in a tent in support; in an army hut you would at least be cut off from the anxieties of the everyday world. But you will find yourself a prey to the worst of all anxieties. You can do very little. But you can do a little and the real agony comes when you have to rack your brains over what, within those pitifully small limits, it is best to do. That is torturing.

A man at this point is subject, in his interests at home, to exactly the same disasters or perplexities as his temperament prepares for him in times of peace. If he is the sort of man to have to put up with the treacheries of others his interests at home will suffer from treasons; if he is the man to incur burdens of debt, debts there will unaccountably amass themselves; if he is a man destined to be betrayed by women his women will betray him exaggeratedly and without shame. For all these vicissitudes will be exaggerated by the more strident note that in time of war gets into both speeches and events. . . . And he is indeed, then, *homo duplex*: a poor fellow whose body is tied in one place but whose mind and personality brood eternally over another distant locality.

It was this stress that I had to take into account when I thought of my central character.

I carefully avoid the word "hero." I was in no mood for the heroic. My character would be deprived of any glory. He was to be just enough of a man of action to get into the trenches and do what he was told. But he was to be too essentially critical to initiate any daring sorties. Indeed his activities were most markedly to be in the realm of criticism. He was to be aware that in all places where they managed things from Whitehall down to brigade headquarters a number of things would be badly managed—the difference being that in Whitehall the mismanagement would be so much the result of jealousies that it would have all the aspect of the most repellent treachery: in brigade headquarters, within a stone's throw of the enemy, it would be the result of stupidities, shortage of instruments or men, damage by enemy activities, or, as was more often the case, on account of nearly imbecile orders percolating from Whitehall itself.

These things he must observe. When it seemed to be his duty he would criticise. That would get him, even at the Front, into many and elaborate messes. . . . So I should get my "intrigue" screwed up tighter and always tighter.

It came then to the choice of rank and social status. He could not be a private soldier, although many private soldiers serving in the trenches were equipped for disastrous criticism of their superiors. But, for the necessities of the intrigue his criticisms must filter through to headquarters. The criticisms of no private soldier, however intelligent, could do that. He must then be an officer of sufficient authority to make reports that would get through at times to the higher commands.

The British Army during the war was, in the officer's mess, socially divided into quite rigid, if insensible, stages. Theoretically every man wearing H. M.'s uniform is a "gentleman" and, in the mess, the social equal of everyone else. In practice a superior officer is apt to remember that he is superior .and it is just as well for a subaltern to remember it too. But, on the private, social side, the rigid barriers between class and class that have always subsisted continue to subsist. You may, at mess, sit next to the son of your milkman. He may be a fine fellow of faultless deportment and as such you will treat and even respect him. But the moment you go to your own quarters—and they may be merely a hole in the mud—the normal civilian hierarchy reasserts itself.

For reasons that I will later dwell upon I did not wish my central character to be merely a "gentleman." By the time I had arrived at St. Jean Cap Ferrat I had arrived at the stage of finding the gentleman an insupportable phenomenon. . . . But, separated from and absolutely above the merely gentlemanly class, there is in England another body. They are the Ruling Classes. This body is recruited as a rule from the sons of landed proprietors, old titled families, the sons of higher Army officers and what, in England, one called Good People. They are distinguished by being authoritative, cynical, instructed in the ways of mankind. They are sometimes even educated and not infrequently they are capable of real, cold passions for some person or some cause. It is they who monopolise and distinguish the First Class Government offices—the War and Foreign Offices, the Treasury, the Diplomatic Corps. They are permanent unless they come personal croppers over a woman, or through overintelligence or on account of financial disasters. As such they are really the Ruling Classes. A politician may rise high and have the aspect of governing but almost always he is the slave of the permanent officials who control his activities and his utterances. . . . It is the "gentlemen" of the country who control elections deciding whether the country shall be temporarily conservative or liberal. But the Permanent Official is almost always either Whig or Tory and sees to it that the services of the country run along the lines of its ancient traditions. . . . So at least it was before and during the War—and it was with those periods alone that I meant to deal.

The "Waring" of whom Marwood and I had talked in the railway carriage between Ashford and Rye had been of pretty good family and, but for his disaster, would have been in the Foreign Office. But he had taken the affair lying down and, utterly unmanned, was leading the alcoholic existence of one of those poor beings who manage golf or social clubs anywhere between the Riviera and Rangoon. His disaster, then, was alone useful to me.

And, curiously enough, almost before my feet as I stood in Harold Munro's garden was the villa of a poor fellow who had had almost Waring's fate. He was a wealthy American who had married a wrong 'un. She had been unfaithful to him before and after marriage. He had supported these wrongs because of his passion for the woman. At last she had eloped with a ship steward and had gone sailing around the world. The husband being an American of good tradition considered himself precluded from himself taking proceedings for divorce but he would gladly have let the woman divorce him and would have provided liberally for her. She however was sailing around the world and he had no means of communicating with her. Almost simultaneously, after a year or so, he had conceived an overwhelming passion for another woman and the wife had returned. . . . What passed between them one had no means of knowing. Presumably she had announced her intention of settling down again with him and had flatly refused to divorce him. So he committed suicide. . . .

The dim sight of the roof of his villa below me over the bay gave me then another stage of my intrigue. My central figure's wrong 'un of a wife must return to him just after he had fallen for another woman. . . . The wife of course would be upstanding and in a golden sheath gown. Marwood had said she was a thoroughbred with congenital vices—a member of the Ruling Class . . . but reckless. . . . The "other woman" would be, equally naturally, the Suffragette.

But my central figure could not commit suicide. He must live his predicament down. It suddenly occurred to me to wonder what Marwood himself would have thought of the story—and then what he would have thought of the War. He had died before the opening of hostilities: otherwise his views would have had immense value. . . .

I imagined his mind going all over the misty and torrential happenings of the Western Front—his tolerance for the military even when they were intellectually childish and his complete and vitriolic contempt for the politicians at Whitehall. . . . Above all for Dai Bach. . . .

It was he who for the first time had said, speaking as a Tory:

"We ought to have had Lloyd George to do our dirty work. We have to have someone. We bought Disraeli: we bought Chamberlain. We ought to have bought Lloyd George!"

. . . And immediately, on that remembrance, I had my central character. Marwood had died before the war but his knowledge of the world's circumstances had been so vast and so deep that, as it were, to carry on his consciousness through those years seemed hardly to present any difficulties. I seemed, even as I walked in that garden, to see him stand in some high place in France during the period of hostilities taking in not only what was visible but all the causes and all the motive powers of infinitely distant places. And I seemed to hear his infinitely scornful comment on those places. It was as if he lived again.

There he was, large—an "elephant built out of meal sacks." Deliberate, slow in movement and extraordinarily omniscient. He was physically very strong and very enduring. And he was, beneath the surface, extraordinarily passionate—with an abiding passion for the sort of truth that makes for intellectual accuracy in the public service. It was a fascinating task to find him a posthumous career.

Actually he had no career after a brilliant beginning. An internal tuberculous condition made it impossible for him to live in a town. So, in the country he followed the career of a philosopher. He had his mysticisms. When he talked of Higher Mathematics it was as if he were listening to the voice of angels. I suppose he saw waves round the throne when he considered the theory of waves and that he saw resurrections when he thought of recurrent patterns in numbers.

He died in the fulness of his strength and no death ever seemed to me to be more regrettable. To the best of my ability I gave him life again and for me he lives still, in Avignon, and I shall have a letter from him tomorrow.

. . . I do not have to say that no incident in this book had any parallel in his actual life! He lived the life of a Yorkshire squire that an inherent physical weakness compelled to inhabit the South and to eschew all the privileges of his birth. So he was the Permanent Official turned hermit, but unsoured!

There remained then for me, under Munro's olive-trees, a final struggle with my courage. This was the question of details. For me, before I can begin a book, it is necessary for me to have got together an immense number of details that might bear upon the circumstances of the story that I am about to relate. It is really quite immaterial whether Army G.S. limbered waggons have brakes that screw down or brakes that act by leverage. It is a million to one that I should never have to mention a G.S. limbered waggon and the question of the nature of its brake could quite easily be avoided. I have at least skill enough for that. . . .

But what had put me into a panic on that afternoon in Notre Dame was the sudden fear that the quality of my memory might have deteriorated. Usually I can be fairly sure of my memory—particularly for material details and the conversation of other people. What I say myself I forget rather easily and what I write usually goes out of me with astonishing rapidity. All names also go. But the speeches of other people remain to me with singular clarity and so do, say, the details of machinery. So my mind is cluttered up with an amazing amount of useless detail. But to me it is not useless for without it I should feel insecure. I may—and quite frequently do—plan out every scene, sometimes even every conversation, in a novel before I sit down to write it. But unless I know the history back to the remotest times of any place of which I am going to write I cannot begin the work. And I must know—from personal observation, not reading, the shapes of windows, the nature of doorknobs, the aspects of kitchens, the material of which dresses are made, the leather used in shoes, the method used in manuring fields, the nature of bus tickets. I shall never use any of these things in the book. But unless I know what sort of doorknob his fingers closed on how shall I—satisfactorily to myself—get my character out of doors?

So, in that garden above Villefranche bay, I put myself through a regular Staff Examination. I found I knew still every "detail" of Infantry Drill, of musketry practice as set forth in the textbooks and could repeat them word for word in English and fairly well in Welsh. I found I still had by heart all the paragraphs of King's Regulations and Military Law that a regimental officer could be required to know. I went over in my mind every contour of the road from Bailleul to Locre,

Locre-Pont de Nieppe, Nieppe down to Armentières—
and of all the by-roads from Nieppe to Ploegsteert,
Westoutre, Dramoutre. And I found that I could remember with astonishing vividness every house left, in
September 1916, along the whole road, and almost
every tree—and hundreds of shell holes!

I will here make a confession. I have always had the
greatest contempt for novels written with a purpose.
Fiction should render and not draw morals. But, when
I sat down to write that series of volumes, I sinned
against my gods to the extent of saying that I was going
—to the level of the light vouchsafed me—to write a
work that should have for its purpose the obviating of
all future wars.

War to me was not very dreadful. I would, for my
personal comfort, far rather go through another similar
war than face an eternity of writing endless books.
But the desperation and horror that war caused to other
people impressed me with such mass and such vividness
that I was ready to put my principles behind me. . . .
I was not going to go against my literary conscience to
the extent of piling horrors on horrors or even of ex-
aggerating horrors. That policy, in the end, always de-
feats itself. After you have seen two or three men killed
or mangled your mind of necessity grows a carapace
round itself and afterwards witnessing the slaying of
thousands hardly moves you unless those men belong to
your own unit. And the mind of the reader does the
same thing. . . . To read the words of that tablet in
Notre Dame excites emotions. I never read them my-

self without tears in my eyes—and even merely to think of them I find at times unbearable. . . . But the emotions are those rather of pride than of revulsion. One thinks: "The fine fellows!" or one thinks: "How well they must sleep!" One thinks: "They at least are out of it!" One says: "They at least did not die in vain. . . ."

But it seemed to me that, if I could present, not merely fear, not merely horror, not merely death, not merely even self-sacrifice . . . but just worry; that might strike a note of which the world would not so readily tire. For you may become callous at the thought of all horrors of more than a million dead: fear itself in the end comes to rest. . . . But worry feeds on itself and in the end so destroys the morale that less than a grasshopper becomes a burden. It is without predictable term; it is as menacing as the eye of a serpent; it causes unspeakable fatigue even as, remorselessly, it banishes rest. And it seemed to me that if the world could be got to see War from that angle there would be no more wars. . . .

So it was my duty to be sure of my details. For technical facts as facts I have no respect whatever. Normally I rather despise myself for playing for factual accuracy in a novel. It did no harm to Shakespeare not to know that Bohemia has no sea-coast or even to believe in the fabled virtues of the mandrake. I would just as gladly make such slips as not. But they give weapons to fools and if, in this case, I failed in factual correctness, I should betray the cause for which I was working.

So for two or three days I mooned about, testing my memory as to all sorts of technical facts and geographical minutiae. I tried myself out on Nordenfelt and Maxim and Stokes guns as on the stoppages of the collection of bits of tin and hairpins that we infantry were given to use as machine guns—and precious good they were too! I tested myself as to strengths of units, as to supply, as to cyphers, as to the menus for troops and the stabling of mules. In each case I checked myself by such textbooks as I still had and in nearly every instance I found that my memory was correct enough.

So one day I sat down at Munro's grandfather's campaign-secrétaire—it had been on the field of Waterloo—I took up a pen: saluted St. Anthony who looked down on me, in sheer gratitude for his letting me find my pen at all and I wrote my first sentence. The scene took the shape it did out of remembrance of how Marwood and I had conversed in the railway carriage between Ashford Junction and Rye where they play golf. It ran:

"The two young men—they were of the English public official class—sat in the perfectly appointed railway carriage."

Harold Munro's villa stood high. It has always been my fate to have to climb when returning home. Even my apartment in the rue de Vaugirard was on the seventh floor of the beautiful old house that the Senate in its madness is now pulling down. I luxuriate in views and generally get them before I think of the climb. Even now there is sixty feet difference between the top and bottom of my garden so that if I have to water the cabbages I have to descend those sixty feet and then climb up again to get the wrench to turn the hose-attachment, and then in turn my cigarettes, matches, black spectacles and garden hat. . . . Thus before I have finished that simple gardening operation I shall have climbed and descended six hundred feet. . . . I suppose destiny arranges these things for the benefit of what Archbishop Warham in the suppressed preface to the Bible called one's haughty and proud stomach. It does!

And at St. Jean Cap Ferrat the mountainous hinterland comes so close to the sea that if one wanted to take a walk from the Villa des Moulins one had to descend to the Lower Corniche, dash across it to escape

being knocked down by one of the innumerable auto-
mobiles and immediately begin a precipitous climb, between olive trees planted as if on a house-side. To
return one had to descend as precipitously, dash back
across the Corniche and then decide whether one would
reach the Villa by the long, agonising path called the
Chemin des Moulins or whether one would climb on
hands and knees up poor Munro's stone staircase that
rose perpendicularly from the Cap Ferrat road. The
staircase was more agonising—but it was sooner over.

I was once toiling up the Chemin des Moulins when
an elderly, fiercely white-moustached gentleman with
a sort of lustre all about him, standing on the bank
above me, said:

"Seen my motor-car with Mrs. Hammerdine in it?"
—The name was not Hemmerdine.

I realised that I must be in the presence of at least
a Field Marshal so I put a "Sir" into my answer that
I did not know his motor-car. He said—as if I must be
obtuse indeed.

"Got no number on it!"

I understood then where I was and offered to go and
look for his car. He said it was not necessary. He had
told Mrs. Hemmerdine where he was going. He added:

"Women always keep you waiting. They shouldn't
do it. How do they know you may not have important
things to do? I hate keeping people waiting to give me
tea!"

He said:

"I see you're stopping on through April! . . . That's

the sensible thing to do, young man. . . . I always tell people the year doesn't begin to get perfect till April. . . . I try never to come here before April. . . . But they make me, you know."

I got soundly rapped over the knuckles—but yet not contradicted—for in my last lot of reminiscences reporting the *ipsissima verba* of the King. I hope it is not treason to report the words of His Majesty's uncle who was in all but name the monarch of those regions. For the Riviera year does not get perfect till April. . . . Here at the gate of the Côte d'Azur it does not get really warm till April is over and perhaps one should not come here till May. . . . But the greater truth is that one should not come here at all. One should live here all the year round and go away from the end of January till March. In the North, poor devils, they have to know how to heat houses. Here they build their houses against heat and it can be cold on occasion to people softened by living here. Once every ten years or so they even have frost and, in the winter when I was in hospital at Cap Martin, as I have said, the snow even lay and the cold cut down all the olive and lemon trees so that they have only this year begun to bear again. It completely killed the immense mimosa whose limbs, covered with roses and ivy, still tower over the tiny bastidon.

But for the greater part of the year you can, here— and I am doing it today at noon on the feast of St. Servais—sit without clothes in the shade and be unaware of your corporal existence. The air will be exactly flesh-heat so that you are at one with the universe. That is why I have said that all the calamities of our poor civilisation come from humanity's having left these shores. If you are conscious of either heat or cold you cannot think justly and it is the final carrying out of the curse of Adam that men should have to work at the pit-face or in an atmosphere of crude mineral oil in order to keep humanity overwarmed in regions that are not fitted to support human life.

Outside a radius of a hundred miles from these shores —to North or South—barbarism is always creeping in with the North or South winds. Here those deities are the great Mistral and the horripilant Sirocco!

Down in the town at the foot of my hill it can be hot enough. It can be so hot that you can hardly drag your feet along the blistered pavements, the very shade of the plane trees is an offense and the Negro troops in their scarlet fezzes stagger beneath their rifles, rivers of sweat coursing down their faces. You would say it was Africa—and indeed it is Africa for the dreaded Sirocco is the fetid breath of the Sahara. It is in short Africa come to take a look at us and to make us understand that, pink as we may be, it is but a few degrees of temperature and barometer that separate us from the most abhorred anthropophages of the central Congo.

Up on our hill we wake up one morning in what seems the breath from an oven mouth. Everyone we see, the most cherished member of the household, the most attached domestic, the most faithful hound, the cat of the house and the very canary in its cage, wear hateful faces. The garden is a wilted desert, the sea a hideous disk of black steel, the very dophins and tarpons that spring from it, seeking in the air, in vain, a moment's relief from the tepid bath—even they are outrages to the eye. To serve the salad at lunch is to transport hopeless burdens across vast spaces; in dressing it one struggles against the temptation to substitute Prussic acid for the vinegar. But that one cannot drag oneself about one would do murder or be murdered by the whispering conspirators that are one's household familiars. . . . Disaster, treachery, pestilence, fill the heavy air above the drooping flowers. . . . So it goes through the dreadful day.

And then suddenly, towards six, there is a little rustle from far away behind the house! You perceive that your garden smiles; the sea is innumerable little laughs; your companions recline above it in Hellenic serenity; your hound is fit to run with the coursing dogs of Diana; your cat is a black leopard of the breed of Circe; your canary shakes the sky with his notes. With a roar the great Mistral springs at the throat of his eternal enemy! And you thank the beneficent deities who have made the world so fair and so full of laughing motion. . . .

That was the Sirocco—the South Wind of Mr. Norman Douglas.

Fortunately his visits are few. The great feasts of our year are the St. Sylvestre which ushers in the Jour de l'An; Easter; the Ascension; Pentecost; the 14th July; the Assumption; the Toussaint which is the eve of the

feast of All the Dead; the Fête des Victoires which cele-
brates those who died in the War—and so Christmas.
Ten in all. The visits of the Sirocco are about as many.
It is as if the beneficent deities to please whom we must
live a life of frugality and high thought, allowed one
ten days on which to *faire la bombe*, which you may
translate into the Nordic "go on a bust." . . . And
then they send the Sidocco ten times a year—to learn
us to be toads. Or perhaps to make the return from
our Saturnalia less hard. For the feasts are lovely: but
after the visits of the Sirocco our frugal life seems even
lovelier.

Of course it can be hot without the Sirocco. Hot
with a natural torridity that no taking off of garments
can even temper. It is then that one should learn to appreciate the natural wisdom of the Moor who piles
garment on garment upon himself—to keep out the
heat. One does not however learn that. Some years ago
when I was merely writing and not, as is normally my
habit, part writing, part market-gardening, I used to live
for some months of each year in a hotel in the town. I
was still writing away at the work which began in
Munro's bastide.

One day of unspeakable heat I was sitting writing
in my hotel room, with all the jalousies closed and
in the garb in which I had got out of my bath—or all
but. It was the costume that Achilles might have worn
on a hot day in his tent—except that the Greeks didn't
wear running shorts. I was writing quietly and con-
tentedly when the door was slightly pushed open by

the *valet de chambre*. He said someone wanted to see me. He was one of those polygot White Russians of the rank of ex-Colonel who wear striped waistcoats and neither understand nor speak any known Occidental language. He said the name of my visitor was something like the bubbling of a pot for a second or two and then something like Monsieur Geese. . . . It might have been any one of three painters whom I saw nightly in the café down the main street—poor Juan Gris who died next year, or M. Othon Friesz who is now my next door neighbour or even M. Matisse. . . . Their names all contained an "eese" sound and any one of them might well have called on me. I told the waiter to send up whoever it was and went on writing. I may make the note that, fortunately, my ante-room which was lit from the corridor fairly blazed with light, whereas my writing room was as dim as a cavern.

When the knock on the door sounded after the hollow mumbling of the elevator I cried: "Entrez!" and then made one spring for my bathroom. My ante-room was crammed with ladies and gentlemen all in the white of tropical costumes—but all in costumes that must have come from Fifth Avenue above Thirty-second Street. And there were more in the corridor.

They cannot have seen me for they completely filled my room—that is to say there were twenty-seven of them and I gave them audience from my bathroom door. I was enveloped in a voluminous bathrobe of white towelling and I hope that, against the light behind me, I looked a little like the Emperor Nero. . . .

They were introduced by a charming and very elegant stranger who comes back to me as exactly resembling the American narrator of what I consider to be my best book. He was like a gentle and reduced imitation, in his white ducks and with his white, pointed beard and the beautiful Panama straw in his hand, of the Southern Judge of the Broadway melodrama. He said—These things *do* happen!—in almost the immortal words of Mark Twain's, that they were a deputation of American citizens from the good ship So and So that was on her way to the Isles of Greece. That was no doubt the "Eece" sound of the *valet de chambre*, or it may have been "Nice." Their ship had touched at Villefranche and they had seen that I was stopping where I was in the local paper. So, each of them having a copy of my then latest book on board, they had taken the train from Nice in order to say nice things to me and to ask for my autograph. . . . And each one defiled in turn before me and offered his or her copy and his or her fountain pen. They were nearly all from the states of Missouri, Ohio and Illinois—which was near enough to my imagined audience for that book! And what touched me most was that the last lady who came from Memphis, Tenn. asked me to keep the fountain pen with which I signed her copy and, if I liked it, to go on writing that work with it.

So I made a little speech of gratitude. And it really was gratitude for, since I do not have press cuttings, that was the first intimation I had that the book was, as the saying is, getting over, and just to the audience

235

to which it had been addressed. So I told them that, if from the deck of their ship, in Villefranche harbour, they would look almost vertically up and to the East, they would see the ceiling under which I had written the first words of that work and the terraces of the garden beneath whose olive trees it had been planned. And I said that that nice little bundle of coincidences might well have been kindly planned by Pallas Athene who if she had occupied herself a little longer with the affairs of us mortals would have been, with her emblem of the olive, the patron saint of writers—and of readers! so that if, when they got to Athens, they would release an owl before the statue of Minerva they might well for the rest of their lives be inspired to read nothing but very good books!

They went away pleased, I think. Certainly they left me pleased. . . . For myself I like these demonstrations. Higher and more stern natures find them superfluous. They may be impulsive—but it is better to act on your generous impulses than to wait, finger on your pulse, until you do not act at all. They may be, in part, inspired by hypocrisy, lip-service or even the desire to profit—but hypocrisy and lip-service, those homages paid to virtue, are at least homage to Literature. And if ten thousand people think that by making autograph collections they may make a little money, two per cent of them may, in that pursuit, be turned towards a real liking for good books. And literature has so hard a row to hoe that two hundred readers of good things are not to be sneezed at on Parnassus. In any case writing is a lonely job and out of these tributes, illusory as you may know them to be, you may get, precisely, the illusion that, somewhere in the world, are friendly hands that might be held out to you. For myself, if I pass many days without two or three requests, at least for my autograph, I feel lonelier!

As for the fountain pen. I should now be writing this manuscript with it. But, alas, at the moment it was given to me I was suffering from writer's cramp and had to write with a machine—to the considerable deterioration of my work. So I put the pen carefully away somewhere—and have never been able to find it again!

. . . My mother had a watch she much valued. My father had bought it for her in Strasburg and it had belonged to Marie Antoinette. It had that queen's portrait surrounded with diamonds in a plaque on its back. One summer she was going into the country, leaving her house in Chiswick unoccupied. She put the watch away carefully. Remembering the advice of Inspector Trench at the time her house had been burgled by the emissary of the Russian Embassy, she left all her cupboards, drawers and closets unlocked. You lock your receptacles, the Inspector said, against the members of your household. When there are none in the house you should unlock them all. No fastening you have will stand against the tools of a burglar and he will smash your best pieces in opening them. On the other hand give the constable on the beat half a sovereign and every night he will tie a piece of black cotton across your garden gateway. . . .

My mother came back from her holiday and the watch was nowhere to be found. There were no signs of burglarious entry: not once had the piece of cotton been disturbed. She remembered distinctly having put the watch somewhere. She searched the house for months and months. No watch! . . . In the family we lamented that beautiful thing. It became a legend.

Years after—fifteen, I think—she moved further into town. In turning out her lumber-room she found under an old bedstead a pair of old shoes. In the toe of one was something heavy and hard. . . .

I must have inherited that talent. At a moment's notice I can—and do—invent completely burglar-proof hiding places. But I never remember them afterwards so I leave the world full of treasure. On such occasions it is of no use to appeal to St. Anthony. On leaving the Bank of England you go up the steps of St. Paul's Cathedral and throw away a thousand pound note, putting your cigarette carefully in your note-case. You are warned of your loss by heat in your breast pocket. You mutter a short invocation to St. Anthony, and, in the gutter below the steps, you find your note. That is mere absence of mind. I have told so many times how, on a Sunday in Blois, I left all my money in a wallet on the telegraph desk in the chief Postoffice, that I will not tell the story again. . . . The Saint in fact is kind to those who lose by absence of mind. But if your haughty and proud stomach leads you, not trusting to his offices, to devise caches of your own, it is useless to appeal to him. . . .

With regard to methods of writing. . . . For myself I dislike writing with a pen. My writer's cramp has never completely left me and every word I write is accompanied by a little pain. Towards the end of my morning's work it will be a very severe pain running from the knuckle of my third finger to my elbow. But for me, it is worth while. . . . After the volume I began at St. Jean Cap Ferrat the cramp became so severe that I could not hold a pen at all. I took to writing with a machine and then, worst of all, to dictating! I am not to that extent machino-phobe—or even a hater of stenographers—that I consider the one or the other below my dignity. It is that the one—and still more the other!—make me become too fluid. It is as if they waited for me to write and write I do. Whereas if I have to go to a table and face pretty considerable pain I wait until I have something worth saying to say and say it in the fewest possible words.

The very ease and speed of a typewriter makes tautology thus likely. And, in myself, there is something worse. On a machine corrections whilst you are writing are relatively difficult to make. You must rub out words and replace them and your rubber is somewhere else. . . . Then, too, I detest a typewritten page showing any corrections. Horrible as it may seem, if I happen to type an entirely wrong word,—say "almanach" when I mean "autograph" I will go through the most excruciating mental gymnastics sooner than erase the word and make the correction. I am quite capable, I mean, of writing, when I want to say: "He asked me for an autograph"—"he asked me for an almanach on which, with a red stone, he might mark the happy date of his receiving a specimen of my handwriting." . . . I do not say that I do this very often. But I do do it.

The patient and faithful secretary is even more fatal. With his or her services you become a perfect fountain of words. It is so easy to try on any effect that you try them on galore, hoping that, if they do not come off, you will have the strength of mind to correct or eliminate offending passages. But often you do not find the strength of mind to correct or eliminate. Then you will have a terrible page or two of *longueurs*. Or if you do correct, the passage will lose all spontaneity. . . . Elimination is always good. . . . Conrad and I used, in humorous moments, to shut our eyes—and, at random, scratch out passage after passage of our work in hand.—The result was always improvement. It was the Beau Christ d'Amiens who gave the casting vote for verse as against prose. Because there are fewer words to the page!

Then too there is the personal element. The creature of doom rings your bell at ten. If you are in a base mood you say: "I pay this creature to write for me. . . . Quick then, let me give him or her something to do. . . . In better moments the mere aspect—the reproachful air—of that amanuensis makes you plunge into work. . . . I have even had secretaries who sighed when I did not keep them busy!

And, worst of all, there is the almost irresistible temptation to write at the secretary—that, I am convinced, was responsible for the decadence of Henry James's prose in its latest and most *faisandé* developments. . . . You have the silent back or the emotionless face of the doomful creature presented to you. You dictate for a little while and nothing happens. And nothing and nothing. It gets to be like being in the presence of a marble block. At last you say: "Damn it all I *will* make that creature smile. Or have a tear in its eye!" Then you are lost. . . . When I was dictating the most tragic portion of my most tragic book to an American poetess she fainted several times. One morning she fainted three times. So I had to call in her husband to finish the last pages of the book. He did not faint. But he has never forgiven me. Having since become an eminent English literary critic he attacks me with a hatred and acridity that surpass all those of my worst detractors—with or without occasion. I don't wonder. I should hate anyone whose secretary I was forced to become. I should think I could write so much better than that fellow. . . .

So one day—it was on board the *Berengaria*—I was correcting the typescript of a book I had finished some months before. It was a horrible experience. Partly I had typed the book; partly I had dictated it to a secretary who wrote longhand, partly to another who used a machine, and partly to a third who was a remarkable stenographer. At the time of my final correction the book was about six months old. It is six months after finishing a book that it becomes most like stale fish to you. In ten years' time you may be wondering

241

how it was you used to be able to write so well! There are these bitter compensations!

The *Berengaria* rolled towards Paris over the winter seas. . . . No, I have never been sea-sick! . . . I slashed at that horrible prose. I cut out miles of passages intended for one or another of those secretaries. As if with a chaff-cutter I cut into five or six sentences that, fluidly, I had composed on my new Corona. Time after time I threw that typescript from end to end of the smoking room at six in the morning. Then one's head is at its clearest and there is no one to mark your despair. . . . Even nowadays I almost cry when I see the back of that book and of others written in New York at about the same period. So I have locked all my own books that I possess in a press of which I have mislaid the key. . . .

And then one day, just before breakfast, at the hour most fitted for morning prayer and virtuous resolution, I swore solemnly that I would never write a book again save with a pen. And I never have. . . .

I think it is best to write with a pen—or with a pencil if you dislike the grating of metal on paper. My friends—who are all American and all of whom were born after there were machines with which to write—raise their eyebrows if they happen to see a sheet of my manuscript lying about. They say:

"Oh, you write with a *pen*!" According to their natures they will become patronising, as if it is because of my great age and growing feebleness that I employ that obsolete instrument. Or they will grow rather cold—as if I were high-hatting them.

But I am certainly not high-hatting them. Even in the age of the triumph and decadence of the machine it is as unreasonable to say that you *must* use a machine for your art as it would be if one said that a machine is a vulgar instrument not to be seen in the purlieus of a devotee of the muse. It is indeed a matter of expediency alone—a matter of the mechanical difficulty of correction with the machine and of creative difficulty of composition pen in hand. If I had to give advice to a writer that is the advice I should give: In composing make your circumstances as difficult as possible but in correcting let not so much as a shadow or a whispered sound interfere between you and your sheet of paper. And erase with bold, remorseless black strokes that hiss as the pen traverses the lines. So you will know virtue. . . . You will have the fewest possible words on your page.

I have used this digression about the mechanics of writing to indicate the lapse of time that I spent at St. Jean Cap Ferrat, writing away at the first part of my book.

And though I was on the Riviera at the height of the Season I did little else but write and take uphill and downhill walks. A Riviera Season is an annex of Coney Island, Blackpool, Hampstead Heath and all the Magic Cities and Luna Parks of a polyglot and *"rasta"* world. There is, perhaps, no reason why they should not be, these Occidental yoshiwaras. But it seems a pity that they should have chosen for their ephemeral saturnalia the most beautiful, the most legendary and the most nobly historical strip of seacoast in the world. An afternoon at Rockaway Beach or Southend, a couple of days in one of the marble caravanserais that the French call Palaces may, on occasion, be salutary. *Cela change*, perhaps, *les idées*, as they say here. But more prolonged sojourns must be anodyne—and there are too many refuges from thought already in the world. Jazz-dancing is an admirable and health-giving pursuit. But if you dance jazz in the moonlight on the Acropolis you display indifferent taste and Apollo, god of Harmony and father of Aesculapius will probably see that your health suffers.

For me, whilst disclaiming any doctrinaire connection with nudism and deprecating sunbathing as being dangerous to the unskilled, I like to be able to sit in the shade of an olive tree, on a flat rock, extremely lightly clad. And then to think. It seems to me that that is the proper occupation of a proper man. And when Humanity leaves shores where such a passing of the time is practicable or, still more, when Humanity converts such shores into arenas for competitions in dispendiousness and brayings, Humanity makes a mistake and offends the gods. The story of Pompeii, the pleasure-city of the Romans, sufficiently confirms that view. . . . But Humanity must make mistakes and there will always remain above the Mediterranean enough flat stones and a sufficiency of the shadows of olive branches. . . .

And I will confess to not being as highbrow as all that. I made my excursions from the Villa des Moulins mostly in the company of local French residents. And there were occasions when their frugality disconcerted even me. I found it, for instance, very trying, to sit on a public seat beneath the bandstand on Mentone parade with the Professor of Senatorial rank and the heiress of Judith Gautier whilst all the *beau monde* of the Côte d'Azure butterflied it in the sun around us to the strains of music. For those two insisted that there we should eat hardboiled eggs and slices of smoked ham from pieces of brown paper spread on our legs. And, similarly, when going to call, at Antibes, on the niece of Flaubert in company with the grand-niece of Lamartine and the grand-daughter of Turgenev it was trying to spend more than half the time allotted for our visit in the midst of a small crowd, mostly Anglo-Saxon, whilst these highly descended ladies denounced the driver of a fiacre who had demanded of me—not of them!—two francs fifty more than his legal fare. But it was worth it, to be within sound of such names. And who knows? That minute attention to a few sous may have been the heredity of the men who paid such minute attention to little, valueless words that they made of their country the cynosure and the glory of the Western World. Artists—witness Cézanne whose father died a banker— are not infrequently descended from economists. Then why should not the descendants of the greatest artists be economical. . . .

So the year wore on and it became time to drift

through Provence northwards to Paris. And indeed at that time I still thought that I should end up on the Northern side of the Channel. So the drifting was reluctant and, as I drifted I continued to write furiously on great sheets of foolscap. For a time I wrote in a great dim old room with alcoves in a great, dim old hotel at Tarascon—the city of the good King René and of St. Martha; the city that I have always loved best in the world. . . . It would be then May; the jalousies tight closed against the sun and the nightingales singing like furies. . . .

I have jeered against the nature-love of the English. But I will confess that I am never completely easy unless I have the sense of feathered things near me. . . . In the garden of the studio that I was soon to occupy in Paris there was, positively, a nest and brood of white blackbirds. And I stayed much longer than I should have in that horrible and dank abode—it was on the site of a temple to Diana. It is not that I have the patience, like Hudson, for spending hours looking at a bird. . . . But I like to think that one—or two—are sometimes near, creeping through a hedge or a vine. And New York was always a little sad to me for there seemed to be no birds there except the insupportable sparrow. But one day, a couple of years ago, in the hospitable study of the New York doctor to whom, and his wife, the predecessor of this book is dedicated, I looked aside from my writing and saw, in the vine that trailed down an outside staircase, a couple of birds, creeping and examining each tendril. For all the world as if it had been here in

Provence. Both were quite unknown to me. One was as big as—and rather like—the European shrike, grey, with a black head and bill, and the other black and as small as the European tomtit. It was at the rear of a house in West 12th Street just off Fifth Avenue and there are neither shrikes nor tomtits within four thousand miles of those *parages*. But then I understood why I had been writing rather happily and felt sure that what I was writing would be liked by men of good will.

The nightingale heard from quite near—as I hear no less than three of them at this minute, one being certainly not ten yards away—has a voice of amazing volume for so small a bird, so that how such a quantity of air can come from such a small throat is incomprehensible. Yesterday Mrs. Worthington, the authoress of "Mrs. Taylor," said that the first time she heard the nightingale she was disappointed.

I said:

"I suppose you expected to be handed a box of candy and five free tickets for the movies."

And she answered:

"Well—ye-es! . . . I suppose I did."

. . . I think that is what is the matter with most people who are disappointed. One should not hear the nightingale for the first time—only for the first time of the year! One should be born while a nightingale is singing and never know when one first realises that it is a nightingale. Then it is as if the bird's song was a part of oneself. And, when for the first time of the year, you hear through the breathless stillness of the

247

black night down the hill, that amazing bouquet of sounds that are like an incredible spray of sparks from an anvil, and the following intolerably prolonged wail of agony—ah, then you know that, come what may, the year is sanctified for you.

So the nightingales of Tarascon did not disturb my tranquil penmanship, any more than the bird that, five yards from my head, wakes me most mornings a little before five, much harasses me. I do not mind sounds that I cannot prevent when I am writing though if someone or something over whom I have authority make the smallest sound I can become very nasty indeed! But I can bow to—and forget—the inevitable so that I can write as well in a railway carriage as elsewhere. But twelve steam organs under my Tarascon window did drive me away at last. . . . The yearly world-fair at Beaucaire across the Rhone lasts two months and such showmen and gipsies as come from the East spend a preliminary month in the *Place* of that little city where, as I have said, I hope to die.

So I drifted away, rather imprudently, to St. Agrève, a little market town that I did not know, on the highest point of the plateau of the Massif Central. I was recommended to go there by Maître Laurent, the Notaire of Tarascon. Maître Laurent, in spite of living in that crumbling city, is one of the most elegant of men and in a house that looks as if it must have been mouldering away before the Conquest, has the most perfectly elegant office, the most elegantly shining typewriters, manifolders, dictaphones and secretaries so ravishing in their elegance that you would think that it would be impossible to find them outside the millionaires' offices round Wall Street.

With him and the Avocat, Maître Montagnier and some long, silent officers of the famous Fourth Cavalry that was once the regiment of Ney but is now disbanded, I used to pass all my evenings—except one when, as I have related, I passed some hours consoling a mournful Englishman who had been driven from his home in Ottery St. Mary's by an elephant. Those evenings were usually tranquil. But now and then Maîtres Laurent and Montagnier would discuss a point in French Grammar. Me. Montagnier was an Anglophil—the most amazing I have ever met. He wore a cricket cap of the kind worn by professional cricketers in the early 'eighties; he was extremely short and his figure was exactly that of a cricket ball mounted on two wax vestas. When he was not discussing grammar with the Notaire he instructed me for hours on my habits as an Englishman. But when he could get me to his home—and he had the most marvellous *vins du Rhone* of his own growing and a cook who would have ravished the palate of Gargantua—but when he got me planted immovably in an armchair he would read me pages and pages of Dickens.

His accent in French was more amazingly Marseillais than was even Conrad's. I have never heard such an accent. And with exactly that pronunciation he read— or made his unfortunate little daughter read:

"E weell nayvair . . r . . . re dayser . . r . . re

249

Meestai . r . re Micko . . . baire . r . e . . ." the child's voice would pipe . . . And:

"Sapr—r—r—isti! Magnifiqu . . . . ë! R—r—r—avis-sant . . . ë! E weell nayvair—r—r—re dayser—r—re . . . ." her father would roar.

His voice gave the effect of an earthquake and when he discussed, what tense should follow the substantive preterite with Me. Laurent or asserted that it was just as correct to say "*causer à*" as to say "*causer avec . . .*" all the strangers in the town would rush to that café. I really might have learned some of the nice points of French as it is used in the lawcourts if my whole time had not been given to keeping the glasses on the table. And meanwhile the poor cavalry officers pulled their long moustaches or inspected the spurs at the ends of their shining leggings. I don't know what they got out of it.

So those two kindly men of the robe advised me to go to St. Agrève. They said I should escape the Tarascon heat. I did. The snow still lay at St. Agrève and, on my second day there I was so badly hit by my old lung trouble that I almost lost all chance of dying in Taras-con. The year on those Cevennes heights is a very extraordinary and kaleidoscopic close up. I am no good at estimating or recording heights, but I know that St. Agrève is at a respectable altitude as compared to Mont Blanc, all the Alpine peaks and their eternal snow being visible from there.

There, the snow disappears towards the middle of May. Immediately the fields are covered with grass of an amazing emerald green and enamelled with blazing flowers of primary hues so that the grass disappears. The beasts are let out of their stalls and byres; the birds pair and nest with furious haste and seem to hatch out far faster than in the valleys. The woods are green and filled with foxes; the rivulets teem with otters, trout and crayfish. The shop windows are full of pelts—fox, otter, mole, squirrel, badger. In a moment the hay is cut and the fields are brown: in a moment the same fields are green for the second haycrop. The markets swarm with the different sects—for there are different religious sects in each of the innumerable valleys. There are Macdonaldites, Brunonians, Campbellites, Adventists, Huguenots, Lutherans. . . . Each of these wears a different headdress. . . . In a moment the corn is golden, in the next the rays of the sun are white, like magnesian light. They say that here there are more violet rays in the sunlight than anywhere else in the world except for the Mediterranean littoral. It is perhaps true. . . . The streets, the houses, the fields are filled with holiday-makers from Marseilles, Lyons, Valence, Avignon. . . . It was in the hotel dining room here that I heard the whole roomful violently debating the respective merits of the styles of Paul Bourget, Barrès and Stendhal. They were all small shopkeepers. . . .

And then—they are all gone. The skies grow heavy; the first flakes fall. The cattle are hurried back to the byres and stalls which they will not leave again till May. Every garret and every inch of roofspace is crammed with fodder. It falls and falls. The entire earth is bedded and softened by a mantle of soundless white. . . . The living year here lasts from May to the beginning of September. There are, in the hidden valleys, whole families who, snowed up, never set foot outside their houses from September till May. I saw a woman whose husband died in the early fall. They had to live with him there for eight months. They could not get out to bury him. . . .

I was sitting one evening after dinner in the hostess's private room playing, I think, dominoes when a familiar voice boomed out from the passage. It demanded a bedroom for less than I could have imagined possible and got it. It was rich, fruity of the soil and oratorical. It went straight up to bed. It was the voice of Mr. Hilaire Belloc. I saw him next morning at the other end of the market talking to a farmer and punching a fat bullock as if he had been a grazier all his life. Before I could get round to him he had gone and when I got back to the hotel he had left—to my regret. . . .

Some days afterwards I read in the *Morning Post* a full page article—I am not sure there were not two. It was all about St. Agrève and it was signed by Mr. Belloc. It recounted not only all the history of St. Agrève but the most intimate gossip about its inhabitants and singular details about their habits, clothes, ancestry. . . . All with profusion and in the admirable writing of that genius. Now Mr. Belloc reached that town a little after nine and left it before seven. So he was there not more than ten hours, some of which must have been devoted to sleep. How did he do it? . . .

It became time to get back to Paris and afterwards to Mr. Belloc's country of Sussex where I intended to finish my first volume. I finished it however in the studio in the Boulevard Arago—or rather in the pavilion in the garden where the white blackbirds lived. . . . And I have been a resident of Paris ever since—except for the fact that I have passed the greater part of the intervening years either in New York or here on the Côte d'Azur.

I have said that I do not like Paris. That statement needs qualifying. I *detest* the Quartier de l'Étoile,—the region not so much of the idle rich as of the too industrious rich—the bankers. I dislike all the boulevards built by Haussmann and his imitators. On the other hand I really love the real Quartier Latin, the Faubourg St. Germain, the streets between the Sorbonne and the Pantheon. I can even support the Boulevard Montparnasse though my Paris ends with the parallel rue Notre Dame des Champs. It is a grey, very quiet quarter with the gardens of the Luxembourg like a great green jewel on its breast. That I love and I am never quite content if no string attaches me to it. It may be the merest one-room *pied à terre*: as long as I have that I feel a complete man. Without it I sit forlorn. But I do not want to be there too long or too often. The highest thoughts in the world have been thought in those grey buildings and streets and I find it too tiring to keep that pace. There you may dress like a tramp and no one will look askance at you: but you may never even to yourself let your thoughts stray about in dressing gown and slippers. They must be precise.

For me, I like to be precise when I am in the mood—but to have to be so when that mood is not on me is rather torturing. It is not merely the French language. It is that there every stone calls up the memory of a great artist. Nay, every table in a restaurant does. At that one, Cézanne sat: at that other, Verlaine. Before them you cannot sit in your dressing gown and slippers. Even the chimney pots spur you on. From the back window of my apartment in the rue Vaugirard you could see an incredible number of chimney pots and under everyone a masterpiece had been produced. My apartment itself had housed the servants of the great Condé; beneath its windows Mirabeau had been born. Latterly it had housed Jules Janin and Professor Darmstetter, the philologist. Jules Janin was no great shakes, but beneath his shade and that of a philologist you have to be very careful of your words . . . and your thoughts.

My brain, I think, is a sort of dove-cote. The thoughts from it fly round and round, seem about to settle and circle even further than before and more and more swiftly. I try in the end to let them come home with the velocity and precision of swifts that fly at sixty miles an hour into their apertures that you would say could not let them through. I hope thus to attain to a precision of effect as startling as any Frenchman who is forever on the make. Perhaps I do.

During my first days of each stay I make in that

august Quarter I feel exactly like Dick Whittington. But without even a cat for capital. After directionless wanderings I sometimes find a sou of thought and get along somehow with that. But sometimes I do not.

It is a curious and, to me, a tragically suggestive fact that Paris is equidistant from the Rhine at every point from where it takes its rise to where it loses itself in the sands of Holland. It is also, like London, situated on the first ford from the sea that is practicable for heavy wagons bearing merchandise. But for that the art-centre of the world might have been near the birth-place of all the world—might have been in a clime less rigorous and less open to Nordic dangers. It would have been in the territory of those mighty rulers, the Counts of Toulouse. . . . In Provence!

PART THREE

"E PLURIBUS MULTA"

PART THREE

CHAPTER ONE

THE *Transatlantic Review* WAS BORN AMIDST turmoil and had a tumultuous if sometimes gay career. Foreseeing this, we took for its crest the ship that forms the arms of the city of Paris and, for its motto, the first words of that city's device: "Fluctuat. . . ." "It is borne up and down on the waves." Had its career been prolonged we had intended to add the rest of the device: "Nec mergitur"—"and does not sink." . . . It was not to be.

Before setting out on that tilt against the windmills I had to settle the question of my return to England. I remember the exact hour of my coming to that decision—though the exact date does not come back to me. But I had a date with Mr. Joyce at the old Lavenue's which used to be one of the best restaurants in Paris. As I stood outside it the clock on the Gare Montparnasse marked five and twenty past seven. I can see the spidery black hands on the pallid, opaline face of the dial! I had asked Joyce for seven-thirty; so I bought an English newspaper and sat down to an apéritif outside the restaurant in an evening of golden haze. . . . So it was perhaps in August 1923.

The English newspaper was yelling with triumph. All across the front page it yelled the words: "Big Axe's First Chop!" . . . The British Government had abolished the post of Historical Adviser to the Foreign Office. It was then that I said:

"Perhaps I had better never go back to England!"

A country whose Foreign Office lacks Historical Advice is no country for poets—or for anybody else! . . . It was then 19.h.27.30. . . . The clock had moved on two and a half minutes. . . .

It was not, of course, the first time that such an idea had crossed my mind. On the 12th of November 1922, when I had just reached Paris, I had read—within a hundred yards of that spot—of the fall of Mr. Lloyd George's Government. . . . I had only meant to come to Paris for six weeks but then I thought it safe to go as far as St. Jean Cap Ferrat. And I had said:

"Perhaps I need never return to England."

It was a curious sensation—of relief! I am no David and any slingstones of mine would rebound like peas from the brazen brow of Dai Bach. I am even no politician. I never talk politics except when I get excited by the ascent to power of somebody like Mr. George or his friend Mr. Hitler. Even at that I soon tire of the subject. Once you have said that Mr. Lloyd George was responsible for all the sorrows that now beset our poor civilisation or that Mr. Hitler is the anti-Christ of culture you have said all that is to be said and it is monotonous to repeat even truth. Still less do I ever write about politics, though for purposes of my own I have always followed with deep attention the public affairs of the countries round the Atlantic. So I did not see that my presence in England could in any way help that country.

But, till that November day I had felt as if I were doing what motorists call watching the traffic. As if I had been in an immense public automobile careering above precipices, at the mercy of a mad driver who had never traveled those roads before. One is unwilling to get out and petrified with terror at the thought of staying there. . . . In any case even a rat should not desert a sinking ship. . . .

Mr. Baldwin, the new Prime Minister, appeared to be another nice middle-aged gentleman for a quiet tea-party. Less lugubrious than Mr. Bonar Law—whose face would have wrecked any party—he appeared to be even more inactive. At the same time he was a charming speaker, his pleasant voice and pious, anodyne opinions making of his sentences so many gentle opiates. So it seemed to me that he was what my country most needed—somebody who would do nothing for seven years and let the English people work out its problem for itself.

England at that date—and still!—presented the aspect of a nation divided into two hostile camps by a line running say from the Bristol Channel to the Wash or thereabouts. In the North was an immense industrial city of thirteen million inhabitants. The district between Liverpool and Middleborough was one metropolis, tramways running between uninterrupted houses from one to the other, right across England. In the South was another city of thirteen millions—London and her out-skirts. The North was being ruined by the lowness of the franc; the banking South would be ruined if the gold standard was not maintained.

Of the latter proposition I had no supporting evidence. It was generally stated that the prosperity of London depended on its remaining the banking centre of the world and that it could only be the banking centre of the world if it had the gold standard. How that might be I had no means of knowing. But I had evidence enough of the other proposition—that the industrial North was being ruined by the lowness of the currencies of the lesser breeds. Evidence of that hit me everywhere. In the Paris that I had known before the war the names of British products blazed in advertisements from every wall and from the columns of every newspaper. Now there were none and, if you wanted anything English, you had to seek for a tiny shop in a side street and pay from three to five times as much as you would have to pay for a similar French product. The French product would not be quite so good but, in face of the difference in the prices, what choice had one? . . .

I had made, in the Cevennes, a little tour in the car of a friend who was a French automobile manufacturer. He had told me that he could turn out three automobile wheels of the standard of a famous British house for the same price as that house could manufacture one. So M. Chose could employ three times as many men.

In addition he eventually supplied the British firm—which had hitherto advertised that it sold only British products—with its automobile wheels, thus putting more British mechanics out of work and giving employment to more Frenchmen. In addition the British firm actually re-exported the wheels to France, having made some slight alterations to their attachment and were able, on the strength of their name, to sell them for more than M. Chose's own wheels would fetch. This however was put a stop to by legal action, so that even that slight profit, due to the once famous British reputation for workmanship, was put an end to. . . .

All this was matter as to which I could hardly judge. I was neither captain of industry nor financial leader. My interests went out to the artist and the agriculturist. For me the manufacturer was more pestilential than the banker and the banker more pestilential than the manufacturer. Between those hideous upper and nether millstones what chance had the farmer? and the poor poet! What a hope was his? . . .

A peculiar incident had, even before my leaving England, predisposed me towards expatriation. This was the call of an election agent—a Tory, I think. He asked for my name on his rolls. I said he could have it because I never refused anybody anything that was mine to give and the Liberal agent had never called on me. . . .

I will here interpolate a little anecdote that has always amused me when I have thought of it. And it may be of use to electioneers. . . . I was once returning officer in Sussex. An aged, nearly blind labourer came in to vote. He said to me:

"Which be I to vote for, zur, Conservative or Liberal?"

I expressed proper horror and explained that, presiding at the poll, I had to be strictly impartial. He said:

"Well, it be like this, governer. The Conservative gen'lman come to see me and he never gave me nothing. The Liberal gen'lman never came to see me but what I thinks is: if he had a come he *might* have give me sutthing. So I shall vote for he!"

This Tory gentleman certainly gave me nothing— except food for thought. . . . When he had taken down my name he said oilily: "And what profession shall I put, sir?"

I said: "Writer?"

He exclaimed:

"*What?*" . . . and only after a second remembered to add: "Sir!"

I said:

"I'm a writer! I write books for a living!"

He was appalled and became almost lachrymose. He said:

"Oh, *don't* say that, sir. Say: 'Gentleman.'"

I explained that I was not a gentleman. I was a poet.

He became almost frantic at that. He said:

"Oh, I *can't* say that, sir. It would make my roll look ludicrous. I should be laughed out of my job if you made me say 'poet'. . . . Make it 'gentleman', sir. . . ."

And, sitting there, outside Lavenue's I was reminded of something else. When I was employed in demobilising my battalion after the armistice I had to sort men into categories. There were eighteen categories. They regulated the rate of priority of discharge according to the use of the individual to the community. In the first category you had Administrators—Bankers, Manufacturers, Employers of manual labour. After that you had classes labelled: "Productive"—skilled artisans, coal-miners, blacksmiths, whitesmiths, breeders of animals. . . . When I came in my inspection of the Army Order making these regulations, on the XVIIIth and last category which was labelled "Totally unproductive" I found huddled together and not even in alphabetical order those who were to be last discharged. They were utterly useless to the community. They included:

"Travelling showmen, circus performers, all writers not regularly employed on newspapers, tramps, pedlars, all painters not employed as house, factory, industrial, carriage, or sign-painters; all musicians, all unemployable persons . . ." and, oh irony! "Gentlemen, independent."

I pondered over those things whilst I waited for Mr. Joyce. . . . It was by then 8.10. . . . Indignation took complete possession of me. That artists should be lowly rated was supportable. But that they should be labelled unproductive, being the creatures of God who produce entirely out of themselves, with no material aids and no hope of help! I could imagine, even with sympathy, the honest Army Officer who composed that document in

265

his Whitehall Office. . . . But that the State should, to its eternal shame, let pass such a compilation—that appeared to me intolerable. . . .

And on top of that that Election Agent! It appeared that for me and my brothers there was no escape. One way or other—either as Artists or Gentlemen we had to be in the XVIIIth Category. . . . And more than anything I resented being forced to be a Gentleman. An Artist cannot be a Gentleman, for, if he is a Gentleman he is no artist. The best Gentleman is he who, with the pink cheeks of urban health, inhabits a glass showcase. He at least will never commit a solecism. His clothes at least are for ever perfectly pressed. He at least will never express despair, intelligence, fear, animation or passion! And I on an electioneer's sheet must write myself down —that!

I pondered like that as the hands of the station clock reached 8.15!

And now Mr. Baldwin's Government had moved. They were no Gentlemen, they had allowed themselves to be badgered by the cheap press, into action. With an axe! The cheap press with the voices of jackals demanded Economy. To them Mr. Baldwin's Ministry had, like the Russian mother, thrown to the wolves the Foreign Office Adviser in History. No British diplomat from henceforth was to know what was the Pragmatic Sanction, or what was enacted by the Congress of Rastatt, the Convention of Cintra, the Venezuelan Arbitration award—or the very treaty of Versailles which by then was historic. . . .

Two ladies passed and bowed to me—Miss Sylvia Beach and Miss Nina Hamnett.

They said:

"We shall see you at Joyce's dinner at nine. Opposite!"

I said:

"No: he's dining with me here at 7.30. . . ." It was then 8.37.

They said:

"Joyce never dines with anybody, anywhere but opposite and never at seven-thirty."

I said:

"He is dining with me to-night to try the *Château Pavie, 1914.*"

They said:

"He never drinks anything but white wine."

I said:

"Anyhow I am never going back to England."

They said:

"How nice!" and passed on.

So it will appear to the reader that I have nothing to say against my country which any Englishman would resent. For all that I have said amounts to that the English State and the English social hierarchy believe in keeping the imaginative artist in his place—his place being the XVIIIth Category. The admirable Staff wallah who compiled that schedule would merely shake his head in bewilderment at reading my reasons for living outside his shadow. He would say:

"This seems to be rather tosh. Does Mr. F. really

think that banks are not more useful to—er—the Community than . . . er, novels? . . . Surely not *novels!*
. . . Or that coals are not more necessary to England than pictures. . . . Even handpainted oil ones!" . . . And he will shake his scarlet hatband in perplexity and add: "The johnny must mean something. But what?"

And the tragedy is that that man is an admirable personality inspired by the very best sense of duty. The very best! If you could get him to see that a training in the Arts was as salutary to mankind as Army physical training, he would spend a month of slow arranging and rearranging his schedules so that every Tommy would get at least as many hours a week of Æsthetic and Literary training and exercise as he spends on P. T. And that Staff Officer would see to it that that instruction was the best to be got and that the regimental officers saw to it that there was no shirking.

But the tragedy is that you could never get him to see what every peasant here in Provence knows—that to the properly circumstanced man frescoed rooms are infinitely more salutary than artificial heating—or than anything that is the product of steam driven machinery. . . . So they fresco their rooms with those admirably primitive, local paintings that have had so great an influence on modern art and make no provision whatever for heating. And, on occasion, it can be cold here.

I think I have said enough to make it plain that I regard the British Army as a human machine with so great an admiration that I can hardly write of it without hyperbole. With an admiration almost equally great I regard the British Constitution, the British legal machine and administration of justice. The one and the other are inspired by a deep tradition of humanity that as long as there are wars and laws and rulers mankind would be foolish indeed to let die. England may or may not, in saving France on the 4th August 1914, have saved civilisation by her arms. But there is no doubt that she could now, in the department of life that I have mentioned, save civilisation by her example.

And even in my resentment of her treatment of the artist I bear no personal feeling. It is to me a matter of pure indifference how I am treated by English people. What I should bitterly resent at the hands of a Frenchman leaves me, on the other side of the Channel, completely indifferent. It remains hypocrisy to search for the person of the Sacred Emperor in a low tea house and to expect urbanity from the barely adolescent is to give evidence of ignorance of the nature of man.

No, what enrages me is the thought that the same grossness might be shewn to great artists. Imagine, say, Matisse in England and understanding the social nuances by which, supposing him to be painting a portrait in an English house, he should realise that he ranks a little after the governess and a little above the butler—or that his "*état civil*" is in the company of tramps and the unemployable! . . . To have, when abroad, to blush for one's country is the most painful of all experiences.

But for the rest it was that day at 8.49 my humble prayer that the reigning house might for ever protect the laws of Great Britain; that her arms might be for ever victorious; that her commerce might for ever prosper; that Kent might always hold the County championship; England retain the Ashes, the British Empire the Davis Cup, and particularly I prayed that a British heavyweight might be found to stand on his legs for six rounds out of any ten-round contest, anywhere. Oh . . . and might Mr. Lucas's favourite paper find now and then some really side splitting ones. Then England will, for ever, know happy sunsets. . . .

From that day I began to feel that I had no country and I have gone on feeling more and more convinced that I have none—or that my only country is that invisible one that is known as the kingdom of letters. So that, since that day I live in France where the Arts are held in great honour and as often as I can I go to the United States where the greatest curiosity as to the Arts is displayed. I go there, that is to say, when I can afford it and stay until my money is spent. Then I come back to the shores of the Mediterranean where one can live on a few herbs and for the greater part of the year, in a soft climate, pass the day and night entirely out of doors! . . .

The *Transatlantic Review* arose almost accidentally, though I have said that when I had been passing through Paris on my way to the Riviera an idea had passed through my mind. It was a vague sense rather than an idea. . . . It seemed to me that it would be a good thing if someone would start a centre for the more modern and youthful of the art movements with which in 1923 the city, like an immense seething cauldron, bubbled and overflowed. I hadn't thought that the task was meant for me. But a dozen times I was stopped on the boulevards and told that what was needed was another *English Review*. Then one day, crossing the Boulevard St. Michel up near the Luxembourg Gardens, I met my brother. I had not seen him for a great number of years. The last time had been in 1916 when I had passed his rather bulky form, in uniform, in New Oxford Street. He had been wounded and I failed to recognise him, khaki making everyone look alike. My companion on that day said that I exclaimed—it was during the period when my memory was still very weak:

"Good God: that was my brother Oliver. I have cut my brother Oliver. . . . One should not cut one's brother. . . . Certainly one should not cut one's brother! It isn't *done*."

I do not remember to have uttered those words but I can still hear the ringing laughter that saluted whatever I did say. I ran back along the street after him but he had gone down the tube lift before I caught him up.

Now I met him on a road refuge half way across the Boulevard. He said that he wanted me to edit a review owned by friends of his in Paris!

My brother Oliver Hueffer was a gifted and in many ways extraordinary fellow. From my earliest days I was taught—by my father, my mother and himself—to regard him as the sparkling jewel of the family whilst I was its ugly duckling. My father used to call me "the patient but extremely stupid Ass!"; to discipline my haughty and proud stomach my mother made me surrender to him my rabbits, my tops, my catapults, my stuffed squirrel. My father, respecting the rights of primogeniture, used to give me as pocket money a weekly sixpence and to my brother fourpence halfpenny. My mother however used to insist on my equalising the sums, so I never had more than fivepence farthing to spend. That sum was really insufficient to keep me at school in the position that I might have expected. . . . When we grew to young manhood I could excel him in one thing: I could grow a moustache, which he never could. This used to cause him great heartburnings. And of course I could always knock him down for, owing to his having at the age of six dislocated his hip, he was always slow moving. But as I seldom wanted to knock him down this was small consolation to me.

From an early age I saw little of him except in his more coruscating moments. When I was about nineteen I was standing on the side-walk outside St. George's, Hanover Square, watching the guests go in to a wedding of some member of the Grosvenor family. My brother got out of a carriage of the Duke of Westminster and handed out one of the bridesmaids. . . . He was then sixteen and in a military uniform.

Under my grandfather's reign, after my father's death, Oliver went through a great series of coruscating avatars. My grandfather had to have geniuses for his grandchildren. Of an evening he would go through our names in turn, beginning with the young Rossettis:

"Olive's a genius, Arthur's a genius, Helen's certainly

a genius." Then he would begin with my mother's children: "Juliet's a perfect genius; Fordie is too perhaps. But as for Oliver I can't make out whether he's a genius or mad. . . . I think he's both!"

That was high praise. That all his grandchildren should be mere geniuses was a commonplace to him. But that the gods should vouchsafe to him a mad genius —that was almost beyond his most private hopes! . . .

So, with his aid, my brother, with the swiftness of the succession of the seasons at St. Agrève, ran through the careers of Man About Town, Army Officer, Actor, Stockbroker, Painter, Author and under the auspices of the father of one of his fiancées, that of valise manufacturer!

My grandfather, with his square white beard and his long white hair cut square, exactly resembled the King of Hearts in a pack of cards. Towards the end of his life he used to paint till far into the night—with his left hand because his right was paralysed. He would lay down his palette, take off his béret and go up to bed. He would put on his nightcap and carefully lay in the flat brass candlestick his gold watch, chain and seals, and his gold-rimmed spectacles. . . .

One morning a week the early hours would be pierced by his imprecations. He would send for my brother who would look more than usually cherubic. He would fling his nightcap across the room and shout:

"God damn and blast you, Oliver, what have you done with my watch and chain and spectacles?"

Oliver would say, with an air of ingenuousness:

"Well you see, Granpa, I had to have a couple of quid for debts of honour and I knew you would not want me not to have them whilst I did not want to wake you. So I took them down to Attenborough's. But here are the pawn tickets."

I think my grandfather was, in secret, rather proud of these exploits. At any rate he never locked his bedroom door. . . .

On coming into his money from our *oncle d'Amérique* he set up as a wholesale tobacco-merchant under the auspices of one of our Virginian cousins. This was appropriate because our uncle's money had been gained by tobacco planting in the South. But he soon gave that up and took seriously to the profession of letters. Under the pseudonym of Jane Wardle he published several books which were very successful—one of them, the "Lord of Latimer Street," being enormously so. The press soon got on to the secret and compared his books to my own, always preferring his lightness of touch to my "Teutonic" stolidity. He however drifted gradually into journalism and only occasionally wrote books. Sometimes he would deliberately take one of my own subjects—to shew that he was more brilliant than I. And, in England, he would always be more successful. I wonder no English publisher has thought of resuscitating his work. It had great qualities of fancy.

He went eventually to New York as correspondent for one of the great English dailies. There he tried to found a paper on the lines of what in England is called the Yellow Press. I was told the other day by a New

York journalist who had known him at the time that he actually did succeed—in 1910 or so—in publishing some numbers of a paper that in every way resembled the *Daily News* of New York. New York however was not ready for such brilliances; the paper died, and my brother went through some hard times. . . .

A little after the outbreak of the late war, the War Office rang me up and a voice said:

"There's a fellow here who says he's your brother."

I said that if he said he was my brother he probably was.

The voice continued rather outragedly:

"But he says he's a Mexican General. . . ."

I said that if he said he was a Mexican General he probably was.

With a still greater intonation the voice continued:

"But he says he commanded 3,000 men, 4,500 women, and 6,000 children."

I said that my brother's enumeration of his troops was absolutely correct. The women cut the throats of the wounded, the children went through their pockets when they were dead. I added that they might grant him a commission with perfect confidence. He served through the war with credit and was twice wounded. I never shall forget the sense of rest that my mother shewed when she received the news that for the second time he was in hospital in London. I have never seen greater contentment. She folded up the telegram from the War Office, placed it in the fly-leaf of her novel—it was "Wuthering Heights," folded herself deep into her armchair and shawl, put on her spectacles, said:

"You know, Fordie, I think you're perfectly wrong when you say that Heathcliffe is overdrawn" and so settled down to read for five hours without speaking. It had been many, many hours since she had laid down that work—at page 36.

Two years ago I was sitting on the terrace here, reading the English paper. I noticed that a piece had been cut out. Below the excision I read: "—imer Street etc." Then I knew my brother was dead. I was at the time just finishing a book and at such times I am always depressed and nervous. A finished book is something alive and, in its measure, permanent. But until you have written the last word it is no more than a heap of soiled paper. I fear preposterous things—that one of the aeroplanes that are forever soaring overhead here might drop a spanner on my head. . . . Anything. . . . So a member of my household had cut out from the paper the necrological announcement hoping to hold back the news till I should have finished the book. But I knew that there had been the words: "He was the author of a number of works which achieved great popularity amongst the best known being 'A Book of Witches'; 'A Tramp in New York'; 'The Lord of Latimer Street,' etc." And these were the exact words . . .

I will add a curious fact. My brother's character and temperament must much have resembled my own. He had inherited from my mother and my grandfather a little more of their romantic tendency to take geese for swans—though Heaven knows I too have enough of that. And I got from my father enough of a passion for justness in expression and judgment to rob me of the chance of his undoubted brilliance. So that, in conversation, I am really rather inarticulate whereas when it came to what is called back-chat he was the most amazing performer that I have ever heard, not excluding Mr. H. G. Wells. But what was singular was that whenever we were together alone and silent, when one of us broke the silence it was to say exactly what the other had been about to bring out. I have tested this time and again and it certainly came true seven out of ten times as to the substance of the remark and five out of ten times as to the actual words. The same sort of, I suppose telepathic, *rapport* existed between my mother and myself, but not nearly in so marked a degree.

. . . In 1923, then, my brother stood beside me on a refuge halfway across the Boulevard St. Michel and told me that some Paris friends of his wanted me to edit a review for them. The startling nature of that coincidence with the actual train of my thoughts at the moment made me accept the idea even whilst we stood in the middle of the street. He mentioned names which were dazzling in the Paris of that day and sums the disposal of which would have made the durability of any journal absolutely certain. So we parted with the matter more than half settled, he going to the Eastern sidewalk, I to the West.

Ten minutes after I emerged from the rue de la Grande Chaumière on to the Boulevard Montparnasse.

Ezra with his balancing step approached me as if he had been awaiting my approach.—He can't have been.—He said:

"I've got a wonderful contribution for your new review" and he led me to M. Fernand Léger who wearing an old fashioned cricketer's cap like that of Maître Montagner of Tarascon, was sitting on a bench ten yards away. M. Léger produced an immense manuscript, left it in my hands and walked away. . . . Without a word. I think he regarded me with aversion as being both English and a publisher.

Ezra led me to the Dôme—a resort I much disliked—and provided me with a sub-editor and a private secretary. The sub-editor was a White Russian, exiled Colonel, an aristocrat to his fingertips, knowing not a word of English and more nervous than you would imagine that anyone could be. He saw Communist conspiracies everywhere and, within five minutes, was convinced that I was a Soviet agent. He was a beautiful specimen of his type but he was starving.

The private secretary was also a beautiful specimen of his type. He was an English Conscientious Objector, an apparently mild, bespectacled student. He too was starving. . . . Everyone in the Dôme was starving. . . . I would have preferred not to have a Conscientious Objector for my private secretary or a White Russian aristocrat for a sub-editor. Indeed I was not quite certain that I needed at the moment the services of either functionary.

The Russian produced a contract with a printer and

several manuscripts by friends—White Russians who recounted their martyrdoms under the Soviet: the Conscientious Objector gave me the ms. of a work of his
on German lyric poetry and another on neo-German
metaphysics. Ezra beckoned to a slim, apparently diffi-
dent young man and to a large-boned undiffident young
man. They told Ezra that they had not brought the
ms. he had told them to bring. They had thought I
should not like them. I did not catch their names because
the avalanche began.

Ezra had gone away with the two young men, in
order, he said, that I might have leisure to talk things
over with my two collaborators. But there was no
chance of talking. I have always disliked the Dôme,
mainly because of the facial ugliness of its frequenters.
. . . That only means that the best goods are not always
done up in the most attractive parcels. Taken singly I
would rather have the society of the ugliest man at the
Dôme or the most indigent of the habitués of the
Rotonde than with the handsomest and best got up of
the drinking at either of the smarter cafés of that Boulevard. Individually the Dôme's crowd are apt to prove
at least keen followers of one art or another. Now
and then they will develop into geniuses. But keen followers of the arts and geniuses who have not yet succeeded have not usually—or indeed unreasonably—a
quality of ferocious resentment that shows itself in their
faces. The ferocious resentment of neglect when one
is conscious of great gifts or even of only great industry
has my entire sympathy even when that resentment is

expressed against myself as capitalist or for this or that. That has happened to me often enough. But to be pressed close in on by several hundred beings all, whether geniuses or industrious or merely detrimental and needy—all crushed together, in a fetid atmosphere and an unceasing din—that is apt to disturb my equanimity.

Ezra however had insisted on my playing chess with him every afternoon during my stay—my two stays— in Paris with the result that, bulky and blond and to all appearances opulent I must have been extremely well known in those *parages*. And that occasion was like a riot in the Tower of Babel. The beings that bore down on me, all feeling in their pockets, were of the most unimaginable colours, races and tongues. There were at least two Japanese, two negroes—one of whom had a real literary talent—a Mexican vaquero in costume, Finns, Swedes, French, Rumanians. They produced manuscripts in rolls, in wads, on skewers. They produced photographs of pictures, pictures themselves, music in sheets. Americans expressed admiration for my work; gloomy Englishmen said that they did not suppose I was the sort of person to like their stuff. I was, as a matter of fact, extremely anxious to read the manuscripts. I am always anxious to, and the more battered and unpresentable the manuscript the more hope it excites in me. But I was not to read many of them.

I shared the small sum I had in my pocket between the conscientious objector and the White Russian and ran away. With that small sum the Colonel bought per-

fumes and roses for the Princess his wife. The conscientious objector embarked on a career of martial adventure. I had told him to collect the manuscripts and
bring them round to me next morning. Alas!

When I got home, there were manuscripts—nearly a
wash basketful—already there. And awaiting me were
a very vocal lady from Chicago and an elegant but bewildered husband. It was then ten o'clock at night.
They stayed till two o'clock in the morning, the husband completely silent, the lady—who was very tall and
frightening—threatening me with all sorts of supernatural ills if I did not make my new magazine a vehicle
—of course, for virtue, but also for some form of dogma
connected, I think, with psychiatry. She offered to subscribe for herself and her husband, then and there.

So there I was with all the machinery of a magazine
—sub-editor, secretary, contributions, printers, subscribers. . . .

It had been just before dinner time that I had met
my brother. I had conversed with him in absolute isolation. You could not have greater isolation than a refuge
in the centre of the traffic of the Boulevard St. Michel.
Yet here was an organisation.

It was as if I had been in one of those immense
deserts inhabited by savages who have unknown methods of communication over untold distances. Before I
had met my brother I had had no idea of anything so
tangible as a *Review*; certainly not of a *Review* for
which I should have the responsibility. I had just worked
myself up to the idea of myself writing. You cannot

write and conduct a *Review*, at least, you cannot write
well.

Ezra however had had the idea—that someone else
ought to take on the job. It was an idea that might have
jumped to the eye of anyone in the Paris of those days.
Paris gyrated, seethed, clamoured, roared with the Arts.
Painters, novelists, poets, composers, sculptors, batik-
designers, decorators, even advanced photographers
so crowded the boulevards that you could not see the
tree-trunks. They came from Tokio, they came from
Petrograd; they poured in from Berlin, from Constan-
tinople, from Rio de Janeiro; they flew in locust hordes
from Spokane, from Seattle, from Santa Fé, from all
the states and Oklahoma. If you had held up and
dropped a sheet of paper on any one of the boulevards and had said: "I want a contribution," a thousand hands would have torn you to pieces before it
had hit the ground. . . . At least seven must have come
even from London. . . .

All this clamorous life seemed to call for its organ.
. . . I had discussed that often enough with Ezra. . . .
It was not merely Paris that was alive to the Arts: it
was the whole world. If thousands came from Spokane
it was because there a leaven was working. So with
Tokio, Petrograd, Budapest, and Portland, Maine. It
was the real reaction from the war; the artist making
his claim for glory as against the glory of the warrior.
Mars was to be disgruntled.

So communication should be established between that
Sun, Paris, and the furtherest satellites, and between

them and Paris. St. Louis, Mo., must be told what Picasso was doing and Picasso and Mr. Joyce must be enlightened as to the activities of Greenwich Village. And Lenin reading of these deeds in his palace in Petrograd would be moved to give the Arts a higher place in his body public. It was a fine idea.

It seemed however to be nothing for me. And it was nothing for Ezra, who, at that moment had become both sculptor and musician. Thus all his thoughts were needed for those arts. He had living above his studio in the rue N. D. des Champs a gentleman whom he suspected of being an ex-Enemy, a person obnoxious in himself. He had therefore persuaded Mr. George Antheil, who, besides being a great composer, must be the heaviest living piano-player—he had persuaded Mr. Antheil to practise his latest symphony for piano and orchestra in Mr. Pound's studio. This lasted all day for several weeks. When Mr. Antheil was fatigued, his orchestra played unceasingly Mr. Antheil's own arrangement of the *Wacht am Rhein*. In the meanwhile, turning sculptor, Mr. Pound fiercely struck blocks of granite with sledge hammers.

The rest of his day—his evenings that is to say—would thus be given up in the court of the local justice of the peace, rebutting the complaints of the gentleman who lived overhead. He had some difficulty, but eventually succeeded in convincing that magistrate that he and Mr. Antheil were two pure young Americans engaged in earning their livings to the greater glory of France whereas the gentleman upstairs was no more nor less than the worst type produced by a lately enemy nation. So that fellow had to leave Paris.

It was not to be imagined that, with all this on his hands, Mr. Pound could be expected to give time to the conducting of a *Review* and there the matter had rested. Or I supposed it to have rested. But I knew that Mr. Pound was passionate to have that *Review* and that he was industriously searching for a cat to get those chestnuts out of the fire. He wanted a mild, gentle young man who should provide all the money and do all the work. He in the meantime was to extend his length in the office armchairs and see that that *Review* printed nothing but the contributions of his friends for the time being. . . .

So there I sat, at after four in the morning, in a little garden pavilion on the site of the temple of Diana with the white blackbirds just beginning to warble in the trees. I knew that I was for it. For, even if my brother's scheme fell through the public opinion that Ezra had carefully prepared on the boulevards would see to it. Not even white blackbirds—those fabulous and luckbringing birds of France—not even the *merles blancs*, not even Diana herself would preserve me from their fury if I did not provide harbourage for their composition. I should be torn to pieces as was Actæon by the hounds of that Goddess. . . .

Next day we proceeded—my brother, I, the White Russian, Mr. Pound and others, to see fair play, to an office in the Quartier de l'Étoile. There was no doubt that that office represented High Finance. High

Financiers passed in and out all the time we were kept waiting in the ante-room. I had even a glimpse of the enormously wealthy man, who was said to—and I believe did—own the *Review* it was proposed to intrust to me. He was the principal winning owner of the French turf that year. I didn't much like his looks— I mean as owner of a *Review*—and I gather that he didn't much like mine or those of the helpers who accompanied me. That is not surprising. The cleft between the Left Bank and that quarter is more impassable than any Mappin Terrace, separating wild beasts from avid sightseers.

We were all shown into the office of a gentleman well known in Paris. He was the head of a firm of solicitors though I believe he was not actually a solicitor himself. But he employed English lawyers in that office. That is, I believe, a perfectly proper proceeding and the gentleman himself seemed a very ordinary city man. He certainly knew very little about running reviews and agreed to every condition that I made with such readiness that I made them as stiff as I could. . . . The company to be formed to take over the existing but unsuccessful *Review*—it was temporarily edited by my brother—was to relieve me absolutely of all business and financial responsibilities. It was to pay my staff, provide a business office at that building, on the first of every month to let me have a cheque sufficient to pay all contributions at a flat rate per page. It was to guarantee to continue for at least three years and to pay me, not a salary, but in shares of the company.

In the case of any disagreement between myself and the directors I was to have the right to purchase a sufficiency of the shares to give me absolute control of the company. Most important of all I was to have absolute control of what went into the *Review*, not only in the editorial, but also the advertising pages. The directors were to undertake not even to make suggestions except at my request. The only channel between them and me was to be my brother who was appointed business manager. I was to have my own office which was never to be approached by any of the directors except at my invitation. . . . I go into these details because we seemed to evolve a model agreement for magazine editorship—from the point of view of the editor.

I then gave Mr. P—— an outline of my proposed editorial policy. It seemed to astonish him mildly but not in the least to antagonise him. He had never heard of Picasso, Matisse, Brancusi, Mr. Joyce, Miss Stein, nor Mr. Pound. Not even of Conrad or Thomas Hardy. But he said:

"That's all right. You go ahead. It's in your hands. You get going as soon as you please. We have every confidence in you."

He detained me for a minute when the others left. He said that his friend Mr. Q——, one of the hottest men in Paris or New York, had told him and the race-horse owner an amazing story. Mr. Q—— had never read a book in his life. But one day in Egypt he had been on the *dahabeah* of Mr. R——, the hottest man on Wall Street. . . . I knew Mr. R—— by reputation of course. Mr. R—— had had to go ashore for an evening. He had left Mr. Q—— with a box of his own particular cigars and one of my novels. Mr. Q—— had never read a novel before or since. But he said that that was the happiest evening of his whole life. He couldn't get over it. He could not believe that a mere book could do that to you. He often thought of it. The happiest evening of his whole life. . . . Perfectly blissful!

The book had been my most popular novel. The only permanently popular novel I ever wrote. So it was no great shakes. But there it was. Mr. P—— and the race-horse owner had been pondering over what to do with their unprofitable magazine—which they had taken over as against advertising debts. And Mr. Q—— had told them his rapturous story on the evening of the day when my brother had suggested that the editorship should be given to me. And these simple beings had taken that to be evidence of almost divine inspiration.

"Mr. Q——," Mr. P—— said, "is one of the hardest business heads in two continents and what he says goes. . . . We feel we can have *every* confidence in your judgment."

On the sidewalk I found the White Russian lamenting to Ezra and Ezra with his hat crushed down over his eyes cutting with his malacca the heads off imaginary poppies.

What was the matter with Ezra I did not discover till later. His beard bristled and he bubbled over with little sibilants of his incomprehensible dialect. Besides, the Russian was filling the air with his laments. He had discovered that every man in that office was a Communist!

He knew it by looks in the corners of their eyes, by hidden signs that he had interrupted. He must warn General —— whose life would not be safe. He must resign his own appointment.

Ezra dashed into the traffic, still waving his cane as if he had been Bertran de Born about to horsewhip Henry II of England. I took the Russian to the Café de la Paix and patiently explained to him that those people were financiers, bankers, *commerçants*. They were the last people in the world to be Communists!

He said I was no doubt an excellent person for one not born to the Russian purple. But I was too innocent. I did not understand. He was convinced that one of those people had been an Israelite. The Israelites were one gigantic Freemasonry. They had subsidised the Russian as they had subsidised the French Revolution. He must at once warn General —— of this new conspiracy. He must resign his position as my sub-editor. It was just his luck. The Princess his wife had not tasted caviar or *poulet truffé* for several days. That was the work of malignant fate that beset the path of all loyal Russians. No sooner did he get an employment, however lowly, than his employer turned out to be a Communist. His honour forbade him to remain in such a position. It would always be so.

I told him to go to a colony of White Russians, who, he said, had set up a press in the Gobelins quarter. He could also, if he liked, bring me a White Prince to whom I might offer the nominal post of *gérant*. The *gérant* of a periodical in France is a fictitious manager, a man of straw who appears to any summons that may be brought against the paper and, if necessary, is fined huge sums, which, possessing nothing, he cannot pay. If he goes to prison he gets an arranged indemnity. For these services he receives from five to twenty francs a day.

The Colonel had been the youngest Colonel in the Russian Army and as a Russian officer he was considered to be of exceptional intelligence. He said:

"That will be a splendid arrangement. I shall shew all the proofs to General ——. In that way we can be sure that you print nothing of a communist tendency."

I went to a reception at Mr. Pound's studio that afternoon and there met Mr. John Quinn—who pretended to mistake me for Mr. George Moore. Mr. Joyce was also there and a photographer from the New York *Times*. So we were all photographed together. Then there came in, bearded, thin and as nervous as ever, Mr. William Bird IV. With him was the large-framed young man I had seen at the Dôme. I had played lawn tennis one early morning against him and Ezra, with M. Latapie, the painter, for partner. M. Latapie's studio was next door to mine and the tennis court was on the further side of the wall. Latapie and I used to get straight out of bed towards seven in the morning, get over the wall, play a set or two, have a shower in the clubhouse and then go back to breakfast. If anyone else turned up we would play against them. As those who turned up at so matutinal an hour had usually been up all night we beat them as a rule. I don't remember how it had been with Ezra and that young man, nor had I caught his name.

I didn't catch it then, in the studio. I was engaged in avoiding Mr. Quinn whom I disliked because he had pretended to mistake me for George Moore. I was also engaged in trying not to be near Mr. Joyce. For Mr. Joyce's work I had the greatest admiration and for his person the greatest esteem. I also liked his private society very much. He made then little jokes, told rather simple stories and talked about his work very enlighteningly. But to be anywhere near Mr. Joyce at any sort of reception or public event was embarrassing. I should be at once seized on by the hostess, two stiff chairs would be placed side by side and, surrounded by a ring of Mr. Joyce's faithful, we should be expected to talk. To Mr. Joyce this was by no means embarrassing. He was used to it. But to me, as a young man from the country it was very trying. Mr. Joyce would maintain an easy but absolute silence, the faithful hanging on his lips. I would try to find topics of conversation to which the author of "Ulysses" would reply with a sharp "yes" or a "no." . . . At last I found a formula. I used to beseech Mr. Joyce to drink red, not white, wine.

I was really very much in earnest and not quite without official warrant. I have always held a brief against white wine. Its whiteness is caused by the absence of tartaric acid that renders red wine assimilable. I never drink white wine except when politeness demands it and then, if I take only a small glass, I find myself troubled with depression of a gouty nature. And it happened that, on Joyce's own recommendation I had gone to a great oculist in Nice. The oculist had operated on Joyce. He told me that there was nothing the matter with my eyes, recommended me when I smoked cigarettes to do so at the end of the longest cigarette holder possible. The smoke if it gets into your eyes will damage them—like any other smoke. Otherwise smoking does no harm at all.

He added: "And never drink white wine. It is ruinous to the eyesight. . . ." And then: "If Mr. Joyce had never drunk white wine his eyes would not be as bad as they are. I beg you, if you have any influence at all with Mr. Joyce, to beseech him never to drink white wine. Let him drink three, five, seven, ten times as much red wine. It will not harm him. But white is poison." I fancy that oculist was guilty of professional indiscretion. But his concern for his patient was so genuine that it may well be pardoned to him.

I could not, even for his sake, warn Mr. Joyce against drinking white wine on every occasion that I met him. But I thought the topic would be an admirable one for public ceremonials. I was a little guileful too. I imagined that if some of the faithful heard me they might repeat my plea and, being nearer as it were to the throne, might be listened to. I had of course misestimated the nature of Faith. . . . The faithful would rather see their divinity die than that he should be ministered to by a stranger from without the gates. That was seen when Pope Leo, being very sick, called in secret a Saracen leech who came under safeguard to Rome from Tarascon. The Cardinals poisoned the Pope.

So when on the boulevards I would meet one or other of them and told them that Joyce was dining with me at 7.30 in order to taste my *Château Mouton Rothschild* 1885 they would cry with one accord:

"Mr. Joyce never dines with anybody. He never dines before 9.30. He never drinks anything but white wine. . . ."

On the occasion of the Pound's reception—it was in honour of Mr. Quinn—the Faithful were not present and I found myself at last beside Mr. Joyce. I took the occasion to tell him that I would like to print in my *Review* some pages of the book he was writing. I was going to devote a section of my magazine to Work in Progress of persons like himself and Picasso so as to make it a real chronicle of the world's artistic activities. He said it was a pity that I had not been in time to ask that of Proust. He had been told that a single sentence of Proust would fill a whole magazine. Not that he had read any Proust to speak of. His eyes would not let him read any work of other people. He could just see to correct his own proofs.

I said that I myself had read no Proust. I may add that I have since. A French critic having said that I was one of Proust's closest imitators I was in a position to say—though of course I did not say it!—that I had never

read a word of Proust. And having then worked myself
in my mind into the strategic strongpoint that I desired
to occupy I at once bought a copy of "A Còté de Chez
Swann." I read it and "A la Récherche du Temps
Perdu," in one weekend at Guermantes and I found in
Proust's work all the supernatural hypnosis that his
most devoted followers obtain from it. But I do not
think I have imitated him since. . . .

When he heard me say that I had read no Proust he
confirmed for me a story of his meeting Proust that I
had heard from the lips of the lady in whose house it
had happened. Let her be called, in honour of another
novelist, Mrs. Leo Hunter. . . . The lady had asked
Joyce to a reception to meet Proust. Joyce, knowing
nothing of Proust's habits and no hour having been
named, attended at about eleven. Proust in those days
rose at four in the morning. But in honour of Mr. Joyce
he had got up that night at two and arrived about two-
thirty. Mr. Joyce was then tired.

Two stiff chairs were obtained and placed, facing
the one the other, in the aperture of a folding doorway
between two rooms. The faithful of Mr. Joyce disposed
themselves in a half circle in one room; those of M.
Proust completed the circle in the other. Mr. Joyce
and M. Proust sat upright, facing each other and vertically parallel. They were incited to converse. They
did.

Said M. Proust:

"*Comme j'ai dit, Monsieur, dans 'A Coté de Chez
Swann' que sans doute vous avez lu.* . . ."

Mr. Joyce gave a tiny vertical jump on his chair seat and said:

"*Non, monsieur.* . . ."

Then Mr. Joyce took up the conversation. He said:

"As Mr. Blum says in my 'Ulysses,' which, Monsieur, you have doubtless read. . . ."

M. Proust gave a slightly higher vertical jump on *his* chair seat. He said:

"*Mais, non, monsieur.*"

Service fell again to M. Proust. He apologised for the lateness of his arrival. He said it was due to a malady of the liver. He detailed clearly and with minuteness the symptoms of his illness.

". . . *Tiens, monsieur,*" Joyce interrupted. "I have almost exactly the same symptoms. Only in my case the analysis. . . ."

So till eight next morning, in perfect amity and enthusiasm, surrounded by the awed faithful they discussed their maladies.

PART THREE
CHAPTER TWO

THE STALWART YOUNG MAN WHILST JOYCE
had been telling me that story had retired to a distance
in the vast dim studio and was threatening with his fist
a relic of Ezra's Chinese stage—the rendering in silk
of a fat and blinking bonze.

"That young man," I said to Ezra, "appears to have
sinophobia. Why does he so dislike that. . . ."

"He's only getting rid of his superfluous energy,"
Ezra said.

It appeared like it. The young man was dancing on
his toe points. Shadow-boxing was what it seemed to be.

Ezra said:

"You ought to have had him for your sub-editor.
He's an experienced journalist. He writes very good
verse and he's the finest prose stylist in the world. . . .
He's disciplined too."

I answered:

"He has to be if he's a prose stylist. It isn't like verse.
You can turn that out in your sleep. . . . But you told
Mrs. Levoir Suarez yesterday that I was the finest prose
stylist in the world. . . ."

"You!" Ezra exclaimed. "You're like all English
swine. . . ."

Ezra a few years before had been called the greatest bore in Philadelphia, so ceaselessly had he raved about London and Yeats and myself to uninterested Pennsylvanians. Now he was Anglophobe.

"It's just like you to miss the chance of a sub-editor like that," Ezra fulminated: "Disciplined. Energetic! Trained!"

I said that yesterday he had insisted on my engaging the Russian Colonel. I had engaged him. Ezra said:

"Isn't that like you! . . . of course I was only recommending him. How could you think I wanted you to engage him. . . . Engage Kokulof! . . . You must be mad. He's a Russian Colonel—a *Colonel* Com*pletely* illiterate. . . ."

I said I would engage the young man too. I could easily do with two sub-editors. The young man certainly looked disciplined in a Herculean way. Ezra confirmed my suspicion that he must have been in the Army. I took him to be one of those Harrow-Cambridge-General Staff young Englishmen who make such admirable secretaries until they let you down.

I asked where Ezra's Conscientious Objector was. He ought to have brought those mss. round to me that morning. Ezra said:

"Oh he. . . . That'll be all right. . . . You mustn't keep his nose too close to the grindstone. . . . He's not used to discipline. But he'll be invaluable. . . . That's what he'll be. . . . Only your excremental *Review* will be in the gutter tomorrow. . . ."

Mr. Quinn who had been looking at me over Ezra's shoulder said:

"Poor fellow. . . . Poor fellow. . . . I'm sorry for you. . . ."

Mr. Quinn, tall, lean, perpetually indignant, had, as Mæcenas, conversational licence.

Ezra said:

"I'd never think of letting Ernest engage himself under those English diarrhœas. . . . Why couldn't you have found *French* backers? The French are the only people who have any guts. . . . Look at Tristan Tsara! . . . Why didn't you go to him? . . ."

I said that M. Tsara was a Rumanian and, as far as I knew, was no Crœsus.

Mr. Quinn said:

"Poor fellow. . . . You're an honest man. . . . I hate to see you in that position. . . ."

Ezra said:

"The damfool deserves it. . . . He can't see the difference in merit between Arnault Daniel and Guillem de Cabestann. . . . He *prefers* Guillem. . . . What could you expect? . . ."

Mr. Quinn's resentful eyes fixed me for a long time. He repeated:

"I just *hate* to see you in that position."

I said it was not as uncomfortable as it looked. The chair I was in had been made by Mr. Pound during his cabinet making stage. It was enormous, compounded of balks of white pine and had a slung canvas seat so

large that, once you sat down, there you lay until someone pulled you out.

Mr. Quinn said:

"I'll send Mrs. Foster to you. . . . Have a
cigar . . ."

I struggled on that chair-bottom like a horse that had
fallen down on a slippery seat. Mrs. Foster gave me a
hand. I avoided Mr. Quinn's cigar. It was as large as
a crowbar, black and minatory. It had cost a dollar.
I was not man enough for that. I smoked Alsatians that
cost 40 centimes—1 3/5 cents.

I said I should just love to have Mrs. Foster come
and see me. . . . But I had no pictures to sell. I wasn't,
I explained, a painter. When I had nothing else to do I
wrote a book. . . .

"And fall among thieves," Mr. Quinn said. "I hate
to see it. You're an honest man. . . . I'll send Mrs.
Foster to see you."

Mrs. Foster was the ravishingly beautiful lady who
bought Mr. Quinn's pictures for him. She was an admirable business woman and, as far as they were sus-
ceptible of management, she managed the American
side of the *transatlantic review* to perfection. But I
had only met her that afternoon when she had taken
the opportunity to warn me that Mr. Quinn was very
irritable—as I afterwards knew because of a painful
illness—and that I must not mention Conrad to him. At
the moment I only knew her as the picture buyer of
genius who advised a millionaire. And I thought then
that Mr. Quinn took me for a painter.

Mr. Quinn said:

"Hang it, you mustn't swear at me. . . . I only mean your good. . . . Conrad told me what a violent fellow you are. . . . But I've done nothing to be sworn at for."

I had sworn actually at a piece of Ezra's sculpture. As sculptor Ezra was of the school of Brancusi. He acquired pieces of stone as nearly egg-shaped as possible, hit them with hammers and then laid them about on the floor. The particular piece that had distressed me had, to be appreciated, to be seen from a reclining position in the chair from which Mrs. Foster had just extracted me. In my struggles I had forgotten that piece of work. One should never forget works of Art.

I limped away with the assistance of Mr. Bird. The Mr. Bird of those days was everybody's uncle. He knew everything and could get you everything that you wanted. He was what the *Assistance Publique* would be if it were worthy of its name. In public he was a stern and incorruptible head of a news agency with the aspect of a peak-bearded banker. In private he had a passion for a hand printing press that he owned and his hands and even his hair would be decorated with printer's ink.

On that occasion I asked him if he could find me a private office. That seemed impossible. Paris in those days was as crowded as a swallow's nest that expands and contracts as the young brood breathes inside. You advertised that you would pay thousands of francs to anyone who would find you an apartment. No young couples could get married. Middle-class people slept under the arches of bridges over the Seine. Six artists slept in the kitchen of the Rotonde—by courtesy of the *chef*.

Bird said:

"Certainly. I am taking a second office tomorrow. There will be plenty of room for you."

The next day was Saturday. I sent the White Russian down to the office of the Review Company for the first week's salary of himself and the conscientious objector. The conscientious objector's spectacles had not yet again beamed on me but I thought he might like a little salary.

The Colonel came back from that office raving like a lunatic and unable to speak any language but Russian. I gathered that he had not received his salary and that he was afraid that the Princess would have to go without caviar for another week-end. When he could again speak French he asserted that Mr. P—— the financier had confessed himself a Communist and had threatened to have General —— murdered.

He remembered at last that he had a note from Mr. P. Mr. P—— said that the articles of the Company not having been signed he was not really empowered to pay out anything and the banks were closed. He would however send me a small sum for salaries and petty cash by my brother on Monday morning. . . .

That seemed good enough. I engaged that evening an advertising manager. . . .

I was not as green as I seemed. It was quite possible

that that company might never take shape. I knew enough of business men to know, even then, that it never might. If those were business men the chances were that they would wriggle out of the arrangement somehow or other. Business men have to have enthusiasms—but they have also to have cold feet. . . . If they weren't business men, or if, for the moment, they were not in business frames of mind they might keep their words.

On the other hand the date when the public renews its magazine subscriptions or makes new ones was rapidly approaching. It was important, if the review was to come out, to get out some sort of programme and some sort of prospectus. If the review went on, we should then be in a much stronger position. If it did not I should look like a fool but no one else would be hurt. With the exception of the advertising manager, the people I had engaged were nearly useless but they had no employment and, as far as I could see, had no early chance of ever being employed. So it did them no harm to give them work that might not be lasting and it would keep them going for a week or two. And the loss would actually be very little for there was then so much distress amongst the thousands of incapable foreign artists who had flocked to Paris that one was forced to dispense in charity a weekly sum about equal to what I was to dispense in salaries. It was thus merely concentrating a weekly expense on one or two people instead of doling it out by francs to innumerable beggars at café tables. . . . In the upshot one had to dole out at least as much to the beggars too. . . . But that was human weakness rather than any defect in my possible balance sheet.

The case of the advertising manager was very different. This was Miss Marjorie Reid, now Mrs. Robert Rodes. She was an exceedingly capable journalist and had occupied a number of important posts on New York and Paris papers. At the time she was not working owing to sickness occasioned by domestic or other troubles. She needed distraction rather than employment and was perfectly willing to take the chance of the *Review* coming to an untimely end. Thus no one risked anything save myself. And I was ready to risk looking like a fool. There was too much need for such a magazine. . . .

On Monday at an amazingly early hour Miss Reid turned up with a highly lucrative serial advertisement contract from the French Line . . . the *Compagnie Transatlantique*. How she had got it or at what hour that company opens its Paris offices I have never known. There was great joy in our office—which was an empty bedroom I had hired in another pavilion in the garden of white blackbirds. . . . Miss Reid brought also the almost equally astonishing news that someone else, apparently acting for the existing but moribund review, had secured at least half a dozen quite good serial advertisements for banks, railway companies and fashion houses.

I didn't know whether that money would go to my review or not. But it was at least good news. It seemed to show that advertisements were easily obtainable in Paris. . . .

On the strength of it, I authorised the jubilant White Russian Colonel to order some dummy copies from his White Russian printers. He left me with the speed of an antelope that scents new pastures.

It seemed to me then that everything would turn on the amount of money that my brother would bring from Mr. P.'s office for the salaries and petty cash. If it was a fair sum I might be satisfied that those business men intended to behave according to the generous letter of the agreement. If it were derisively small, I determined, I would at once look for new capitalists. The advertising position had heartened me to that. . . . Miss Reid came in just after lunch with another advertisement from an American bank.

In spite of vigorous telephoning my brother did not arrive till past seven in the evening. He had been away for the week-end. The cheque that he brought was insufficient to cover the costs of the postage stamps I had used. He said that he had had great difficulty in getting it. Mr. P—— was exceedingly irritated by the commotion that the White Russian had made in his office on the Saturday. He was convinced that the Russian was Communist of a violent and dangerous kind. The company absolutely refused to subsidise agents of the Soviet Republic.

That appeared to me to be reasonable as far as it went. But Mr. P—— had himself seen General K——. (The White Russian was a courtesy general.) He had

seen General K—— at our business meeting and had consented to my engaging him. Of course he could not be
expected to distinguish between Russians but I could
not be expected to allow him to interfere with my
staff.

My brother said:

"But he's a very rich man."

I pointed out that if he wanted to be useful to me
Mr. P—— had better forget it except when he was sign-
ing cheques.

My brother repeated shockedly:

"But he's a *very* rich man."

He had a certain engaging naïveté that made him
see an aura round the heads of the very rich. I am
bound to confess that to some extent I share it. When
I see *very* rich men of no special intelligence I feel a
certain awe. I feel that they are favourites of the gods
since they are rich without the intelligence to earn their
riches. And a certain reverence should attach to the
favourites of the gods lest the heart of the gods should
be turned against you. They must have some qualities
or the gods would not shew favours to them.

"Besides," my brother said, "It's his view that you
should be of service to him." His expressive brow was
furrowed as he added: "Mr. P—— is not too pleased
with you either. He says you did not treat him with
the respect to which he is entitled. He's very rich as
I've told you. He says he went out of his way to be
complimentary to you and you did not shew the least
empressement. In fact he said he almost believed . . ."

I asked if Mr. P—— believed that I too was a Communist. . . .

My brother's embarrassment increased. He said he must say that I had treated Mr. P—— very much *de haut en bas*. . . . As if he had been the dirt beneath my feet.

I said that when it came to the Arts he probably was. But did that matter? I need never see him again. He was not coming to my private office and I certainly should not go near his. There was he, my brother, to act as a buffer. And well-padded.

His distress increased. He said that they had decided that I could not have a private office. I must work in their building. They thought they must keep an eye on me. The race-horse owner, passing through the room had not liked my looks much. As for Mr. Pound. . . . Look at his slouch hat, his forked beard, his spectacles. And his extraordinary tie. His malacca cane certainly contained a sword-stick. What else could make you carry anything so out of date as a malacca cane? . . . And his pockets! Why did they bulge? Probably because they contained bombs. . . . And he mumbled. Incomprehensible words! To himself.

That is how the Left Bank looks to the Right.

In short, my brother said, they thought that I might be a worthy person. I dressed passably. My hat of course was a last year's model. Brims were not so wide that year. They had suggested that Oliver should hint that to me. They thought that I was weak. Worthy but easily led astray. . . . I was in the hands of the red-bearded Anarchist and the sham Russian General. . . .

I said: "Get it out. . . ."

"In short," Oliver said, "Mr. X——" —the race-horse owner— "insists that he shall censor the review himself. You must give an undertaking not to print a word that he has not o.k.'d. . . . That seems reasonable. He's finding the money. But fine pie he'll make of Joyce and Pound and Conrad. . . . Not to mention you!"

I felt like cold steel. I said:

"I suppose Mr. X—— wants to insert an article a month. On racing form?"

My brother said:

"Two! He wants to have space for two articles every month. One by himself: on racing form. The other by Mr. P——. That will be on finance. . . . Be reasonable. They're finding the money. They've surely a right to some say about how it's spent. After all they're as keen on their subjects as you are on what you call the Arts. . . ."

Half an hour afterwards Mrs. Foster came in. She said Mr. Quinn wanted me to go to him. He was rather sick. In a hotel on the Champs Elysées. I said:

"No. Let's all go and have dinner somewhere. I've shut the *Review* down."

She said that that was why Mr. Quinn wanted to see me. He had known I should shut the *Review* down. He didn't want me to.

When we were in the taxi she said she wanted to tell me something about Mr. Quinn. After she had said it several times I understood. It was a very old taxi: it must have been in the battle of the Marne. It was no good trying.

We stopped in the rue de Rivoli and went into the Bodega. At least a hundred Americans who were re-acting from Prohibition and at least a hundred others of assorted nationalities who had never known the effects of Prohibition were there already. I could not have learned anything about Mr. Quinn there even if Mrs. Foster had roared in my ears with the voice of Stentor. . . .

We decided to walk the rest of the way. In the Champs Elysées at least it was reasonable to hope for quiet. Alas! . . . I was sufficiently a young man from the country—or an old Parisian—to imagine that one ought to be able to cross the Place de la Concorde as in my day one had done it—from the Tuileries gates to Cleopatra's Needle and from there to one or other of the sidewalks of the Avenue des Champs Elysées. . . . I was used to seeing two or three fiacres drooling along and a three horse bus a quarter of a mile off. . . . It was not like that.

We got as far as the base of the Needle and Mrs. Foster began telling me about Mr. Quinn.

I was watching for an opportunity to cross. I realised that it would not be too easy. I had never seen so many motor vehicles, travelling so fast and in four concentric streams. It was perhaps all the worse that it was night. . . . Mrs. Foster went on telling me about Mr. Quinn. We left the kerb and, crossing a stream of motors com-

ing from the right, we were halted by another that
came from the left. I knew some of the fables recounted
of Mr. Quinn and perhaps a little more. A car bearing
directly down on us just brushed my trousers. . . .
Mr. Quinn was reported to have thrown fabulous sums
into the laps of Conrad, Yeats, Joyce, Ezra, Picasso,
George Moore, Matisse, Seurat, Modigliani—in return
of course for mss. and pictures. Mrs. Foster told me
that Mr. Quinn had come over from Ireland as an
emigrant. He was a wonderful lawyer. . . . We got
across a stream of traffic to find another coming from
the left. We had to stand between the two. I said:

"You'd better take my arm. There's nothing really
to be alarmed at. The Paris motorists are fiendishly
skilful. . . ."

She said:

"What with domestic worries and business worries
he's not. . . ."

I said:

"Now," and we got across the penultimate stream.
. . . That was the worst place of all. We seemed farther
than ever from anywhere. The space between us and
the sidewalk was greater and cars raced each other
instead of going in single file. It was also darker, we
being further from the lights at the base of the Needle.
The drivers therefore would see us less plainly.

Mrs. Foster said:

"So you mustn't think if he talks to you oddly or
sharply it's out of disrespect for you. On the con-

trary, he has the very greatest respect for you because
of what Conrad and Yeats. . . ."

I started to make a break for the sidewalk. I succeeded in dragging Mrs. Foster from in front of an
immense, racing limousine. There we were back again.
. . . Mrs. Foster said:

"So with all that and the dreadful spasms of pain.
. . . And he will have to sell some of his collection. . . ."

As if miraculously the space between us and the sidewalk was a swept desert. There was not a car in sight.
We strolled across.

Mrs. Foster said:

"He burst into tears. . . . I was at the telephone.
. . . And when I told him the Doubledays said that
Conrad wouldn't see him. . . . After all he'd
done. . . ."

I said:

"Conrad was afraid to see him. . . . He was a sick
man himself. . . . And he was told Mr. Quinn had a
violent temper. . . . The publishers advised him not to
see him. . . ."

Mrs. Foster said:

"But Mr. Quinn had been so *good*. . . ."

That evening, before the arrival of Mrs. Foster, in
the depression that had followed my rage over the
race-horse owner's proposals, I had said to myself that
happiness could only be ensured by the possession of a
great deal of money. If you have that, nothing can really

touch you. . . . But, as we reached the kerb I quali-
fied that dogma. . . . I said to myself:

"Nothing can really touch you on condition that you
do good to nobody. . . ."

I did my best. We walked beside the dim trees. But
it was very depressing. . . . I said, which was true,
that the last time I had seen Conrad he had told me he
had refused to see Quinn. But he had felt bad about it.
He acknowledged that Quinn had been a real benefactor to him. He had sold his later manuscripts to
Mc——, I forget the name. He had imagined that Quinn
would be enraged about it. He had really a right to be.
But the war had been on. Conrad had been afraid of
what the German submarines might do. He did not
dare to send the mss. to Quinn in New York and he
had been dreadfully pressed for money. Nobody could
sell books. And Mr. —— had pressed and pressed, offering very large sums. Besides the mss. were not really
manuscripts—not what books were printed from. They
were passages that he had copied out by hand, in order
to make a little money. He had had his family to think
of. . . . It was dreadful for a man like Conrad to have
to descend to that. . . . And he had asked me, if I
saw Quinn in Paris, to explain all this . . . about the
submarines and the distance. And if necessary to
apologise.

Mrs. Foster said:

"Yes. It is dreadful for a man like Conrad to have to
descend to that. And Mr. Quinn quite understood. Until Conrad refused to see him. . . . I do not think you

had better talk to Mr. Quinn about it. It was a great misfortune that Conrad ever came to America. Mr. Quinn has never been the same again."

It was a foretaste of the dreadful mist of cupidity that burst out before poor Conrad's corpse was cold in its grave. I sometimes wish that authors' manuscripts could be destroyed at the printer's sooner than that they should be so dishonoured as articles of barter. But many poor writers would go hungrier if there were none to buy those buckshee products of their agonies. Certainly poor Conrad would have found his grim declining years grimmer and more insupportably anxious but for the real goodness of poor Quinn. Quinn had bought his manuscripts at a time when they seemed to be of no particular value to anyone else. . . .

. . . About him in his hotel bedroom there was a sort of air of forlorn majesty. Perhaps that quality attaches to every man who is bound to die very soon—even to condemned murderers. But about him there was a special shade of that quality—as if he had been a disabled eagle. He had the air of a chained eagle waiting for his old enemy, the sun, to rise and find him no longer there.

His first words to me were:

"They will ruin you. You had better let me handle them. I'll . . ."

I forget what he said he was going to do to them—something picturesque and destructive. But they were just business men and mystified at that. They had really no idea that I might object to their using my name for the rigging of the markets or the influencing of betting prices. And their naïveté was proved by their imagining that articles in a review devoted to chronicling international art-activities could much help their designs.

I said as much and at that that forlorn, lean Quixote went, as the saying is, quite off the handle. His imprecations against Messrs. P—— and X—— would have been exaggerated if they had beggared a thousand orphans. . . . It was indeed as if I had been an orphan. He told me over and over again to leave it to him. He would set his French lawyer on the fellows. He would see that I had my review.

I left it to him all right and he dragged me next day to office after office including that of Mr. P—— himself. Mr. P—— preferred to be represented by a poor devil of an English attorney whom he employed in his business. Him Mr. Quinn certainly left miserable. . . .

The poor fellow was exactly like the sweated Cockney clerks of Dickens's London, old, broken, with a back nearly bent double and it was not the affairs of the review that worried him. He did not like his employer and his employer soon afterwards got rid of him. No: it was the sight of Mr. Quinn that made him miserable. He was a lawyer—and he himself was a lawyer. . . . But Quinn was enormously wealthy and passed for being enormously powerful even in Paris. And that poor fellow could not scrape together enough to pay for his monthly bottle of hair-dye!

Mr. Quinn was not the first very wealthy man I had

met but he was the first I had gone about with for any time. It was impressive. As a supposedly great poet I am always treated with distinguished deference wherever I go in Paris. Anybody announcing himself as a poet will receive the same treatment. But to go about Paris with Quinn was to see the doors of palaces, banks, offices, fly open as if propelled by gunpowder. . . . And before him even the poets prostrated themselves and inflexible notaries departed from the routines of their lifetimes. It was as if he carried about with him the power to make you see fairy tales. . . .

He appeared and at once the poor poets saw their one chance—if he would only glance at them—to realise then their material dreams. The rich refurbished their ideas of fantastic business operations that should make them as Emperors. The starveling London lawyer precipitated himself before him and offered, firstly to become his Paris or London correspondent, then to sell Mr. Quinn his law library. . . .

It was not so much Quinn's reputation for wealth. I do not think he was ever a *very* wealthy man and at that time some fantastic litigation in Scandinavia had considerably impoverished him. His professional income must have been very large and out of that he bought the items of his collection and distributed his largesses. But even his legal income he jeopardised in fighting lawsuits for oppressed poets. . . . It was thus his personal prestige, his fame as the maker of extraordinary combinations and the impatient insolence with the powerful that made up his singular aura and his power to force people to act against their wills. . . .

He once broke a date for lunch with me. I met him a little later with his *notaire*, my friend, the inflexible Maître L——. They were carrying golf-clubs. At an hour when the Law Courts were open, they had been playing and lunching at Versailles! Some time later, Maître L—— having been of considerable service to me—or at least, having put himself to considerable trouble: for no one can be very useful to you if you have any contacts with French commercial law—I asked him to play golf and lunch with me at a club of which I was an honourary member. I rather dislike golf which seems to me to be a futile occupation for a grown man who, if he wants to be in the open would be better employed cultivating a melon patch. But I was ready to sacrifice myself; a lawyer who would play golf whilst the courts are sitting must be a golf-maniac indeed!

Me. L—— froze me. He was an inflexible, hard-fleshed and silent man with an always indignant glance. He asked me if I took him to be mad. What spare time, he said, indicating his magnificent and piled desk—what time had he to spare for the distractions of the imbecile? When, doing violence to his feelings, he tore himself from his desk in the small hours he spent an hour or two in reading poetry or other imaginative literature. A man must keep himself abreast of the Arts and the Thought of his time. . . . But *golf*! That derivative for the half-witted.

I reminded him that I had seen him at three in the

afternoon, in the rue St. Honoré, carrying golf-clubs.
. . . His brow cleared as he realised that I had not
been trying to insult him.

"Oh *that!*" he laughed. . . . "That was to please
that infernal tyrant, old Quinn. That man could force
a cat to take to swimming or an elephant to eat beef-
steaks. . . . But I can assure you I have never felt so
painfully deranged. . . ."

My own association with Quinn was not very fortunate. He forced me to do things that I knew would
turn out to be unfortunate and to avoid courses that I
felt convinced would be propitious. . . . With his legal
keenness he discovered that Messrs. P—— and X——
had put themselves in the wrong—I think by agreeing,
before witnesses, to my terms and he proposed to me
to begin a whole series of lawsuits that both he and
Me. L—— assured me would land at least one of them
eventually in prison. That I did firmly refuse to do.
It is completely against such principles as I have to
take the law against any man—for it is obvious that if
any one wrongs me his necessity to do so must be greater
than my need for redress.

The Company in the meantime took action in order
to forestall any that I might take. They ordered me to
hand over the editorship and office of the *Review* to two
gentlemen they named and threatened to sue me for
the frs. 120 that they had advanced me for salaries. I
took absolutely no notice and two or three days later
I saw Mr. Frank Harris and a gentleman in the worst
Derby hat I have ever seen. They were making their

way, rather gingerly, between the rose-bushes of my garden pavilion. They were coming to take possession of the perfectly empty bedroom which I had taken for an office.

I was always afraid of Mr. Frank Harris. I was conscious of being a just man but he affected me with a sense of the supernatural as if he could mysteriously work with hidden powers so that I committed crimes whilst I slept. I had known him with his high colour, his buffalo horn moustache and his voice of a town bull that was weeping over a sentimental novelette—had known him in the days when he had with infinite brilliance edited the *Saturday Review*. Later, whilst I was editing the *English Review*, he trepanned me into lunching with him at the Savoy. All through that meal he advanced arguments to me to force me to print a story of his so salacious that I thought that if I published it the front of the *English Review* office would become purple. In a case like that—it is the only one—I can be adamant. I *will* not print anything I do not want to print. Mr. Harris went on interminably with his persuasions and even threats. He pointed out that a touch of salaciousness would make the *Review* infinitely livelier. Moreover the ordinary man craved for salacious literature. His story would increase tenfold the circulation of the *Review*. But the great argument that his fruity and cavernous voice brought out again and again was that I was the only editor in the world who would have the courage to print his story.

In his pauses for breath I told him over and over

again that I had the greatest possible admiration for his gifts and that I considered—and it was true!—that some of his short stories were with the best in the English language. But he went on and on pleading until I got really frightened,—as if I should wake up one day and find, in spite of myself, that story in the *Review*.

Suddenly however, he changed his tactics and my near-hypnosis cleared away. He hammered the table with his fist and shouted:

"By God I know why you won't print it! By God I know. . . ."

Everyone else in the Grill must have heard him. I had a strong suspicion that that was what he wanted and that the scene was staged for the benefit of Colonel Harvey, then Pierpont Morgan's representative and afterwards American Ambassador. Harris knew that I knew the Colonel very well as Editor of the *North American Review*. He was two tables away and I had spoken to him as we went in. Harvey was indeed meditating putting some money into the *English Review*. But it eventually came out that he proposed to have a say in the contents of the *Review*. I declined rather reluctantly. I could not consent to let it become an organ of the Morgan interests in England. But I liked the Colonel and believe, contrary to the usual opinion in the United States, that he was one of the best ambassadors that country ever sent to the Court of St. James. He had not the courtly vacuity of Mr. Whitelaw Reid or the moral impressiveness of Mr. Page, but he had a keen sense of public affairs and without the diplomatic lip-service of the other ambassadors or too great a show of Anglo-philism managed to get round more than one difficult corner in the relations of the two countries. I have told elsewhere the story of the curious literary adventure I had with him in Brighton.

Harris banged and banged on the table and shouted:

"By God, I know. . . . It's because you think I'm a financial bad hat. Not safe! Not fit to be trusted! By God, I'll shew you. . . ."

He called at the top of his voice:

"Here, head-waiter . . . *Maître d'hotel.* Whatever you call yourself. Tell the Manager I want to see him. *Et plus vite que cela!*"

The manager hurried to the table.

Harris said:

"Go at once and look at my account and tell me what I owe you. . . ."

When the manager came back he said:

"Four hundred and seventy-three pounds, thirteen shillings and ninepence!"

Harris shouted:

"Four hundred and seventy-odd pounds, that's what I owe you, is it?"

The manager said:

"That's what you owe us, Mr. Harris."

Harris shouted:

"And how much credit will you give me?"

The manager said:

"Unlimited credit, Mr. Harris."

Harris became magnificent. He fairly roared:

"And to how many men in London will you say that—that you will give them unlimited credit?"

The manager said:

"We have to be very careful about giving credit, Mr. Harris. . . . "

I am bound to say that that display made me still more frightened of Harris. If he could thus hypnotise a Savoy Hotel manager, what wouldn't he be able to do to me? . . .

It was this redoubtable figure who was approaching my hide-hole through the rose bushes. Since his Savoy Hotel days he had fallen on worse times. He said he had himself set up as a hotel keeper. He professed to have spent millions on a magnificent palace on a Riviera rock in the Mediterranean. To discover that there was no way of reaching it except at low tide in very still weather! . . . There are no tides in the Mediterranean but I was none the less afraid of Mr. Harris. He must have been in low water indeed to want the editorship of the Company's *Review.*

I saw him enter, dubiously, the passage about ten yards away that led to that abandoned bedroom and I gave orders that if he knocked on my door it was on no account to be opened to him. But he drifted away without calling on me. That was the last I heard of that Company. Its *Review* never saw another number.

Then of course Mr. Quinn proposed to finance a different *Review* for me.

I was very doubtful and apprehensive. I had no doubts of the *bona fides* of Mr. Quinn but I very much doubted if his tyrannous nature would not betray him into interfering a great deal more with the *Review* than at the moment he thought he would. On the other hand he would be in America and I in Paris. But what frightened me most was the thought of having to manage the business affairs of the *Review*. I am a very good business man when it comes to other people's affairs. I know the ins and outs of printing, publishing, and business-editing a review as few others do. But when it comes to managing my own affairs I am worse than hopeless. I do not manage them at all, and if they have any chance of becoming complicated at all they become incredibly complicated.

Mr. Quinn, still pathetically conscious of his notion that I was an honest man who had been struggling with knaves was determined that I must have my review. And I was convinced that at that juncture some such review was a necessity. It is the greatest blot on the face of Anglo-Saxondom that it has never been able to support a review devoted entirely to the Arts. Anglo-Saxondom consists of four hundred million subjects, citizens and variously coloured dependents, yet it cannot find ten thousand to display a glimmering of interest in what differentiates man from the brute creation. It seemed therefore my duty, if there was any chance of the existence of such a periodical, to do all I could to bring it into being.

Mr. Quinn appeared to smooth away most of the difficulties. The French business affairs he said Me. L—— would manage; the American branch he would manage himself. Then Mr. Gerald Duckworth, who had published the *English Review*, consented to take over the London side. Mr. Duckworth was one of my oldest friends; he had been losing money over my books for over thirty years and I would have trusted him with my purse, my life and almost with my reputation—that being the last thing one should entrust to anyone not an archangel or a deaf-mute. . . . I consented at last. It seemed to me that if Mr. Quinn put his extraordinary powers of organisation into the American side of the business the fortunes of the *Review* were made.

We came to an arrangement. I stipulated that I was to find 51% of the capital and should hold 51% of the shares. I had no doubt of Mr. Quinn's integrity but I did not know anything about his heirs or assigns. I also stipulated that neither he nor I should touch any of the profits of the *Review* if it made any profits. It did not seem to me decent that either he as Mæcenas or I as writer should benefit by the labours of artists. He stipulated the *Review* should be turned into a limited company according to French law. It was this that really proved the undoing of the *Review*. The charges for founding and registering that company exhausted nearly half our original capital and the exasperation and minute formalities insisted on by Me. L—— caused me more labours and loss of time than all the rest of the *Review* together.

On the face of it the *Review* should have prospered. The costs of production in Paris were ludicrously small; contributors aware that the proprietors were not to make any profits worked at the tiniest of rates; even distribution was very cheap and office expenses were almost nothing as compared with those of any journal in London or New York. All out, a copy cost between two and three cents, and was sold to the public for fifty! . . . You would have thought that there must be a fortune in it. . . . Alas, I have not yet succeeded in liquidating the debts it caused me to incur. I do not suppose I ever shall.

For a time it was fun. Mr. Bird's "office" turned out to be exactly what I craved for—a great wine vault on the banks of the Seine in the Ile St. Louis. The ground floor was occupied by his great iron, seventeenth-century hand press and his forms. In a sort of kitchen he kept the books he printed and the spare copies of the *Review*. The *Review* office was in a gallery that covered half the vault. It was sufficiently large as to floor-space but it was not much more than five feet high and Miss Reid and I had permanently contused skulls. Every time anybody who looked like a purchaser rang the door bell we would spring up from our tables. Miss Reid—who is very tall—had then become the *Review's* admirably efficient secretary. . . . And it was fine, sitting there in our swallow's nest looking over the Seine to the grey houses on the other bank. The stove below made our gallery sufficiently hot even for a New Yorker like Miss Reid and far too hot for me who had most times to sit in my shirt sleeves. And, across the space occupied by the press with its gilt eagle atop, we could watch the plane leaves drifting down into the river; and then the thin sifting of snow; and then the young plane leaves growing green again. And then dusty!

And the excitement when somebody bought a copy of a *Review*! . . . I never sold anything in my life but my emotions when I actually received seven francs fifty for a wad of paper that existed because of the labours of Miss Reid and myself made me think that to be a shopkeeper must be the most glorious of fates. And there was an old, broken London printer to make and bring me up cups of tea and Mr. Bird bending over his types below. . . . And the wonderful manuscripts!

For me all manuscripts by unknown writers are wonderful until I open them and every time that I open one I have a thrill of anticipation. And I may say I have read every manuscript that was sent to either the *English* or the *Transatlantic Reviews*, except for a few that Mrs. Foster weeded out in the New York office. Of course if a manuscript is by an obviously illiterate person I do not read every word of it: on the other hand I have accepted manuscripts by unknown writers after reading the first three lines. This was the case with D. H. Lawrence, Norman Douglas, (Percy) Wyndham Lewis, and H. M. Tomlinson. In the case of Mr. Hemingway I did not read more than six words of his before I decided to publish everything that he sent me. Of course he had been recommended to me. He was the young man who had been shadow dancing in Ezra's studio. In the case of Ezra, in the days of the

English Review I read three verses of his *Goodly Fere*; in that of Mr. E. E. Cummings I had decided after reading ten lines of his that I would open the *Transatlantic Review* with the poems he sent me.

There then was the *transatlantic review*—without capitals. I had no motive in printing the title without capitals. I had seen the name of a shop somewhere on the Boulevard without capital letters and had rather liked the effect. Then, by a mere coincidence, Mr. Cummings' poems had no capitals. The conjunction made a great sensation. It was of course taken to be a display of Communism. We were suspected of beheading initial letters as if they had been kings. The American Women's Club in Paris solemnly burned the second number of the *Review* in their hall fire, thus giving a lead to Mr. Hitler. Their accusation was that we were not only Communists but indecent—that, on account of a really quite innocent story in French by my extraordinarily staid friend M. Georges Pillement. But one of the scenes took place in a . . . bathroom. It seemed to me that it would be better if some American ladies did not read French. It might cause international complications if they set up a censorship in Paris. After I had written that the Club cut off its subscription.

Bringing out the first number was rather hectic. The misprints made by the Russian printers were natural, but their corrections made the pages look like a Soviet battlefield and their procrastination was without parallel. The White Russian Colonel almost went out of his mind because he read communism into every incomprehensible English sentence. Finally everything was ready except for the proof of my editorial which conveyed a slight *aperçu* of the Arts in Paris at that moment. It had cost me a good deal of work. There seemed to be no way of getting this proof from the printers.

The White Russian Colonel now resigned. He said with a great deal of dignity that he would probably starve. But it was inconsistent with his honour to go on taking money from an organ that was now definitely proved to be an agency of the U. R. S. S. I didn't argue with or even question him. The Soviet Republic loomed enormously large in the Paris of those days for Paris is an excitable city and the finger of Lenin was traced to the most unlikely things. Even the mark of a newly invented rubber boot-heel! It was taken to print a trail by means of which Soviet agents could follow each other's movements. . . .

I had nevertheless, within a week, offers of every kind of service from every kind of White Russian noble or army officer or their wives. I refused them.

I was in rather a hole. The only person at the printer's who spoke comprehensible French or seemed reasonably sane was the manager. He had taken the opportunity to go sick. The rest of the staff who appeared to be mad flew into frenzies whenever I entered their office. My Russian is very limited and Miss·Reid was afraid to go near that madhouse. As far as we could make out that firm was run by near relatives of Grand Dukes. As soon as Miss Reid or I appeared one of them would insinuate that another was an Israelite. A free fight would ensue.

About that time Mr. Pound strolled into my studio and said that my secretary was next door and would like to see me. I was a little confused because I thought that Miss Reid was at the office in the wine vault of the Quai d'Anjou. I had quite forgotten the conscientious objector. "Next door" was the Santé prison.

The ten shillings or so that I had given that studious and bespectacled young man as earnest money had proved his undoing. He had been really near starvation, having been earning what living he did earn as an artist's model. So, instead of spending the money on a square meal he laid it out on the normal products of the Dôme. That is not a good thing to do.

When he got home he found that his concierge's lodge had been moved to the other side of the passage: its furniture was quite different and the concierge was a new man. In his own room an aged gentleman was sitting on the bed. The aged gentleman threw him down the stairs. The kindly *agent* to whom he told this unusual story patted him on the back and recommended him to go home as a good, spectacled student should.

The young man walked round a block and tried again. Things were worse. The strange concierge blocked the way. The young man knocked him down. . . . The aged gentleman was still on the bed. This time he held a gun. Outraged by their offences against the laws of hospitality the young man smashed some windows, defiled the staircase, yelled at the top of his voice and got into bed with the concierge's wife.

When the *agents* arrived in great numbers the young man made a spirited attempt to bite off the nose of the sergeant in charge of them. He was carried, spread-eagled, to the Santé. Next morning a kindly magistrate told him he had acted very wrongly. Poets have a certain licence but his deeds were not covered by that indulgence. The concierge pleaded for him; the old gentleman pleaded for him; the sergeant, who was a poet too, if a Corsican, asserted his conviction that the prisoner was an excellent young man. He had indulged too freely in the juice of the grape—but to indulge freely in wine was in France an act of patriotism.

He was ordered to pay frs. 15 for injuries to the aged gentleman; frs. 12 for the broken window; frs. 5 for the cleaning of the staircase and frs. 9 to the wife of the concierge, all these with *sursis*—the benefit of the First Offender's Act. He expected to go free and unmulcted.

Alas, a much more dire offence was alleged against him. He had been found to be in possession of a prohibited arm! The weapon was a penknife, three inches long. But the blade could be fixed. It was one of those Scandinavian, barrel-shaped affairs that some gentlemen use for cleaning their finger-nails. The unfortunate young man was remanded in custody.

The kindly sergeant did his best to lighten the irksomeness of the young man's captivity. He visited him in his cell, declaimed to him his own *vocéros* and other poems to the glory of the vendetta. He listened with attention to the poems of the young man and to the music of Mr. Pound who had brought his bassoon and rendered on it the airs to which the poems of Arnaut Daniel had been sung. That sergeant even brought half bottles of thin wine and slices of the sausage called *mortadella*. With this he fed the captive. It is good to be a poet in France.

The Higher Court before whom the case was tried was less placable. The poor young man had just, when Ezra visited me, been sentenced to a fine of frs. 4 with frs. 66 for costs and, it having been discovered that as conscientious objector he had been in prison in England, he was sentenced to expulsion from France:—Ezra's proposition now was that I should pay the fine and approach the authorities with assurance of the excellence of the young man's poetry and of my conviction that he would no further offend. . . . I had never read the young man's poetry and had only seen him for ten minutes at the Dôme, so I knew little about his character. But I perjured myself all right. I did it rather reluctantly for I dislike the militant sides of the characters of conscientious objectors and, having once seen a man's ear bitten off by an American trooper, I felt some distaste at the idea that my own nose might leave my face between the teeth of an English poet. . . . Eventually, on the assurance that the young man was in my service, the authorities decided that as long as he kept that job he might stay in Paris.

I was glad, for I did not like the idea of France expelling poets. So that young man became sub-editor. He assisted me to get out the first number. He made the discovery that what was delaying the printers was the fact that that White Russian Colonel had carried off the manuscript of my article and had never returned it. He had taken it to the General who was the Chief Organiser of the Counter Revolution in Paris and, between them I suppose, they had puzzled out that my account of the Dadaists, Surrealists, Fauves, Cubists and supporters of M. Gide was really a Soviet guide to the houses of White Russian organisers in Paris. . . . The idea does not really seem so mad when you consider that that General was, actually, a year or so later, "taken for a ride" in the streets of Paris in full daylight—and murdered.

I never saw that ms. again and had to substitute for it something I had written for a sort of prospectus. I am sorry for, beside the week it cost me, it was, I think, rather a good "constatation" of the ideals of the plastic artists of those days. But perhaps it wasn't!

The first number of the *Review* came out thus about six weeks late. And even at that it did not properly get out. The printers being apparently unable to pay their papermakers had bound the two or three copies that they sent to the office in a fairly substantial paper. But for those they supplied to the trade they provided a binding made apparently of white toilet paper. So, two days after the *Review* had been out for notice I had to face the fact that the trade refused to take it. I had to have it bound all over again. As soon as he saw that cover, enraged cables began to come from New York. Mr. Quinn must have spent more on cables than he spent on the *Review.* . . .

As soon as the first number was out the social life began. It came like an avalanche. I had arranged to give a modest Thursday tea to contributors after the time-honoured fashion of editors in Paris. The broken down London printer was to make the tea and there would be biscuits whilst we sat on benches round the press and talked of the future policy of the *Review.* It is a useful function as it is arranged in France.

But you never saw such teas as mine were at first. They would begin at nine in the morning and last for twelve hours. They began again on Friday and lasted till Saturday. On Sunday disappointed tea drinkers hammered all day on the locked doors. They were all would-be contributors, all American and nearly all Middle Westerners. If each of them had bought a copy of the *Review* we should have made a fortune. Not one did. They all considered that as would-be contributors they were entitled to free copies.

I had to shut these teas down and to admit no one except contributors to the current numbers and instead of a Thursday tea I gave a Friday dance. I do not mind giving dances. I can think my private thoughts while they go on nearly as well as in the Underground during rush hours—and if any one is present that I like and there is a shortage of men I dance. I would rather dance than do anything else.

It was during one of these festivals that I had my first

experience of Prohibition. I was dancing with a girl of seventeen who appeared to be enthusiastic and modest. And suddenly—amazingly—she dropped right through my arms and lay on the floor like a corpse. I was, as it were, shattered. I thought she had died of heart disease.

No one in the room stopped dancing. They were all Americans and nearly all from the Middle West. The girl's mother came from another room and, helped by her brother, carried the girl away. She expressed no particular concern and hardly any vexation. I had never seen a girl—I don't believe I had ever seen a woman or even a man—in such a condition before.

. . . Prohibition made these Friday dances noisy and sometimes troublesome affairs. I didn't much mind. I have a large presence and can overawe troublemakers as a rule. And I like to see people enjoy themselves and Heaven knows some of these poor devils needed to enjoy themselves. There was one poor nice boy—without the beginnings of any talent who had come to France on a cattle boat—to paint. He committed suicide when he found that he would never paint even passably and I learnt that the sandwiches and things at those Fridays had, for several months, been his only regular and certain food. To some devotees the Arts can be very cruel goddesses.

The dances gradually became burdensome and then overwhelming. In the beginning I had asked about thirty couples, all writers or painters with one or two composers. On the second occasion there were perhaps

forty-five, on the third, sixty. . . . So they increased.
By May as the tourist season commenced they became
overwhelming. I had to shut them down.

I did it with reluctance. It seemed to me that the
Review and everything connected with it was—I venture the statement—a burden of public duty laid on me.
And the dances, burdensome as they were, gave the
Review a certain publicity. I do not mean that I was
so naïf as to imagine that any of those who danced
would afterwards subscribe and as a matter of fact not
a soul amongst all those that came did subscribe to the
Review. Not one. . . . But a very large proportion
of those who have real merits as artists are painfully
shy. They are shy of submitting their work and still
more shy of personal contacts. So it seemed to me that
if for such shy persons there could be a little, intimate
function they might be drawn from their shells and
establish contacts not merely with those responsible for
the *Review* itself but also with each other. Thus one
might evolve an atmosphere of artistic friendliness and
intimacy such as is extremely beneficial to the population of an art centre on its æsthetic side.

In that way the *Review* and its social sideshows did
its work. The dances had changed their character almost too soon and the greater number of those who
crashed them being not only not artists but having no
connection or concern with any Art. Indeed towards
the end the dancers were in the majority people like
State Senators and up-state bankers and publishers who,
passing through Paris, came as it were to a dance straight

from a boat-train, made themselves offensive, and caught the next morning's train for Monte Carlo, Berlin or Vienna. That of course froze out all my French friends and nearly all the practitioners of the Arts.

The work however had been done and I do not think that there could ever have been an artistic atmosphere younger or more pleasurable or more cordial than that which surrounded the *Review* offices and the Thursday teas when they were again instituted. It was now possible to keep them intimate. They were not festivities for State Senators or up-state bankers and the purely derogatory bringers of manuscript had by then made the discovery that neither my assistants nor I myself were pigeons easy to pluck. There came to these frugal feasts regularly, Mr. Bird and Mr. Pound before he set up as a musician and, discovering with startling rapidity that all Frenchmen were swine and all French art the product of scoundrels, shook the dust of Paris from his feet. On most Thursdays Mr. Hemingway shadow boxed at Mr. Bird's press, at the files of unsold reviews, and at my nose, shot tree-leopards that twined through the rails of the editorial gallery and told magnificent tales of the boundless prairies of his birth. I actually preferred his stories of his Italian campaign. They were less familiar. But the one and the other being supposed by Ezra, Mr. Robert McAlmon and others of the Faithful, to assist me by making a man of me, Mr. Hemingway soon became my assistant editor. As such he assisted me by trying to insert as a serial the complete works of Baroness Elsa von Freytag Loringhofen. I generally turned round in time to take them out of the contents table. But when I paid my month's visit to New York he took charge and accomplished his purpose at the expense of cutting a short story of Mrs. H. G. Wells down to forty lines—and the London Letter of an esteemed correspondent down to three.

The baroness too was a fairly frequent visitor to the office, where she invariably behaved like a rather severe member of any non-Prussian reigning family. So I thought the stories of her eccentricities were exaggerated. Her *permis de séjour* which she had somehow obtained from the British Consulate General in Berlin expired and she asked me to try to get the Paris Consulate General to extend it. The Consulate General in Paris is made up of most obliging people and I made a date with her to meet me there. I waited for her for two hours and then went home. I found the telephone bell ringing and a furious friend at the British Embassy at the end of it. He wanted to know what the hell I meant by sending them a Prussian lady simply dressed in a brassière of milktins connected by dog chains and wearing on her head a plum-cake! So attired, she that afternoon repaired from the Embassy to a café where she laid out an amiable and quite inoffensive lady and so became the second poet of my acquaintance to be expelled from France. The Embassy discontinued its subscription to the *Review*.

The conscientious objector had had to go. He had worked quite well till Xmas. I sent him to England to do some private work for me and to get a rest. Whilst there he discovered inside himself that I regarded him as an object of charity and resigned his post in a letter of great expletive violence. I had never regarded him as an object of charity but as one who was by turns quite useful and a great nuisance. As he had had nowhere to go to after he left the Santé I had taken him to live with me. His salary was rather small so he was really under no obligation to me. . . . He was eventually arrested and conducted to the frontier. I regretted it because he appeared to be a young man of real talent. He has since pursued the career of a poet and savant in a country bordering on France. . . .

His going severed the *Review's* last editorial contact with England—except for a day when a young Eton and Oxford boy took over the duties. He didn't return on the morrow. The duties were pretty hard and without glamour. A bewildering succession of sub-editors then helped me and Mr. Hemingway. They had all been cowboys so that the office took on an aspect and still more the sound of a Chicago speakeasy, invaded by young men from a Wild West show. The only one whose identity comes back to me is Mr. Ivan Bede who wore large, myopic spectacles in front of immense dark eyes, wrote very good short stories about farming in the Middle West and boasted of his Indian blood and the severe vastnesses that had enveloped his childhood. I take that to be much the same thing as being a cowboy.

Mr. Hemingway had, I think, been a cowboy before he became a tauromachic expert: Mr. Robert McAlmon the printer author certainly had; so had poor Dunning, the gentle poet; even Mr. Bird had been a rancher in his day and Mr. Pound had come over to Europe as a cattle-hand!

That a great literary movement—for a really great literary movement was there beginning—should have originated in the Middle West which is usually regarded as the culminating point of materialism is not really astonishing. It was a matter of reaction, the young reacting violently against the frame of mind of the sires. I went to Chicago some years ago to persuade the father of one of my contributors to permit his son to take up literature as a profession and to let him have a little money while he made his way. Chicago is the butchering metropolis and this was a Chicago magnate—not at all a gross or illiterate person—but adamant. I argued with him for some time. I said his son had great talent and might well one day ornament his family and name. . . .

He said—almost pathetically:

"Mr. Ford, on the tombstones of three generations of my family there is a statement that they left honourable records in the trade I follow. Would it not be a dreadful thing if my son had to have on his gravestone the fact that he was a mere inkslinger? . . ."

I pointed out that a butcher's son whose epitaph began "Dear Friend for Jesus's sake forbear . . ." had for three hundred years conferred on his country and mine, since they had a common origin, the greatest lustre that they could shew.

That produced no effect on him. He said that Shakespeare was different. His father was no doubt not a very important butcher. He understood, too, that he had given his father and his family great cause for concern. He himself would rather see his son starve than that he should become a writer. . . . And starve the boy did for several years in Paris. . . . Another boy from Chicago who came to me for encouragement, whose parents had the same pride in their trade, ran away from home and worked his passage to France. He had seen a translation of Gourmont's "Night in the Luxembourg" and when he got to Paris had just enough money and just enough French to take a taxi to the Luxembourg. He spent the night wandering round and round the gardens, seeking for the entrance. He had of course a hard time for some while but he is now, I understand, as a painter, one of the ornaments of his home-town.

I will add as a contrast a story, that I do not remember to have told before, because it lets me mention a very charming personality. . . . On my second morning in Chicago during that visit the telephone bell rang. A voice said:

"Mr. F——, I see you are in this city. I am Mrs. ——. Mrs. ——, don't you know? The debunker. . . ."

I said that for years it had been one of my chief longings to hear the voice of Mrs. ——.

She continued:

"I want to tell you something—to give you advice. . . ."

She went on to say that she was Ernest Hemingway's confidante and adviser, and one thing she begged me . . . she begged me! . . . not to call on Hemingway's father and mother. I should have a most frightful reception. They regarded me as having horns and a tail. . . . Because I had encouraged Ernest to become a writer. I must promise! . . . Promise!

I promised and hung up the receiver. Before it was well on its hooks the instrument gave cry again. A voice said:

"I am Hemingway. . . ."

It was so exactly Hemingway's voice that I exclaimed in astonishment that I had thought he was safe in Paris. The voice said:

"No—not Ernest. It's his father." He said that he and Mrs. Hemingway wanted me to stay with them for the time I was in Chicago—because I had given Ernest encouragement to become a writer. He was an extraordinarily gentle, swarthy, bearded man who should have been an Elizabethan poet-adventurer. . . . May his ashes know peace!

In any case what I had predicted to myself in my Sussex cottage had by the time of the *transatlantic review* days become fully true. The Middle West was seething with literary impetus. It is no exaggeration to say that 80% of the manuscripts in English that I received came from west of Altoona and 40% of them were of such a level of excellence that one might just as well close one's eyes and take one at random as try to choose between them. It is true that a great propor-

tion of them were obviously biographical in conception
and all of them local in scene. But a just perception of
one's surroundings and of one's own career form the
first step towards a literature that shall be great in
scope. Local literatures are as a rule a nuisance, the
writers devoting to local distinctions of speech without
interest and to local ill-manners that would be best forgotten, talents that might, in a wider scene, develop
comprehension and catholicity. But a wave of literature
that in a few years produced—to mention them without
out apprisal and at random—Mr. Hemingway's "Farewell to Arms," Mr. McAlmon's photographic reports
on Berlin night life; Mr. Nathan Ash's "Love in
Chartres"; Miss Katherine Anne Porter's Mexican
stories side by side with Mr. Glenway Wescott's
"Grandmothers"; Mr. Davis's "The Opening of a
Door"; Miss Elizabeth Madox Roberts' "My Heart and
My Flesh" and Miss Caroline Gordon's "Penhally"—
such a wave of literature cannot, whatever else can be
said of it, be called parochial. . . . And I don't know
what else can be said against it.

So that, try as I might, to divide the space of the
Review into equal portions devoted to French, English
and American writings, the preponderating share of
its pages went to the Middle West. There was no difficulty in finding French contributions or even French
pictures to reproduce—though as a matter of fact most
of the reproductions came from the brushes and pencils of foreigners like Picasso, Juan Gris, Brancusi. . . .
The level of literature and the Arts is in France always

amazingly high though from time to time there will be no great outstanding figure. That was the case in the days of the *transatlantic review*. Anatole France having died unhonoured, Loti forgotten and Proust amidst the lamentations of a people, there were no great outstanding peaks. But outstanding peaks are not of much benefit to the general run of literature. They destroy perspective so that whilst the public read one applauded book they ignore a hundred others that are as good or better and thus the community loses. Certainly with the help of M. Jean Cassou, M. Georges Pillemont, M. Ribemont Dessaignes, M. Philippe Soupault, the *transatlantic review* managed to have as good French pages as anyone could desire who wished to know how good and clear the French writing and the French mind can be.

Thus through no volition of my own but I daresay partly through the patriotic coercion of Mr. Hemingway the *Review* was Middle Western as to a little more than half and a little less than one third French. The remaining sixth, mostly consisting of chronicles, came from the Eastern States, New York, and England.

It was singular how few manuscripts came from England. This can hardly have been due to dislike of the youth of England for myself for the youth of England knew nothing about me. Nor can it have been due to want of knowledge of the existence of the *Review* for with a population about equal to that of the Middle West England consumed a good many more copies of the *Review*. That fact was owing to better distribution.

Yet I did not receive from all England one tenth of the number of mss. that came from Chicago alone. Of what we did print I remember only a beautiful story by Mr. Coppard, a couple of delicate ones from Mrs. H. G. Wells, a story by Miss Ethel Mayne and two or three by a lady whose name I am ashamed to have forgotten. I cannot refresh my memory because my last set of the *Review* was carried away by a gentleman from Chicago. He professed to be a bibliographer but, though it was some years ago, he has neither made the bibliography nor returned the borrowed set. A full set of the *Review* is now rare and, at any rate until the crisis, was rather expensive. . . . But those short stories were very good or I should not after ten years so closely remember them.

I should like to make the note that in my opinion, for what it is worth, the real germ of the Middle Western literary movement is to be found in the Three Mountains Press, Paris, of Mr. William Bird who worked in conjunction with the Paris Contact Publishing Company of Mr. Robert McAlmon. Mr. Bird, an almost hypersensitive dilettante, when he was printing, produced a series of beautifully printed specimens of new prose. These books were edited by Mr. Pound and were mostly American. Mr. McAlmon published a number of uglyish wads of printing called the "Contact Books." These were nearly all Middle Western in origin and included Mr. Hemingway's first work.

These two printing establishments formed a centre and established between young writers contacts pre-

cisely that were, in the early twenties, more than invaluable. The young writer may find himself without
being actually published but he cannot do so without
contacts with ardent fellows in his art. Neither indeed
can an old writer. The claim is made on the point of
one or another noncommercial publication—including
the *transatlantic review*—that it "discovered" this or
that writer because it published his first lispings. It is
not for me to deny the service to literature of, say, the
Little Review, or, in its more opulent way, of the
Dial. But for myself I could not claim that the *transatlantic* discovered anybody. It would like to have, but
the spadework had already been done by the gentlemen
and enterprises that I have had the honour above to
mention.

PART THREE

CHAPTER THREE

AFTER THIS I DRIFTED INTO THE SPHERE OF influence of New York as inevitably as a soapsud in an emptying bath drifts towards a plughole. The attraction of that city lies in the fact that, for me, she is the expression of hope. She is the expression of the hope of all humanity. And she is the negation of the thing I hate most—of nationality. New York is not America because she is the expression of an ideal vaster and more humane. There has been nothing more disastrous for humanity than the conception of nationality. For the sense of race something may be said. But that men living on one side of an imaginary line called a "frontier" should automatically hate people born on the other side of that line is a conception of madness—of the madness that the gods send to people whom they are about to destroy. I was crossing the Rhine at Kehl the other day. On one side of an invisible line the ripples in the water, the fish, the reeds are French—on the other *echt Deutsch*. It was as curious to remember that as to recollect that in a certain township in Indiana a committee of people called Staubenheim, Racockski and Svendsen are engaged in teaching people called

343

Adams and Whittier . . . to be American! The Americanisation committee at least is dignified by the one set of names, the list of raw material on which they work contains the others. A certain race consciousness on the other hand may benefit the individual and help the state. If you can be sure that you are pure-blooded Pole, Jew, Gaul or Anglo-Saxon you may realise your limitations and try to modify your race-exaggerations so that you may live in peace with the Franco-Italian-Bohemian-Slav hybrids that live round you. You may even be conscious of ancient roots, traditions and histories of which to be proud so that, not to shame them, you may become a better and no narrower citizen of a conglomerate land.

For myself I am of such a mixed blood that I have no race consciousness to help me and I have as little national consciousness. Only one thing will arouse any national or race feeling in me. It is to hear one national express hatred for another nation. If I hear a Frenchman express contempt, say, for American art, I find myself become excitedly American of New York. Or if an Englishman by his bearing implies contempt for either of the other two nations I go, as the saying is, completely off the handle. Still more, whilst an American is abusing France I shall for that moment find myself actually French or if the Frenchman abuses England I shall find myself defending my compatriots with a passion of which few indeed of them will be capable. I suppose the only body of men for whom I have anything approaching a settled dislike are the subjects of

Mr. Hitler—if it be not the subjects of Mr. Mussolini. And that is because it is impossible not to believe that both nations have designs on France and one at least against the peace of Poland. Yet if I hear a Frenchman or a Pole uttering diatribes against either nation I cannot avoid pointing out the terrible nature of the Prussian's necessities in his dreary and infertile landscape as I point out the glorious traditions of the Italian.

This is in the main because I have a hatred for hatred —the most maiming of all the passions. Murder, backbite, rob, torture if you will. These are normal human occupations and may be conducted without loss of self-respect. But to hate is not only to lose your sense of proportion but to become a monomaniac. It is to curtail your powers. To combat a man or a rat you must understand the nature of the individual or the rodent. Great generals win battles because they know instinctively what is going on in the minds of the commanders opposed to them, never because of hatred! Prussia lost the late war because she completely misunderstood what was passing in the minds of her opponents and she has handicapped herself for a generation in even the unnamed contest between nations that will for long obtain because she has not understood that though Christendom is vague in its boundaries yet by the tradition of centuries and the gradual growth of a conscience a little sense of chivalry has arisen in us. It is centuries since—with deference to a certain club and to the British and American customs services—it is centuries since a civilised body of human beings burned a book. This is because a book is a living thing and to burn a book whilst taking credit for not murdering the author is to put yourself outside civilisation. If you burn the author you earn at least some respect for having the courage of your convictions. It is to be reminded once more of Louvain! And what have you done when you have wreaked your hate? . . . For myself I believe I can say that I never hated a human being in my life—for more than half a day. That is what makes a novelist. He is a person who must not side with his characters so, in his life, he must not side with himself. Nor even with his own side. He is therefore the only person who is fit to rule our world. Or to put it more acceptably: it is only the statesman with the gifts of the true novelist who could teach this world how bearably to run itself. That was proved nineteen hundred years ago. Since then we have not got *much* further.

I permit myself this little excursion into the field of the moralist which is one I seldom tread. I have lived a long time and thought constantly about these matters. And I have seen, gradually—at least the Western World veering towards that point of view. So one day these words may find themselves preaching to the converted.

New York when I reached there in 1923 seemed more than half way towards that ideal. I had on landing no sense of crossing a frontier though I am sensitive to these things so that if I cross the bridge into Brooklyn I feel myself very sensibly in the foreign.

There are of course customs and emigration authorities like beads on a string behind the Lady who stands with uplifted torch. But these amiable people—they have never treated me at least with anything but paternal kindness—these people so completely defeat the purpose for which they exist that they might just as well not be there. For they are there presumably to keep out the undesirable. But the undesirable will always get in by means of forged papers whereas the desirable are always inconvenienced and are not infrequently excluded. It is for instance obviously better for a state to contain, say, truthful polygamists than lying ones. Yet by the present systems a lying polygamist has only got to deny that he is one and in he will go. Before the polygamist who does not lie there will stand the angel with the flaming sword. But if you know that a man is a polygamist—or a woman a polyandrist—you can always watch them and prevent their obtaining more than their share of life partners. As for smuggling. . . .

I only twice in innumerable crossings smuggled anything. It seemed easy to do—the trouble coming afterwards. In each case the crime was an act of benevolence by which I in no way profited. In the first place I was taken in hand by a bevy of young things who knew that side of the world far better than I. They insisted that I must smuggle various embroidered articles of attire. I refused to be a party to breaking the law of any country not my own. But at last they forced me to give them the keys of my cabin and my trunks. I had no difficulty in getting through the customs but the trouble came then. The young people had scattered to cities distant from New York and from each other. They ordered me to forward whatever I found not belonging to me in my trunks. It cost me several weeks of correspondence and forwarding and re-forwarding of parcels. I did not know the English or French names of most of these articles of attire—and as for the American! . . .

The second occasion was less reprehensible but more expensive. A dignitary of the Anglican Episcopalian Church being sick, asked me to bring him a couple of bottles of Courvoisier 1860. It was a perfectly proper proceeding on his part for the consumption was authorised by his doctor, the alcohol supplied by the State aggravating his complaint. I arrived in New York with the two bottles and at once set off for Park Avenue with one of them. I had to pay a call on the way and left the bottle in the first taxi. I then decided that I was not fit to be trusted with the remaining bottle so I asked the bishop's daughter to come and fetch it. And she left it in a taxi.

I had then to buy two other bottles—which I made the bootlegger deliver and Courvoisier 1860 being rare in Manhattan it taught me a lesson. But as I imagine I should do exactly the same once more if I were asked I suppose the lesson not to have much profited me.

At any rate I set foot in New York just before the Democratic Convention without any more strangeness of feeling than if I had just been going round the corner anywhere to buy a packet of cigarettes. It is possible that the perturbation of mind in which I found myself obscured my powers of observation, but I do not think so. I have never found New York strange. . . . And to me she seems singularly unchanging. That is because the lines of the streets are never altered and I do not walk with my nose in the air looking at the sky-lines. So that in New York I feel safe. The moment I set foot on the ground from a steamer gangway tranquillity descends on me. Paris a little frightens and London saddens me intensely. But little old New York I imagine will go on being—ah how much too good for me to the end of the chapter! . . . What wouldn't I give to be crossing Sheridan Square at this moment! Yet, if I look over my shoulder I shall see through the leaves of an olive tree red sails on the Mediterranean. The other day the editor of the magazine that asked Mr. Joyce to write an article on how it feels to be going blind asked me to write one on how it feels to be an expatriate. . . . Pretty bad! I shall, when I have finished writing this, eat food such as appears on few New York tables and drink wine that few but New York millionaires could procure. . . . But I would give all I shall have here for a glass of hot milk at a tiny cafeteria beside a filling station on Lower Sixth Avenue with the bootleggers' lorries thundering by, after one at night, between an Esthonian Jew and a Magyar veterinary surgeon. . . . Poor modest dreams!

Certainly my perturbations were sufficient to obscure boundaries for me. They formed a double tragedy—that of the *Review* and that of poor Quinn. In the British Museum there are the wonderful clay *bas-reliefs* of Sardanapalus hunting. One of the marvellous little clay cameos shews a lion dying with its spine above the hips pierced by an arrow of the King's. In his last months Quinn was like that lion. He had the sense of power and power was leaving him. His threats were like the roaring of a lion, but they no longer had the power to terrify.

As against that there was the tragedy of the *Review*. To see a *Review* die is as painful as to have an intimate friend die under your eyes. It is a very similar process. They grow weaker and weaker. People rush round the bedside; they rush away to find nostrums; to find infallible physicians. They rush in and say they have found the never failing nostrum, the infallible leech. All the while the man and the periodical die. . . .

I had rushed to New York like that . . . to find the infallible nostrum. The infallible nostrum would have been some way of really managing the business affairs of that undertaking. From the beginning they had been in a state of pie. . . . Printer's pi.

On the face of it there was no reason why the *Review* should not have paid its way. The price of production was ludicrously small, distribution cost almost nothing, subscribers were not difficult to get and really first-class contributors easy. But the business arrangements were impossible to handle. One had three markets. But two of them were barred by fantastic barbed wire entanglements. In England things went quite smoothly.

After we had got the copies printed and bound an English forwarding agency would pick them up. The House of Duckworth distributed them—without enthusiasm. But they distributed smoothly, efficiently and satisfactorily. They even lent us money to run the *Review* with whilst I went to America. Surely no publishers could have shewn greater love!

Indeed the poor *Review* was very largely financed by Duckworth. That is to say that I had put into it all the money earned in England by the first instalment of my large work. Curiously enough the first instalment sold, as the saying is, like hot cakes, in England whereas the second and subsequent volumes fell absolutely dead. I presume the English reader took the first volume for light comedy and with the second discovered that I was in deadly earnest. I can think of no other. The English press received all alike with rapture that, since the death of Lord Northcliffe, it has always exhibited over my work. For certainly, if I had any grudge against the country of my birth it would not be against the press or, really, against the publishers. It is professional to call them names but I only know of one publisher who ever treated me dishonestly and he makes up in literary intelligence what the others supply in an honesty that lacks æsthetic sense.

In America on the other hand the first volume of my work sold relatively very little. It got through however three editions—for which I received three hundred dollars, that too disappearing into the coffers of the *Re-*

view. The second volume however—I suppose the American reader had by that time made up his mind that I was in deadly earnest—sold in New York an amazing number of copies. It came too late to help the *Review*. . . .

I have already said that Mr. Quinn and his lawyer had undertaken to relieve me of all American and French business affairs. Alas! . . . One evening whilst Mr. Quinn was still in Paris I returned home to my pavilion and in that small room shining in the light of candles I found Mr. Horace Liveright. Mr. Liveright was—and I daresay is—so darkly handsome that, when his presence radiates upon me, I always hear the strains of Mendelssohn on the air. Even when I merely think of him here I smell orange blossoms. Of course my orange trees are only a few yards away. But he suggests to me the perpetual bridegroom and it is a great pity that he has gone out of publishing.

He was sitting there, waiting to tell me that he was ready to take over the publication of the *Review* and even, if necessary, to put a little money in it. . . . It was as if Apollo had descended into a poet's garret!

I ran right over Paris to find Mr. Quinn. But Mr. Quinn objected.

I protested that Mr. Liveright was an extraordinarily capable and energetic publisher, publishing exactly the type of work that the *Review* was to promote. It would make a sort of nucleus. Nothing is better than a sort of nucleus. An able and energetic publisher who can really sell good work is of infinite service to literature. He brings good work into the limelight usually reserved for commercial fiction and he proves to other publishers that good work can be made to sell.

But Mr. Quinn still objected.

I have never discovered why I was the only honest man in the black world of Mr. Quinn and Ezra. I seemed to move amongst dark abysses, like the child in Swiss pictures. In a white nightgown, in a single beam of white light! Above me hovered those two, whispering guidance amidst the gloom. . . .

Then, soon, I was in New York, at the National Arts Club, taking tea every afternoon between Mr. William Allen White and Miss Mary Austin who told me, the one, all about the Democratic Convention and the other all about the American Indian. I all the time was wondering what was the matter with the American business side of the *Review*. It had an American publisher of Mr. Quinn's appointment. Mr. Quinn however was too ill to see me. At the same time he did not wish me to call on the publisher before himself seeing me. I had not had any accounts of the American sales of the review; neither, apparently had Mr. Quinn. As American editor Mrs. Foster had a room in the publisher's office but beyond reports of the conversation of a lady accountant of that firm she too could give me no definite information. In moments of elation the lady accountant would talk of sales and subscriptions that would have made us all permanently rich. When

sad, she declared that the cost of carting to the office
the copies which we delivered to Twenty-Third Street
docks was ruining the publisher.

It was sad to think that those poor copies that at
the cost of such desperate labours we in Paris succeeded
in getting on time to New York should have ruined
anybody. I could myself have piled them all into a
couple of taxis and have delivered them at that office
for $2.50. But carting in New York was expensive as
we were to discover when we at last got the imaginative accounts.

No one could have any idea of the labour it cost me
to get those copies there. The printer was fairly punc-
tual. He would deliver them to the binder. I would sit
at the binder's while they were being bound. I would
go to the *emballeur* and see them packed in cases, then
I would sit on the tail of the waggon and see them delivered to the special train that was to take them to the
Paris or the *Ile de France* at Havre. . . . At Havre
they would miss the boat. All that in addition to reading the manuscripts, seeing the *Review* through the
press, because at those times my sub-editors always resigned—and writing, writing, day and night to get
enough money to pay the contributors with. Heaven
knows what in that day I didn't write—articles for the
most unknown papers as long as they only paid. For one
I wrote whole weekly showers of reminiscences, travel
pictures, wise cracks. Thousands of words a week. That
just paid Miss Reid's wages. . . . There were, I can
assure you, some hair-raising Saturday afternoons. Then

that paper shut down on me. The Editor said that he could not stand the way I always came out second best in all my stories. He said his public could not stand it. It is the legitimate pride of the American that he always comes out top dog. If he does not he says he does. . . . . I said he could never have heard of the pride that apes humility. So I think I scared *him* off. . . .

It was of course none of my business to go to the printers, buyers, packers and forwarding agents. By rights Me. L—— should have done it. Mr. Quinn had said that Me. L—— would take all the business affairs off my hands. Alas: what Me. L—— had done had been to attend to the formation of Mr. Quinn's limited liability company. That arduous undertaking took up all the rest of my time. It was not finished when the *Review* expired. Day after day and day after day seven good men and true of us would file into that beautifully appointed office with the heavy curtains, the Wingless Victory and the carnations in a vase on the perfectly beautiful ormolu table. Behind it would be Me. L—— with his perfectly elegant figure, perfectly manicured hands, perfectly, perfectly fitting clothes and perfectly implacable manner. We seven would sit around him with the airs of shabby conspirators and he would lecture us on our duties. There would be Mr. Bird, Mr. Pound, the conscientious objector, myself and any three other people we could pick up in the street: Me. L—— would become furious over the fact that here was a company being formed in France without a Frenchman on its board. But I would have taken a Frenchman if

I could have got one. . . . A Frenchman! . . . I
would have taken a Cochin Chinese! Every time anybody fell out we had to begin the formation of the
company all over again and just before every meeting
broke up Me. L—— would inform us that we all risked
going to prison for life if so much as a comma in the
prospectus was misplaced. The French people very
properly do not want anybody to do business in their
fertile land. The French people are peasants and prose
writers. They regard all business men as swindlers: So
shareholders must be so protected against directors that
no director can do any business. In this case Quinn
and myself were the only real directors. We were also
the only shareholders. So we had to be protected
against ourselves.

One day everything really appeared to be fixed up,
thanks to Mr. Robert Rodes, by then fiancé of Miss
Reid. This astoundingly energetic young man with
the aspect of a rifle bullet romantically manufactured
powder puffs in an old old house in an old old street
near the Comédie Française, and once engaged to Miss
Reid he just took me under his arm and made things
move. His rooms were like the oldest apartments in
Greenwich Village and all hung over with extrava-
gantly romantic lambskins on strings. He knew all
French law, all English law, and all the laws of all the
49 States and he could get round all of them. Such
bright beings are not really meant to bless mankind and
all too soon Mr. Rodes married Miss Reid and carried

her off to Stamford, Conn., there to manufacture stove-pipe elbows.

In the meantime we had our company. The prospectus occupied forty pages in the *Journal Officiel* and we had to pay for them. Mr. Bird printed the most beautiful share certificates that can ever have been printed and we didn't have to pay for them. They were on vellum in the most beautiful and most minute type to be imagined. The whole forty pages had to go on them. I even sold four at a thousand francs a piece—to Miss Barney, Miss Gertrude Stein, a lady whose name I cannot call to mind and the Duchesse de Clermont Tonnerre. I thus became a financier and those ladies had the right to be protected from me by all the rigour of French Law.

Alas: suddenly there came a thunderbolt from Me. L——. His clerk had used the wrong formula for that prospectus and he warned us that we all ran the risk of imprisonment for life if we went on publishing the *Review*. . . . So that was how Mr. Quinn's representative managed our business affairs in Paris. . . .

I was never to know what had happened in New York. After many days of waiting I saw Mr. Quinn once. It was awe-inspiring to go into his shrouded apartment where there were the Picassos and Seurats and Brzeskas and the dim African blacknesses with, hanging over them all, the sense of the hastening doom of their owner. But Mr. Quinn was in no condition to talk about the business of the *Review*. He was gentle and almost apologetic. He confessed that the publisher had been too much for him. Apparently to him too the publisher had reflected the moods of his temperamental accountant. When he had been feeling good the sales had seemed to him more than satisfactory and the subscriptions unprecedented for a periodical of the sort. When depressed he had seen himself being ruined by the enterprise.

By the time he had told me that much poor Quinn was too tired to say any more about business. He went on for a short time to talk in a whisper about Jack Yeats and W. B. and George Moore and A. E. and Mr. Joyce. . . . He said I should see him again soon when he was better able to talk about things. . . .

I went back to the National Arts Club and began once more furiously writing articles to keep the *Review* going. A New York paper—I think the old *Evening Post*—had got to hear of my existence. I found as secretary in the Club a young woman from Seattle. She was as amazing as Mr. Rodes and afterwards of the greatest service to me, even when she had become the dictatress of the shoe and leather trade. At the moment I dictated articles on literary criticism to her in the mornings and Mr. William Allen White dictated his dispatches about the Democratic Congress in the afternoon. Mr. White took me to a sitting of the Congress. His dispatches were said to render it to the life— so what the inside of that young lady's head can have been like it is difficult to imagine. I was at that time writing rather fluidly.

Miss Kerr's successor had the laugh of me—or I of

her—next year. I was living in one of those rambling, old, gloomy apartments in West Sixteenth Street that I so love. Miss Kerr had found it for me. It had a lot of rather rude, very early Colonial furniture and some fine prints of birds and flowers. After I had been there three months, with Miss Caroline Gordon as my secretary, I decided that I must give a large tea-party. I had given tea to one, two, or three Thursday guests at a time and Miss Gordon had made tea on a gas-ring in one of the two parlours. But I wanted to have fifty or sixty people and I thought it would be better if the tea was made in one of the other rooms. So I sent Miss Gordon to ask the janitrix if she could not lend me an electric kettle or at least a spirit lamp. The janitrix said, "Why doesn't Mr. F—— use his kitchen?" The front door which I always used opened into the larger parlour. To the left was a door going into a passage that I had never explored. In the passage was a kitchen! . . . Miss Gordon said:

"Imagine a man who is in an apartment for six months and does not know that it has a kitchen!"

I said:

"Imagine a young lady who makes tea every day for three months on a gas-ring in a parlour and does not know she is in command of a perfectly appointed kitchen!"

. . . During that tea-party a representative of the chief transpontine newspaper tried to interview me. I pointed out that I had a tea-party on and that I was also packing my trunks to go to Chicago. He said that did not matter to him but I pointed out that it did to me. He went away—and wrote an interview with me. It ended:

"Mr. F—— is one of the most ill-favoured men I have ever seen. But he has a kind smile."

One day while I was dictating there came a thundering knock on the door. Mr. Edgar Lee Masters burst in. He said:

"Have you any postage stamps?"

Miss Gordon and I exclaimed simultaneously that we had none.

He said:

"Why haven't you any postage stamps? You ought to have postage stamps!" and slammed the door.

He must have taken me for the janitor. I suppose I ought to have replied:

"I have no postage stamps but I have the honour of having written the first article about you that was ever written in England!"

A few days after Mr. Quinn's secretary rang me up and said that Mr. Quinn would see me on the day after the morrow at two. At nine that morning I received from Mr. Quinn a letter of incredibly violent abuse. He had expected me at two the day before. Whether the secretary made the mistake or I I do not know. He said that there would have been no sense in his making the date for a day after the morrow. I do not follow the reasoning but it may have been so.

That was the end of the *transatlantic review.* I

understood from Mrs. Foster that Mr. Quinn wrote his letter just before being put under morphia and that for the rest of the time he lived he was kept under that stupefiant. He died whilst I was still on the High Seas returning to Paris—or maybe just after.

I have said that mankind is divided into those who are merely the stuff to fill graves and those who are artists. If that dictum is to be accepted it will be necessary to include Mr. Quinn among the artists. For along with the generally accepted primary arts there goes another great art—that of life. If you so live your life as to be in harmony with your tenets, of a clear vision and of benefit to your fellows and to the advancement of truth you may account yourself as of the Ruling Class. . . . Long, lean, burning like a coal with passion, Mr. Quinn by the practice of a learned profession became a very rich man and then relatively impoverished himself in the passionate pursuit of beautiful things and in championing oppressed artists. In his quest for beautiful things he got together a treasure the thought of which is a delight as of an august monument that will not easily be forgotten. In addition he was of infinite service to a whole world of artists and to a whole school of art.

My own contact with him was unfortunate but the essence of the misfortune was that I came upon him too late in his life. Had he then retained his great abilities and been fated to live longer he would have added great service to his other great services to the arts.

I never understood what happened as regards the

Review on his return to New York. I gathered that it had been his intention to get one of the older houses to take over the publication but that, finding them difficult to persuade and being worn out by suffering, he had pitched upon one of the newer publishers that he had so wholeheartedly denounced. This gentleman who possessed a certain *flair* for good writing was, when it came to the business of publishing, apparently quite uninstructed. He nevertheless drove with Mr. Quinn a bargain that nothing but his extreme exhaustion could have let him make. My provisional sketch of an agreement with Mr. Liveright had been that I would deliver to him at the quayside free of duty a certain number of copies at a very low rate but one that would still have left a satisfactory profit. After that Liveright, Inc., was to dispose of them how it pleased. This would have been a very equitable arrangement avoiding all confusion of accounts and placing the burden of expense where it should naturally fall.

The other gentleman apparently persuaded Mr. Quinn that we ought to pay the cost of carting from the quayside to his uptown office. He then persauded Mr. Quinn that the cover was unsuitable and obtained his sanction for the rebinding of the copies. They thus had\to be re-carted from the office to I imagine Garden City—judging by the cost of the transport; the covers were ripped off and they were re-bound and they were re-recarted to the publisher's office. All this must have been highly profitable to somebody, but in the event a

Review produced for three cents a copy and selling to the American public for sixty continued to run up a debt balance against us in the publisher's books.

At the Paris office of the *Review* we received from all over America such a continuing volume of correspondence and such innumerable manuscripts and Mrs. Foster in New York had to deal with so many more that there must have been some sales. Indeed on one occasion the publisher asked us to reprint a number. This may explain a puzzling fact. We published only twelve numbers of the *Review*. After it had died we received some figures from New York. These furnished accounts of the sales of thirteen numbers. Each shewed practically no sales and each shewed a heavy debit against the *Review*.

Heaven forbid that I should be taken as impugning the honesty of the publisher. The mere nature of the entertainment that he offered me would have been sufficient to disarm the most suspicious. He took a taxi-cab and shewed me Brooklyn Bridge which I must have crossed a hundred times before then and the Aquarium on the Battery where I had gone courting when I was a child, and the Woolworth building and the Flat Iron corner where, when ladies wore skirts, the skirts used to be whisked over their heads. And he enjoyed these wonders with the ingenuousness of a New England schoolmarm and we finished up the day at a bone-dry night-club where more than a hundred Russians in national costume sang the "Boatsong of the Volga." . . .

Didn't someone once say that Russia was the only country in which to live because there there was only one man who sang the "Boatsong" and him they executed?

So that all I took away from New York on that occasion was a sufficiency of speakeasy cards to fill a small card-index box. Everyone I met gave me speakeasy cards—the bootblack at the corner of West Tenth and Sixth; the man I bought my papers from; strangers in the streets and tubes. . . . On my first visit to New York when she was still little and old every fifth man in the street would stop me and ask: "Well, and what are your impressions of New York?" . . . The handing out of speakeasy cards took the place of that diversion.

I may say that, during that visit, so great was my respect for the laws of a foreign country I didn't go to any speakeasy except for one call at a house in Washington Place. To this I had been taken years ago when it had been a blindpig frequented by the more lively of the Four Hundred. . . .

I may be asked why I did not take legal proceedings to obtain proper accounts for the *Review*. . . . In the first place, as I have said, my principles will not allow me to take legal proceedings against anyone—and then, it is useless for a foreign writer to take proceedings against a New York publisher. The courts in New York are so congested that any such action takes at least two years to come to trial. The plaintiff during that time can publish nothing, either in Europe or America—for he will not continue to publish with the firm that he considers to have wronged him and that firm can obtain an injunction preventing him from publishing with any one else until the trial of the action. He cannot in the meantime publish anything at home because if he does he will lose his American copyright. Thus, if he is dependent on his pen, he will be ruined. . . .

I may say that, in spite of this and similar experiences, by August 1929, I had saved enough on my publications in New York—my books had ceased to be published in England and three of them written at that date have never appeared in London nor do they even appear in the catalogue of the British Museum Library— I had saved enough to consider finally paying off the debt I had incurred over the *transatlantic*. That had become considerable because after the death of Mr. Quinn I had continued to run the *Review* out of my own pocket, being determined that for the credit of the Arts the poor thing should run its twelve numbers. On the first of that month I lunched—I think with the W. C. Bullitts in their little house off Fifth Avenue. There were present Professor Erskine and a Professor of Economics at some university of the first eminence. He was, I was told, the first economist in the United States. He was going to lecture that afternoon on Prosperity and, since I was unable to go to the lecture he was good enough to give me an *aperçu* of the situation. I was inclined myself to be pessimistic and had said as much in an article in the *Herald-Tribune*. It appeared to me that the President and the Federal Reserve Bank between them had for purposes of their own frozen out the small speculator. I did not see how the Stock Market differed from any other market. The small speculator in his millions kept up the price of stocks just as the small buyer in his millions kept up the price of commodities. I asked: what would the proprietors of the five and ten cent stores say if the Executive succeeded in freezing out their customers? . . . And indeed, the gains of the small speculators going largely into the pockets of those stores and of the manufacturer of the cheaper car and domestic labour-saving implements, would not the action of the President and the Bank seriously injure these industries?

I was overwhelmed as the amateur in economics is always overwhelmed by the professional. I was told that I was speaking un-Americanly and un-American nonsense at that. I was in effect denying buoyancy to the American people. The President and the Federal Reserve Bank had acted prudently and with foresight in checking the extravagance of the small speculator. Their motive had been to get the control of the wealth of the country into the hands of the thirteen or fourteen great families who had always steered the finances of the United States with skill and wisdom. The slight check that the markets had experienced early in the year had in no way endangered Prosperity. It had been merely the momentary disturbance naturally attendant on the transference of power from one to another set of hands.

The Professor of Economics said that he had that morning been talking with Mr. Lamont on that very point. Mr. Lamont had said that there was no fear for the continuance of Prosperity. The price of a stock did not depend on the earning value of the company that issued it. That was a consideration solely for bondholders. The price of a stock was created by demand, as is the case with every other commodity and the demand was created by the country's confidence in its own Prosperity. . . . And, look where you would you could see no sign of the slightest check in public confidence. . . .

I pointed out that the building trade was not in very good fettle and that a slump in the building trade was always a precurser of depression. . . .

Then I *was* overwhelmed. Professor Erskine and the other Professor were both big men and they and all the lightweights at the table joined in convincing me of my imbecility, of my being a traitor to the Republic and of my un-American-ness. . . .

I never back my opinion in matters over which I have no mastery and I just hated to be accused of un-American-ness. For, if I am psychologically speaking un-American what in the world am I? So I let myself be convinced.

I let myself be disastrously convinced and I have suffered from it ever since. I took the advice of the only immensely great financier whose advice was at my disposal and next day invested my money exactly according to his instructions. I was told that I was to sell out on the 17th December and then my money would have increased by an exactly prophesied sum—and the increase would make up exactly the difference between the sum I had and the sum I needed. The addition of that coincidence to the other that my birthday—O Sapientia!—was on the 17th December was too much for me. Why should Minerva or someone not want to make me an appropriate present? I omitted to observe that the date on which I made that investment was the 4th August—the 15th anniversary of the declaration of the war. . . . Alas, poor dung beetle!

On that 17th December. . . . But I will spare the reader the rest of the story . . .

In Paris, in 1924, the *Review* staggered on its way towards death. The attendants rushed in and out looking for the nostrum or the leech. . . . Someone—Hemingway I should think—brought in the usual young financier who was to run the *Review* for ever. But the young financier, as is usually the case, turned out to have no money—or only so much as was allowed him by his female relatives. So we got to the twelfth number and I called a meeting of the four shareholders in Miss Gertrude Stein's studio and there, surrounded by the Picassos and Matisses and the pictures of whoever was the latest white hope of modern painting—I think it was then M. "Baby" Bérard—I told that valiant four that they had lost their money.

In spite of the limitation of that company I paid all the debts of the *Review* . . . and then of course there was the usual incident of the unpaid contributor.

There was a writer for whose work I had the greatest admiration. I did not know him very well personally. I bought some of his work and, since he was very, very poor, I paid for it considerably more than the standard rate of the *Review*, which was very small. In such cases I paid for the contribution out of my own pocket, debiting the *Review* with the standard page rate. I received in due course a receipt for my cheque. . . . Two months or so later, just after the *Review* had stopped, I received a mild little letter from Mr. X—— . . . asking when I intended to pay for his contribution. . . . I looked at the receipt and then got my cheque back from the bank. The receipt and the indorsement were not in Mr. X's handwriting. . . . I understood at once what had happened. Mr. X—— was in domestic difficulties, he had left home and a member of his family without his knowledge must have taken the money.

I did not wish to make mischief for Mr. X—— so I wrote to him and said that the *Review* had stopped but as soon as its affairs were wound up I would send him a cheque. I could not do anything more for at the moment I was quite penniless and living on borrowed money. I received from him a tart letter reproaching me for trepanning him into contributing to a moribund *Review*.

Shortly after that I went to New York and sent Mr. X—— his cheque. It cost me exactly what I received for two articles that I contributed as "Visiting Critic" to the *Herald-Tribune*. Three weeks later I received by the same post a letter from an editor asking me to write an article about Mr. X—— whose first book was just appearing in New York and a letter from Mr. X—— from which there dropped out a cheque. I have never received such a letter. Mr. X—— began by saying that he had denounced me to every literary paper and to every author's society in England and America.

I was a thief, a rogue, a swindler. I got writers to write for me and robbed them. He had been persuaded to write for my filthy *Review* because people said it would do him good in America. What good had it done him? From the first he had been against writing for a fat, capitalist brute like me. There I was, rolling in money, with my gross thumbs stuck into the arm-holes of my bulging white waistcoat, a huge cigar dripping from my foul lips, basking in glory! And that glory had been bought with the sweat of the miserable wretches I had deluded! It was the glory of the dung-heap that was my natural and unspeakable habitat. . . .

My secretary—there *are* fatalities!—in making out that cheque had dated it a year ahead and I had not noticed!

I got dollar bills, registered them to his address, and marked the envelope: "To be delivered into addressee's hands and to no other." I never heard that he got it but I suppose he did. I never heard either whether he actually sent out his denunciation of me. I daresay he did.

I sat down and wrote my article about him. In it I expressed my great admiration for his marvellous power of language and his great genius. . . . There *is* a pride which apes humility. . . .

But I asked myself, naturally: What price glory! Then I went back to writing my long book.

PARIS, JAN. 12TH—
TOULON, JUNE 11TH, 1933

P. S.

I have not found occasion to explain why it was that my father pre-disposed me to see glamour in the city of New York. . . .

I was rising seven when I first made, in company naturally with my parents, the Grand Tour, London, Paris, the Rhine, Alsace-Lorraine, the Midi and so back through Paris to London. In Paris we had seen my *oncle de l'Amérique*. He had fascinated my infant eyes with his engaging breakfast-table manners. So, when we were lying off Bonn, on the Rhine steamer, I broke my breakfast egg on the edge of a glass. . . . My father, who for an English gentleman *was* an English gentleman, let out one roar. I can still see my egg and glass flying through the porthole into the sunlit Rhine. . . . When he had recovered himself he explained that no-one who expected to grow into an English gentleman could do anything else with his breakfast egg than delicately to slice off its top with a knife and extract the contents with a tea-spoon. (You must of course, if you wish to prevent the witches from flying over the sea, make a hole in the bottom of the shell when you have emptied it.)

So for years I had a "complex" of my father's provision. My longing to eat eggs out of a glass, their gold mingling with that of butter and with pepper and salt, was something in which you would not believe. But something subconsciously paralysing rendered my hand powerless when I faced eggs on a breakfast table. . . .

Then, on my first crossing of the Atlantic in relatively green-salad days, at my first breakfast, I observed that the company in the saloon divided themselves into opposing groups, like the guests in Tartarin's pension on the Righi. . . . The smaller body were provided with egg-cups; the larger, with glasses. I agitatedly called the table-steward and asked him who those people were who were breaking their eggs into glasses.

"Those ladies and gentlemen, sir," he said, "are New Yorkers!"

INDEX

A

Abbey, Edwin A., 49
Adversity, 104, 108
Air-raids, 85, 93, 96, 97
Alcestis, 148-151
America, 155, 157
America and the Arts, 270
American Review, 317
American visitors, 234-237
American Women's Club, 324
Anglo-Saxondom and the Arts, 320
Anglo-Saxons in Paris, 203
Animals, thoughtfulness to, 107
Antheil, George, 283
Antibes, 245
Antoinette, Marie, 237
Army duty, 100
Army service, release from, 17
Art, the business of, 51
Arts, honour of, 176
Arts in Paris, 17
Ash, Nathan, 339
Athenaeum, 29
Austin, Mary, 353

Autographs, 236, 237
Azores, 143

B

Baldwin, Stanley, 261
Bankers, 142, 143
Barker, Granville, 150, 211
Barney, Nathalie, 203
Bax, Clifford, 123
Beach, Sylvia, 200, 267
Beau, the dog, 121
Beaucaire, 248
Beaulieu Point, 191
Bécourt Bécourdel wood, 113
Bede, Ivan, 335
Beerbohm, Max, 26
Béhaine, René, 214
Belloc, Hilaire, 252
Bennett, Arnold, 18-20
Bérard, "Baby," 368
Berengaria, 241, 242
Berthelot, Philippe, 18
Bird, William, IV, 289, 300, 323, 333, 341
Birds in New York, 246, 247
Boulevard Arago, 253
Boxing, 184, 186-189

Braddon, Miss, 88-91
Brakes, 195
Brancusi, 286, 339
British Army, 218
British Embassy, 334
Brother, Author's, 136, 271-277, 284, 303-306
Brzeska, Gaudier, 157, 180
Buckshee, 147
Bullit, W. C., 365

C

Caine, Sir Ralph Hall, 179
Calais, 206
Campden Hill, 48, 49, 63, 70, 79, 98, 100, 104, 149
Cannen, Gilbert, 51
Cardinals' Consistory, 178
Carpentier, 185, 187, 188
Casson, Jean, 340
Cat, the, 129
Catullus, 191
"Celebrity, The," 186-189
Cézanne, 245, 254
Chamberlain, Joseph, 222
Chicago, 169, 170, 336, 337, 341
Cobbett, 88
Collier's Weekly, 178
"Colonel, the," 278-280, 287, 289, 296, 300, 303, 324, 325, 329
Comfort, 141, 142, 183
Condé, 254
Conrad, Joseph, 30, 35, 36, 45, 75, 89, 129, 150, 208, 286, 308-311

"Conscientious objector, the," 278-280, 300, 326-329, 334
Cooking, 111
Coppard, A. E., 141, 173-176, 341
Corn-growing, 125
Country Life, 60, 61
Craig, Gordon, 182
Crane, Stephen, 118
Crays, 135
Crémieux, Benjamin, 202
Cubists, 329
Cummings, E. E., 324
Cunard, Miss Nancy, 34, 57

D

Dadaists, the, 202, 329
Dai Bach, 20, 221, 260
Daudet, Léon, 214
Dead as a writer, 25
Democratic Convention, 353
Dessaignes, Ribemont, 340
Detective novels, 213
Dial, 342
Dickens, 249
Dignity, 203
Digressions in a novel, 213
Disraeli, 222
Dôme, the, 278, 279, 328
D. O. R. A., 99
Dostoiewsky, 215
Douglas, Norman, 232, 323
Dreiser, Theodore, 31
Dressing for dinner, 184
Dressing-gown, 157
Drinkwater's Repertory Theatre, 151

Driscoll, Ted, 185
Duckworth, Gerald, 137, 202, 321
Dung-beetle, 105, 117, 205, 368
Dunning, Ralph Cheever, 336

E

Earnestness, 169, 351, 352
Edge, S. F., 117
Eighteenth Amendment, 52
Elgar, Sir Edward, 161
Elimination, in writing, 240, 242
England and The Arts, 75-77, 264-270
English dead, 65, 68
English liberty, 100-104
English Politics, 260-269
English Review, 35, 39, 50, 60, 209, 271, 316, 317, 321
"Epipsychidion," 211
Epitaph in Beaulieu Churchyard, 118
Epstein, Joseph, 180
Erskine, Professor, 365, 367
Evans, 193-196, 202
Ex-soldiers, 187
Eyesight, 291

F

Father, author's, 135, 137, 138, 271, 272, 372
Fauves, 329
Federal Reserve Bank, 366
Fittleworth, 158, 159

Flatiron building, 91
Flaubert, Gustave, 38, 57, 245
Fleet street, 174
Flint, F. S., 156
"*Fluctuat nec mergitur*," 80, 259
Forged cheques, 151
Forman, Harry, 178
Forman's dinner, Mrs., 185
Foster, Mrs., 298, 299, 306, 307, 309, 310, 323, 353, 363
Foster, Mrs., advises Quinn, 298
France, Anatole, 57, 198, 340
France and Art, 268
France and literature, 198-202
French frugality, 245
French Impressionists, 76
French writers, 57
French writing, 340
Friday dances, 330-333
Friesz, Othon, 234
Frogs, 206

G

Galsworthy, John, 30, 32, 33, 41-62, 128
George, Lloyd, 20, 21, 183, 184, 222
Gide, André, 201, 202, 329
Goldring, Douglas, 61
Gordon, Caroline, 339, 360
Gosse, Sir Edmund, 35, 39
Gourmont, Rémy de, 203
Graham, Anderson, 60, 61
Graham, Cunninghame, 171, 172

Grandfather, author's, 117, 184, 206, 272-294
Greek scholarship, 149, 191
Gris, Juan, 339

H

Hamnett, Nina, 267
Hard-luck story, 209
Hardy, Thomas, 75, 286
Harris, Frank, 26, 315-319
Harvey, Colonel, 317
Haussmann, 253
Hecht, Ben, 88
Hemingway, Ernest, 32, 182, 295, 323, 333, 335, 338, 339, 341, 368
Herald-Tribune, 365, 369
Hitler, 260, 324, 339, 345
Hog-raising, 127, 133, 141, 158-161, 170
Hokusai, 140, 141
Hollywood, 134, 140, 143-145
Hudson, W. H., 75, 107
Hueffer, Oliver, 136, 271-277, 284, 303-306

I

Imagism, 166

J

Jaloux, Edmond, 202
James, Henry, 24, 35, 36, 49, 59, 75, 104, 133, 150, 161, 162, 190
"Jane Wardle," 274

Jo, the boy, 120, 127, 128, 158
Joyce, James, 181, 200, 203, 259, 267, 286, 290, 293, 294, 308, 349

K

Karns, Fred, 125
Kemmal Hill, 194

L

"Lady novelists," 84-88, 90
Lamartine, 245
Lamb, Charles, 71-75
Lamont, Thomas W., 367
Larbaud, Valéry, 201
Latapie, the painter, 289
Latin Grammar, 204
Laurent, Maître, 248, 250
Lavenue, 259, 265
Law, Bonar, 261
Lawrence, D. H., 323
Left Bank, 305
Léger, Fernand, 278
Lewis, Kid, 185, 187
Lewis, Percy Wyndham, 157, 323
Lewis, Sinclair, 178, 185, 189
Lewis, Mrs. Sinclair, 178, 187
Literary agents, 146
Little Review, 342
Liveright, Horace, 352, 361
Liverpool, 261
Lloyd, Marie, 197
London, 103, 104, 189, 197, 262
London, back to, 178

London, ease of, 98
London, passion for, 78
London suburbs, 102
"Lorna Doone," 95
Loti, Pierre, 340
Louvain, 346
Lovinghofen, Baroness Elsa Freytag von, 333
Lucas, E. V., 71-76
Lungs, damaged, 155, 192, 250
Luxembourg, 31, 253
Luxuries, 141, 142

M

Madox, Tristram, 74, 135
Maître L——, 314, 315
Marwood, 39, 51, 184, 207-210, 220, 222, 227
Masterman, Charles, 93
Masters, Edgar Lee, 360
Matisse, Henri, 234, 269, 286, 308
Maupassant, Guy de, 35, 36, 47, 57
Maxwell, W. B., 89
Mayne, Ethel, 341
McAlmon, Robert, 333, 335, 339, 341
McClure, S. S., 169
Mediterranean, 108, 130, 131, 157, 176, 191, 192, 244
Memory, loss of, 80, 194, 195, 223, 224
Meredith, George, 75
Middle West, 169, 171, 172, 214, 235, 331, 335-340
Minto, Dorothy, 210

Mirabeau, 254
Mistral, 231
Modigliani, 308
Monroe, Harriet, 158, 160
Montagnier, Maître, 249, 278
Moore, George, 32-36, 38, 40-43, 289, 290, 308
Morning Post, 252
Mother, author's, 95, 118, 138, 139, 271, 272, 275
Mother's watch, 237, 238
Movie-play, 145
Mr. X——, 369-371
Munro, Harold, villa, 192, 205, 220, 221, 228
Murrell, Lady Ottilie, 88
Mussolini, 345

N

Name, change of, 132-137
National Arts Club, 353
Nationalism disastrous, 343-346
Nationality, 74
Nature love, 246
Nature quotation, 131
New York, 102, 139, 253, 343
New York and the *transatlantic*, 343-371
New York, love of, 349
New Yorkers and eggs, 372, 373
Nightingale, 177, 247, 248
Northcliffe, Lord, 61, 157
Northwestern University, 170
"Not English," 73, 74

Notre Dame, 116, 193, 195, 202, 223
Nouvelle Révue Française, 201, 202, 205
Novarro, Ramon, 145
Novel, characters and subject, 206-211
Novel, details in, 223-227
Novel-writing, 193, 211-212
Novels, construction of, 165
Novelist of commerce, 144
Nudism, 244
Nutriment to plants, 122

O

Offices in Paris, 299, 300
Omens, 109, 127
One thing at once, 112
Onions, Oliver, 213, 214
"O Sapientia," 128, 368

P

Paris and the Arts, 282
Paris, arms of, 80
Paris Contact Publishing Company, 341
Paris in winter, 32
Paris, old, 253-255
Paris, traffic in, 307-309
Party at French Embassy, 17-25
Paterson, N. J., 97
Peasant mind, 117
Pen Club, 201
Penny, the goat, 120
Personal likenesses, 42

Picasso, 180, 286, 292, 340
Pillement, Georges, 324, 340
Pinker, literary agent, 133, 134, 145, 151
Playfair, Nigel, 148, 149
Poetry, 157, 161
Poets, 186-7
Porter, Katherine Anne, 339
Potato-growing, 122-124
Pound, Ezra, 42, 51, 155, 156, 166, 203-205, 278, 279, 283, 286, 287, 288, 292, 305, 308, 326, 333
Pound, Ezra, in Philadelphia, 296
Prayer, 115
Price, Professor Marsden, 183, 184
Prohibition, 307, 331
Proust, Marcel, 213, 214, 292-294, 340
Proust, Marcel, death of, 197-202
Provence, 108, 131, 160
Pulborough Flower Show, 124
Pulborough market, 161
Punch, 73, 128, 270
Pure thought, 71

Q

"*Quelque giroflée*," 130, 131
"*Quelque moineau*," 130, 131
Quinn, John, 42, 289, 290, 292, 297, 298, 306, 308-312, 319

Quinn, John, and the *trans-atlantic*, 320-361
Quinn, John, death of, 361

R

Red Ford, 23, 25
Red Ford, life at, 107-151, 156-161
Red Ford, visitors at, 164-169
Refugees from thought, 244
Regan, 58-67
Regent Street, 90, 92, 94, 103
Reid, Marjorie, 302, 303, 322, 323, 325
Reid, Whitelaw, 317
Reinach's Greek villa, 191
Rendal, Stuart, 28
Riviera season, 243
Riviera weather, 230-233
Roberts, Elizabeth Madox, 339
Roman Catholic training, 115
Rossetti, D. G., 95
Rotonde, the, 279
Rue de Vaugirard, 228, 254
Ruined author, 108
Ruling classes, 219, 221
Ruskin, 104, 105

S

Sales in America, 351
Sargent, John S., 75
Saturday Review, 25, 27, 173, 174, 316
Secretaries, 240, 241
Seurat, 308

Shallots, 110, 116, 118, 119
Shaw, George Bernard, 26, 150
Shopkeepers and literature, 251
Simenon, Georges, 213, 214
Sinclair, May, 178, 185-188
Sirocco, 231-233
Smuggling, 347, 348
Snow in France, 192
Somme, 113
Soupault, Philippe, 202, 340
Speakeasy cards, 364
St. Agrève, 248, 250-252, 273
St. Anthony, 205, 227, 238
St. Jean Cap Ferrat, Life at, 192, 206-246
Standing, Mr., 158, 159, 160, 167, 168
Stein, Gertrude, 179, 180, 181, 203, 205, 286, 368
Stendhal, 131
Stevenson, R. L., 86, 87
Strasburg, 184
Style, in writing, 179
Surrealists, 329
Sussex, 158, 253
Swinburne, 47
Swine-fever, 121

T

Tarascon, 24, 192, 246, 248
Thackeray, 72, 181
Thursday tea, 330
Time-shift, 161, 165, 212
Times, London, 139, 157, 289, 290

Times, New York, 161, 213, 289

Times Literary Supplement, 204

Tired people, 117, 118

Tomlinson, H. M., 323

transatlantic review, 259-371

Tsara, Tristan, 297

Turgenev, 38, 48, 57, 215, 245

Typewriters, 239, 240

Tyrrell, Sir W., 18

U

Ulysses, 177, 191

V

Valentino, Rudolph, 145

Verlaine, 254

Villefranche, 193, 206, 235, 236

Vorticism, 166

W

War experiences, 63, 64, 192, 195, 196

War Memorial in Notre Dame, 68, 225, 226

"Waring," 209, 220

War-novel, 162

Watts-Dunton, Theodore, 179

Waugh, Edwin, 119

Wells, Bombardier, 185, 187

Wells, H. G., 26, 150, 157, 178, 186, 187, 277, 334

Wells, Mrs. H. G., 341

Wescott, Glenway, 171, 214, 339

Whistler, 49, 75

White, William Allen, 353

White blackbirds, 246, 253, 284

Whitehall, 217, 218, 221, 266

Wilde, Jimmy, 185

Wines of Provence, 22-23

Wines, Red and White, 290-292

Worry, 216, 217, 226

Writer or gentleman? 264-266

Writer's cramp, 239

Writing for money, 146

Writing in French, 202

Writing, methods of, 239-243

Wyndschaete, 194

Y

Yeats, W. B., 75, 308

Yorkshire dialect, 207